# Latin American Melodrama

# Latin American Melodrama

## Passion, Pathos, and Entertainment

Edited and with
an Introduction by
DARLENE J. SADLIER

UNIVERSITY OF ILLINOIS PRESS
Urbana and Chicago

♾ This book is printed on acid-free paper.

Library of Congress Cataloging-in-Publication Data
Latin American melodrama : passion, pathos, and entertainment
/ edited and with an introduction by Darlene J. Sadlier.
p.   cm.
Includes bibliographical references and index.
ISBN 978-0-252-03464-0 (cloth : alk. paper)
ISBN 978-0-252-07655-8 (pbk. : alk. paper)
1. Motion pictures—Latin America.  I. Sadlier, Darlene J.
(Darlene Joy)
PN1993.5.L3L345     2009
791.43'098—dc22      2009009435

# Contents

# Acknowledgments

The idea for a volume about Latin American melodrama emerged during the 2005 conference of the Society for Cinema and Media Studies in London. There, one evening, Gilberto Perez and I began talking about older Latin American films and our favorite melodramas. The lively conversation made me realize how very little material in English existed concerning Latin American film melodrama, even well-known movies made in the 1940s in Mexico, the country that has received the majority of scholarly attention on the subject. The result of that conversation is the present collection, which brings together essays about melodramas from various parts of Latin America and includes analyses of not only dramatic films but also documentaries and the *telenovela*.

I thank *Screen* and the Brazilian publisher Cosac and Naify for permission to publish Ismail Xavier's essay about Nelson Rodrigues, which has been revised for this anthology. I am also grateful to my colleague Juan Manuel Soto, whose technical expertise greatly facilitated my work as editor. As always, James Naremore provided me with important feedback, editorial advice, and loving support.

# A Short History of Film Melodrama in Latin America

## DARLENE J. SADLIER

In 1990, in recognition of the approaching centenary of film, the journal *Artes de México: Nueva época* dedicated an entire issue to photographs and commentaries about Mexican cinema. Directors, actors, cinematographers, scriptwriters, film historians, and critics from different generations were interviewed about their first memorable cinematic experience, their favorite movies and genres, and their thoughts about current and future trends in Mexican filmmaking. One of the most striking aspects of this special issue is that individual golden-age melodramas, in particular, Emilio "El Indio" Fernández's *María Candelaria* (1943) and *Enamorada* (Woman in Love, 1946) are repeatedly invoked as powerful initiations into Mexican film culture, and major contemporary directors such as Arturo Ripstein continually identify melodrama as their favorite genre.

The distinguished film historian and critic Emilio García Riera, who is interviewed by the journal, regards the year 1933 as pivotal in his formation because of Fernando de Fuentes's *El compadre Mendoza* (Godfather Mendoza) and Arcady Boytler's *La mujer del puerto* (Woman of the Port), two classics whose treatment of the Mexican revolution and the "fallen" woman were to give them iconic status among the golden-age melodramas.[1] Critic Leonardo García Tsao is partial to the melodramas about the revolution, "even if the cinematic version is very often distorted" (91–92), while director Luis Alcoriza and critic Andrés de Luna praise the intimacy and power of Fernández's *Pueblerina* (Little Country Girl, 1948), a melodrama about rape and revenge.[2] Both Matilde Landeta,

Mexico's pioneer female director, and world-famous cinematographer Gabriel Figueroa call *Enamorada* their most memorable film because of its aesthetic sensibility (Landeta) and its powerful ending (Figueroa). The latter, who photographed this film, among many other melodramas, is especially passionate in describing its imagery: "[*Enamorada*] has everything, and in particular an extraordinary visual emotion, as in the scene where the long shadows of the [revolutionary] soldiers are projected onto the heroine's house, and she begins to run among the shadows. That's a very striking scene in which it is not technique but imagination that counts" (85). Director Guillermo del Toro, whose *El labirinto del fauno* (Pan's Labyrinth, 2006) was clearly influenced by classic Latin melodramas, criticizes those who dismiss Fernández's and Fuentes's movies about revolution and romance, advising young directors to take advantage of the "melodramatic elements" of older films: "I believe genre films are extremely valuable because they have concrete rules; you either respect these or break them, but they help you to reach a wider audience" (93).

This anthology of critical writings is devoted to the films of which del Toro speaks and to films like them from other Latin American countries—films not only of the golden age but also of the present that belong in the melodramatic tradition. It may be useful, especially to U.S. readers, if, before I provide background information about the films and the critical essays, I first comment briefly on *melodrama,* a word used not only in the United States but throughout Latin America by filmmakers and historians to describe the films in question.

In Spanish and Portuguese as in English, *melodrama* derives from the Greek *melos,* or "music," and it originally was used to designate early nineteenth-century stage productions in which the drama was interspersed with musical numbers and backed with an orchestral accompaniment that heightened emotional climaxes. By the mid-nineteenth century, however, melodrama had become associated less with music than with plots featuring spectacular action, improbable twists of fate, intense expressions of emotion, last-minute rescues, and vivid conflicts between bad and virtuous characters. Melodramas of this sort typically involved the persecution of the innocent by the powerful, but their endings were usually happy, illustrating the triumph of good-heartedness over every sort of social or moral evil. Whether conservative or leftist in their political implications, they were vehicles for what literary theorist Peter Brooks describes as the "moral occult" (5). Charles Dickens was a melodramatic novelist and, in the United States, David Belasco became famous for directing spectacular stage melodramas. Among the most successful examples of the form in late-nineteenth-century U.S. theater were *Uncle*

*Tom's Cabin,* adapted from Harriet Beecher Stowe's celebrated 1852 novel, and *East Lynne,* adapted from a best-selling novel of 1883 by Mrs. Humphrey Ward. Both became staples of touring-company theaters at the turn of the century and were performed again and again across the country. It was only a short step from such theatrical productions to the cinema of D. W. Griffith, which is profoundly melodramatic. It is significant that long after *East Lynne* had begun to seem outdated, Griffith adapted it for one of his late films, *Way Down East* (1920), which gave new conviction to the clichéd scene of the poor young mother cast out into the snow.

With the advent of modernism and the Jazz Age, melodrama began to take on negative connotations—in spite of the fact that Hollywood cinema is and has always been in some sense melodramatic. Thus, from the 1920s onward, film producers in the United States rigorously avoided using the word to promote their wares because it sounded old-fashioned, the opposite of more attractive and saleable descriptions such as "realistic." Meanwhile, classic Hollywood films explicitly denigrated melodrama, even when they were being melodramatic. In Otto Preminger's *Daisy Kenyon* (1947), for example, Joan Crawford and Dana Andrews, who are involved in an adulterous relationship, have a conversation in which they tell each other not to be so "melodramatic" about the situation. Finally, in the postclassical era, the term was revived and given respectability by academic theorists in the United States and England who used it in discussions of what once were called "women's weepies," "women's matinees," or "soap operas." (Classic examples include *Now, Voyager* [1942], *Mildred Pierce* [1945], *Letter from an Unknown Woman* [1948], and *All That Heaven Allows* [1955].) In their day, such films had often been treated condescendingly by established critics, but with the rise of feminist scholarship they took on special interest and were closely analyzed. One consequence is that in U.S. film studies today, the term *melodrama* is nearly always used to designate films about domestic or family issues. Strongly associated with stars such as Bette Davis and Joan Crawford and with directors such as Douglas Sirk and Vincente Minnelli, it also signifies a kind of emotional or stylistic excess that at least theoretically functions as a release from repressive Puritanism and patriarchy.[3]

Latin America produced and continues to produce many films of this type, but the term *melodrama* has somewhat broader implications in countries such as Mexico, Argentina, and Brazil, where it refers not only to domestic dramas but also to historical epics in which family life is viewed in relation to larger national issues.[4] Furthermore, the domestic films from Latin America are somewhat closer in spirit than their Hollywood counterparts to the original melodramas of the early nineteenth century. Especially in the films from Mexico, musical numbers performed by popular recording artists or nightclub entertainers are interspersed throughout the narrative. Hence the protagonist of a Mexican melodrama is likely to be a wife, mother, and show-business professional all at the same time, or, failing that, the film will simply feature several scenes that take place in a nightclub. (There are roughly equivalent films from Hollywood—see, for example, Susan Hayward in *I'll Cry Tomorrow* [1955] or Doris Day in *Love Me or Leave Me* [1955]—but these are exceptions to the rule.) The special film issue of *Artes de México* to which I referred above repeatedly cites classic Mexican examples of melodrama that have been widely recognized and studied as part of the nation's film history. Unfortunately, films of this type have received far less critical attention in countries such as Argentina and Brazil, which, along with Mexico, have constituted the principal centers of film production in Latin America. Melodramas were also produced in places where the cinematic infrastructure was especially fragile or even nonexistent, including Venezuela, Bolivia, Peru, and Puerto Rico. A complete history of such films would also need to include many silent melodramas that have been lost or destroyed. This was the case in Chile, where, of an estimated eighty features made between 1916 and 1931, only two, *Un grito en el mar* (A Cry in the Sea, 1924) and *El hussar de la muerte* (Death's Hussar, 1925), both directed by Pedro Sienna and both melodramas, are known to have survived (Barnard 217).

In Brazil, the early silent period was rich in melodramatic productions, many of them adaptations of canonical literary works. José de Alencar's popular romantic novel *O guarani* (The Guarani, 1857) was the source text for a short 1908 film adaptation by Antônio Leal. Salvatore Lázzaro filmed a 1911 adaptation inspired by Brazilian composer Antônio Carlos Gomes's celebrated opera based on *O guarani,* which was followed by other film versions in 1916, 1920, and 1926.[5] Gomes's score was used in every remake, which confirms not only the historically close relationship between opera and melodrama but also the pivotal role that *melos* plays in creating the emotional extremes that reduce audiences to tears.

Salvatore Lázarro and Vittorio Capellaro are only two of the many Italian immigrant directors who deserve credit for bringing early melodrama to Latin American screens.[6] Indeed, the whole of Latin American melodrama has been somewhat transnational in style. As critic Gustavo García points out, early silent melodramas in Mexico were heavily influenced by "diva" films from Italy and France, as well as by melodramas from the United States: "The Mexican public suffered as much over the fate of the combating [Mexican revolutionary] armies as it did the misfortunes of the Gish sisters or Francesca Bertini" (154). In the 1930s and 1940s, Colgate-Palmolive and Lever Brothers sponsored Cuban *radionovelas* (radio plays) that were transmitted throughout Latin America, and the popularity of the radio soaps, whose target audience was female, further fueled a demand for screen melodramas that were featured at special matinee sessions, billed "for women only."

The geographic proximity of the United States and Mexico resulted in the exchange of considerable cinematic talent and expertise. Emilio Fernández, Dolores del Río, and Pedro Armendáriz, three of the most famous names in melodrama, worked in Hollywood and in Mexico. During World War II, Nelson A. Rockefeller's Office of the Coordinator of Inter-American Affairs (CIAA) supported "Good Neighbor" Mexico's cinema at a time when Hollywood was busy making war movies. Boosting the Mexican industry while withholding raw film stock from Argentina, the CIAA chastised a "neutral" with whom Good Neighbor relations with the United States were strained, and Argentina's film industry suffered greatly as a consequence.[7]

The sheer number of high-quality Mexican melodramas exported throughout Latin America in the 1940s ensured that country's preeminence as a maker of women's weepies. Nonetheless, transnational collaborations within Latin America's borders were quite common during the classic period. As Luisela Alvaray points out in her essay for this volume, Argentine director Carlos Hugo Christensen was hired by Venezuelan producer Luis Guillermo Villegas Blanco to film *La balandra Isabel llegó esta tarde* (Sailboat Isabel Arrived This Afternoon, 1950), which was Blanco's attempt to establish a film industry in Venezuela. In addition to Christensen, Blanco contracted Mexican actors Arturo de Córdova and Virginia Luque, Argentine star Libertad Lamarque, and Spanish-born José María Beltrán (who was a major cinematographer in Argentina) to work on the melodramatic *La balandra,* which became one of the first Latin American films to win a major prize at Cannes.[8]

Brazil's Vera Cruz Film Company was also transnational in composition. In 1949 Brazilian director Alberto Cavalcanti, who had been making films in France and later at Ealing Studios in England, was invited to head production at the newly created company in São Paulo. Vera Cruz's main objective was to build a studio and produce high-quality, Hollywood-style films for international audiences; it brought in technical talent from outside Brazil, including Anglo-Argentine cinematographer Herbert "Chick" Fowle and Austrian editor Oswald Hafenrichter. Cavalcanti, Fowle, and Hafenrichter collaborated on Vera Cruz's first production, the melodrama *Caiçara* (1950), about an unhappily married woman (Eliane Lage) who is desired by her older husband's business partner (Carlos Vergueiro). In the story, the two men wage a silent war against one another ending in murder; in the meantime, the woman falls in love with a passing sailor (Mário Sérgio). After Cavalcanti's departure as production head in 1950, Fowle and Hafenrichter continued to work together and separately on other Vera Cruz productions, including the melodramas *Tico-Tico no fubá* (Sparrow in the Cornmeal, 1952), a biographical film about composer Zequinha de Abreu (Anselmo Duarte), who is destroyed by his passion for a beautiful circus performer (Tônia Carrero), and *Floradas na serra* (Blossoms on the Mountain, 1954), based on the novel by Dinah Silveira de Queiroz, about the doomed love of a woman (Cacilda Becker) for a fellow patient (Jardel Filho) in a tuberculosis sanatorium. Despite the quality of its eighteen features, among them Lima Barreto's melodramatic western *O cangaceiro* (The Bandit, 1953), which won the prize for Best Adventure Film at Cannes, Vera Cruz's international enterprise was costly and conceptually flawed. The worldwide success of *O cangaceiro* came too late, and the company went bankrupt in 1954.

The transnational character of Latin American melodrama involves not only the border crossing of directors, cameramen and stars, but also of music, a phenomenon that is especially evident in the *cabareteras* (cabaret-brothel films). Argentine Carlos Gardel's 1920s tangos, marketed throughout Latin America, Europe, and the United States, inspired a series of silent features by Argentine director Agustín Ferreyra that often were accompanied by live tango orchestras. In 1936 Ferreyra cast Libertad Lamarque as Luisita in the melodrama *Ayúdame a vivir* (Help Me to Live), which launched her career as an actor and as one of the world's great tango performers. In the 1940s Lamarque had even greater success in Mexico, where she became the country's first female tango songstress, alongside Mexican *charro* sensations Pedro Infante, Jorge Negrete, and Tito Guízar, who also sang tangos. In one of her best films, Lamarque paired with Mexican composer Agustín Lara and with Infante in Miguel Zacarías's 1952 melodrama *Ansiedad* (Anxiety). The plot involves a curious love triangle: two men from different social classes (both played by Infante) battle over the same woman, not realizing that they are actually long-separated twin brothers. Lara and Lamarque would collaborate on numerous songs with wrenching titles such as "Arráncame la vida" (Tear My Life from Me). Beloved by Latin American audiences, Lamarque became known as "The Bride of America" and had a successful later career as a suffering mother and grandmother in Mexican soap operas, or *telenovelas*.

As popular as the Argentine tango were the Afro-Cuban congas, mambos, and, in particular, rumbas (Mora 85). Cuban-born Ninón Sevilla was famous for her lively *rumbera* roles in postwar *cabaretera* films such as Alberto Gout's *Aventurera* (Adventuress, 1949) and *Sensualidad* (Sensuality, 1951) and in Emilio Fernández's *Víctimas del pecado* (Victims of Sin, 1950). Gilberto Perez's essay for this volume makes the important point that fallen women in these melodramas were not necessarily weak or downtrodden, and his detailed discussion of Sevilla's feisty rumbera character in *Aventurera* provides a striking example. Brazilian music and Portuguese lyrics were also adopted by Mexican melodramas. For example, Sevilla performs the song "Chiquita Bacana" in Portuguese as part of her *Aventurera* repertoire. The equally celebrated (and also Cuban-born) rumbera María Antonieta Pons sings "Aquarela do Brasil" ("Brazil"), by Brazilian composer Ary Barroso, to love interest Pedro Armendáriz in *Konga roja* (Red Konga, 1943), by the Mexican director Alejandro Galindo. The film concerns a nightclub romance in the midst of labor union strife at a banana packing plant (124–25).

Diegetic music is fundamental to Latin American melodrama, and, as I have indicated, the spectacular dance numbers and stirring vocals in these films have few equivalents in Hollywood pictures of the type.[9] Zacarías's *Ansiedad* is an excellent example of what is often called the "musical melodrama."[10] In addition to a conventional nondiegetic score, the film contains eleven musical numbers performed by Libertad Lamarque and Pedro Infante, including five songs composed by Agustín Lara and two tangos by Carlos Gardel. The movie shifts back and forth between scenes of the suffering mother (Lamarque) and musical interludes that feature Lamarque and Infante as local theater singers. A dance number that accompanies one of Lamarque's folkloric performances is rather like a low-budget Busby Berkeley performance, complete with stylized peasant costumes.[11] Most of the film's songs, such as "Mujer" (Woman) and "Amor de mis amores" (Love of My Loves), are about romance and suffering, although two numbers performed on the town's theater stage are unusual for their comedic and boisterous qualities. Cuco Sánchez's "Ando muy borracho" (I'm Very Drunk) features Infante and a mariachi band in a cantina; Salvador Flores's "Ingrata perfida" (Treacherous Ingrate) portrays Infante and Lamarque as a wrangling hillbilly couple.

Alberto Gout's *Sensualidad*, which concerns the fatal consequences of *amour fou*, has five musical interludes, two of which are unusual for their hybridity. In "Dixie Mambo," Sevilla does a burlesque-style striptease to rumba and mambo beats; in the more spectacular "Se—você" (If—You), Sevilla performs a Carmen Miranda impersonation replete with Portuguese lyrics, rolling eyes, a bare midriff, and a headdress adorned with two large pineapples. In the middle of the performance, she disappears in a puff of smoke and reappears wearing a more extravagant outfit with bunches of bananas on her headdress and skirt. The title song, "Sensualidad," appears in one of the most effective sequences: one moment Aurora (Sevilla) is dancing with her older lover Alejandro (Fernando Soler) as the song plays on a record in her small, dingy apartment; the music continues without interruption as we cut to a shot of the couple sometime later dancing to an orchestra in a fancy nightclub. (In addition to the Latin music, the club scene also features North American jazz, which serves as background music for tense and emotional dialogue that advances the plot).

Gilda Abreu directed one of Brazil's most famous musical-style melodramas, *O ébrio* (The Drunkard, 1946), featuring popular tenor Vicente Celestino, who was married to Abreu and whom she later eulogized in a 1977 documentary, *Canção de amor* (Song of Love). In *O ébrio,* the eponymous protagonist goes from rags to riches (he becomes a popular radio singer *and* a celebrated neurosurgeon) and then drops back to rags and alcoholism after he is abandoned by his fickle wife (Alice Archembeau). An unusually eclectic melodrama that combines drawing-room theater with slapstick comedy, the film features several songs by Celestino. In the title number, "O ébrio," he sings a chronicle of his downfall for a group of elegantly dressed socialites who are slumming in a tough bar. He is rewarded with a drink and almost immediately afterward is unexpectedly reunited with his wife, who has been abandoned by her lover and who happens to enter the bar at that moment looking for menial work. Their chance encounter is the essence of melodramatic coincidence, accompanied by an emotional coming together that gives way to cathartic tears. The chance reunion, however, does not lead to the typical happy ending. Although the drunkard forgives his wife, he refuses to reconcile and leaves the bar with a tramp friend to continue his downward spiral.

In addition to music and musical performers, Latin American melodramas also gave a great deal of attention to historical events, in particular, the nineteenth-century struggles against colonial oppression. Such films usually involved Manichaean characterizations and emotional upheavals between men and women who were in love but were divided by warfare, politics, or social class. Paula Didier-Félix and Andrés Levinson's essay in this collection examines these and other typically melodramatic themes in a film by the Argentine director Lucas Demare, *La guerra gaucha* (The Gaucho War, 1940), which concerns Argentina's struggle for independence.

The Mexican revolution was also a major event in numerous melodramas. As historians regularly point out, the revolution itself had been filmed and shown as newsreel footage in movie houses; Pancho Villa even signed a contract with Mutual Films Company of the United States in which he agreed to wage battles in daylight for the benefit of the camera, and he reenacted battle scenes that were deemed insufficiently dramatic. Critic Margarita de Orellana describes Pancho Villa as the first actor of the revolutionary film—a star whose international fame ultimately led to biographical films in Mexico and in Hollywood (*Artes,* 88–89). Villa could also be described as the father of revolution-themed melodramas. Fuentes's *El compadre Mendoza, El prisionero trece* (Prisoner Thirteen, 1933) and *¡Vámonos con Pancho Villa!* (1935), which concern patriotism, disillusionment, and martyrdom, are some of the earliest and best of these. Later examples include Fernández's classic *Enamorada,* which features Pedro Armendáriz and María Félix, and Roberto Gavaldón's *La escondida* (The Hidden One, 1955), in which Armendáriz reappears as the handsome peasant–revolutionary leader and Félix as a peasant-turned-courtesan.

Still other national film industries in Latin America turned to history as a source for melodrama. Among Bolivia's first movies was José María Velasco Maidana's silent epic *Wara Wara* (Star, 1930), which concerned the Aymarans' resistance to a romance between their princess Wara Wara (Juanita Tallansier) and a Spanish officer (Maidana) during the Incan conquest. Two years later, Bolivian directors Marío Camacho and José Jiménez made the silent feature *Hacia la gloria* (Toward Glory, 1932), which was about an abandoned child who grows up to be a pilot and falls in love with a woman who is revealed to be his sister; the drama takes place during the skirmishes between Paraguay and Bolivia that precipitated the Chaco War (1932–35). In 1956 Jorge Ruiz and Augusto Roca joined forces to make a semidocumentary melodrama about warring Chipaya and Aymaran communities in Bolivia. *Vuelve Sebastiana* (Come Back, Sebastiana) is the story of a young Chipaya (Sebastiana Kespi) who leaves her village to live among the enemy Aymarans. Her grandfather (Esteban Lupi) follows her and beseeches her to return to her community, but she refuses, and he dies on the way home. The partly recovered Colombian film *Garras de ouro* (Dawn of Justice, 1928) by P. P. Jambrina, is the story of a love affair between a U.S. journalist and a Colombian woman against the backdrop of U.S. military intervention that led to the building of the Panama Canal.[12]

In Brazil, Carmen Santos directed *Inconfidência Mineira* (1948), which is about the failed 1789 attempt by Minas Gerais rebels to overthrow the Portuguese monarchy and its impact on the love lives of the condemned poet-revolutionaries. The sixteenth-century cultural encounter between the European and the Indian had reappeared as the topic for José de Alencar's 1865 novel *Iracema,* which, like his earlier *O guarani,* was repeatedly adapted. Perhaps the most successful version was Vittorino Cardinale and Gino Talamo's 1949 remake, which starred Ilka Soares as Iracema and Anselmo Duarte as Martim. The stars married shortly thereafter and became Brazil's top celebrity couple for most of the following decade (*Dicionário* 437). The 1972 epic *Independência ou morte* (Independence or Death), directed by Oswaldo and Aníbal Massaini, took its title from the famous proclamation by Prince Regente Pedro I that liberated Brazil from Portuguese rule in 1822. Against the background of the liberation movement, the film tells of the love story between Pedro I (Tarcísio Meira), who was married to Dona Leopoldina of Austria, and Domitila de Castro Couto e Mello (Glória Menezes), who was also married and whom Pedro raised to the title of Marquise of Santos.

Although the majority of Latin America's historical melodramas feature revolutionary figures who are associated with liberation and with other progressive movements, Cid Vasconcelos's contribution to this book discusses the way a few Brazilian melodramas advanced Getúlio Vargas's agenda for women during his Estado Novo (New State) dictatorship. In films such as Adhemar Gonzaga's *Romance proibido* (Forbidden Romance, 1944), women are still victims of their passions, but they forestall and even sacrifice love in order to fulfill the nation's call for educators and mediators between the poor and the middle classes. Melodramas were also inspired by the teachings of the Catholic faith and by Catholic rituals that focus on the centrality and sanctity of the family. The virgin and the prostitute, the suffering mother and the all-powerful father, the sacrament of marriage and the sin of unholy alliances, self-sacrifice and martyrdom rather than personal satisfaction and gain, are only a few of the character types, themes, and moral lessons treated in the genre. Emilio Fernández was particularly effective in summoning up the struggle between good and evil in rural (sometimes called indigenous) melodramas such as *María Candelaria,* in which Edenic peasants in the countryside valiantly resist malevolent village types.[13] Gabriel Figueroa, who filmed *María Candelaria, Enamorada* and other Fernández films, was unparalleled in his creation of a paradisiacal rural landscape that was no less visually stunning than the baroque cathedral interiors that appear in *Enamorada* and *La malquerida* (Passion Flower, 1949), the latter concerning the tyranny of a stepfather (Pedro Armendáriz) over his wife (Dolores del Río) and stepdaughter (Columba Domínguez). Figueroa's domestic and jailhouse interiors were often decorated with crucifixes and other religious iconography, and he was especially adept at filming shadows from windowpanes and prison bars that stretched across rooms to form a cross.

Fernández's *Río escondido* (Hidden River, 1947) is a paean to Catholicism in the form of a village priest (Domingo Soler) who supports and defends a schoolteacher (María Félix) sent by the president to educate poor indigenous children in the countryside. An image of the veiled Félix with a child in her arms and a large, rough-hewn cross in the background melds the Virgin and Child with the cross of Calvary. A large crucifix with an El Greco–style bleeding Christ becomes the centerpiece of a village processional, and Figueroa's shots of a landscape barren except for a tree with two massive dead limbs also give a spiritual atmosphere to the film. Here and elsewhere Fernández and Figueroa imbue nature with solemnity and religiosity.

The sanctity of the mother-child relationship is repeatedly explored in melodramas, as is the theme of the abandoned child who is found and raised by a surrogate mother. The Bolivian film *Hacia la gloria* evokes the story of Moses in its plot concerning a baby left on a riverbank. A darker urban version appears in Fernández's *Víctimas del pecado,* which is about a baby left in a trash can who is retrieved just prior to the arrival of a garbage truck. In Zacarías's *Ansiedad,* a mother (Libertad Lamarque) takes in an abandoned child but also must give up one of her own desperately ill babies to a family that has the financial means to treat and save him.

Like the popular musical comedy, or *chanchada,* as it was known in Brazil, the melodrama came under heavy attack in the late 1950s by young left-wing filmmakers and intellectuals, who criticized it as sentimental, Hollywood-style entertainment that ignored many of the sociopolitical and economic realities of Latin America.[14] Postwar Italian neorealism's portrayal of the urban proletariat had a particularly strong impact in Brazil, where director Nelson Pereira dos Santos initiated a Cinema Novo, "New Cinema," with the neorealist productions *Rio, 40 Graus* (Rio, 100 Degrees, 1955), which concerned children from a Rio *favela* (slum), and *Vidas Secas* (Barren Lives, 1963), which concerned rural migrants and grinding poverty in the drought-ridden Northeast. The desire for a socially responsible left-wing cinema grew throughout Latin America after the 1959 Cuban Revolution, resulting in a range of radical, antimelodramatic films, including *La hora de los hornos* (The Hour of the Furnaces, 1968) by Fernando Solanas and Octavio Getino, *Yawar mallku* (Blood of the Condor, 1969) by Jorge Sanjinés, *La batalla de Chile* (The Battle of Chile, 1975) by Patricio Guzmán, *Memorias del subdesarrollo* (Memories of Underdevelopment, 1968) by Tomás Gutiérrez Alea, *Reed, México insurgente* (Reed: Insurgent Mexico, 1971) by Paul Leduc, and *Deus e o diabo na terra do sol* (Black God, White Devil, 1963) and *Antônio das Mortes* (1969) by Glauber Rocha. Despite their lack of popularity at the local box office, these and other productions won acclaim as well as prizes at Cannes and other major international festivals, and they remain among

Latin America's best-known films today. In my own essay in this volume, I show that despite their different politics and audiences, Cinema Novo and melodramas now reside alongside one another in Latin America's cinematic archive, and, as Nelson Pereira dos Santos's *Cinema de lágrimas* (1995) suggests, Cinema Novo films such as Rocha's *Deus e o diabo na terra do sol* can provoke emotional responses on the order of those elicited by the very melodramas that they reacted against and often critiqued.

Despite the desire of New Cinema filmmakers to create an "authentic" Latin American cinema, audiences preferred melodramas and musical comedies to neorealist films and political critiques. In Mexico, Emilio Fernández continued to make movies about idealized peasant lives, including *Pueblito* (Little Town, 1961), *La Choca* (Clash, 1973), and *Zona roja* (Red Zone, 1975). In *Los hermanos de Hierro* (Hierro's Brothers, 1961), Ismael Rodríguez cast melodrama star Columba Domínguez as the suffering mother who encourages her sons (Antonio Aguilar and Julio Alemán) to avenge the murder of their father (Pedro Armendáriz), and in *La soldadera* (The Woman Soldier, 1966), José Bolaños used the Mexican revolution as the setting for the emotional travails of a young villager (Silvia Pinal). In Bolivia, Jorge Ruiz made his first dramatic feature, *La vertiente* (The Watershed, 1959), which concerned a love affair between a schoolteacher (Rosario del Río) and an alligator hunter (Raúl Vaca Pereira) in the tropical interior. Transnational collaboration on melodramas also continued, as exemplified by such films as *María* (1972), a Mexican-Colombian co-production that was directed by Chilean-born Tito Davison, photographed by Figueroa, and adapted from Colombian writer Isaacs Jorge's nineteenth-century novel about sweethearts (Taryn Power and Fernando Allende) separated by distance and illness.

In Brazil, where melodrama also thrived, bandit films inspired by Barreto's *O cangaceiro* were especially popular. Wilson Silva's 1962 *Nordeste sangrento* (Bloody Northeast) was one of many *cangaço* (banditry) films to feature dramatic shoot-outs alongside stories of tortured love in the backlands. *Um ramo para Luísa* (A Flowering Bough for Luisa, 1964) by J. B. Tanko is a story about incest between a brother (Jece Valadão) and sister (Vera Viana) that ends in tragedy; in 1963 Tanko had adapted Nelson Rodrigues's play *Asfalto selvagem* (Savage Asphalt), which also explores interfamilial sexual relations. As Ismail Xavier explains in his essay for this volume, Rodrigues's complex psychological portraits of middle-class desires and sexual repression became popular cinematic vehicles for exploring and critiquing the patriarchal family unit. But around this same time in Mexico, an antimelodramatic critique emerged that was centered on the patriarchal family. In his contribution to this anthology, Marvin D'Lugo analyzes Luis Alcoriza's *Mecánica nacional* (National Mechanic, 1971), a film that satirizes certain melodramatic themes including that of the iconic suffering mother, who in this case is played by none other than the diva of maternal angst, Sara García.

Since the 1960s the telenovela has been the principal purveyor of melodrama in the region. In 1964 Brazil's TV Tupi adapted a 1950s radionovela to make the highly popular *O direito de nascer* (The Right to Be Born), the story of a single mother (Nathália Timburg) in early-twentieth-century Havana whose baby is despised by the father's family, especially the grandfather (Elísio de Albuquerque). Fearing for the baby's safety, the mother's servant (Isaura Bruno) flees with the child and raises him while the disconsolate mother enters a convent and becomes a nun. Despite TV Tupi's auspicious entry into the telenovela industry, neither it nor any other network could rival TV Globo, which has dominated the Brazilian marketplace with novelas about middle-class Cariocan domestic crises, as well as stories based on popular literary works. Among the most popular in the 1970s were *Gabriela* (1975), based on Jorge Amado's best-selling novel about Bahia's African-Brazilian community, and *A escrava Isaura* (The Slave Isaura, 1977), an adaptation of Bernardo Guimarães's nineteenth-century antislavery novel about plantation society. Unable to compete with Globo's polished productions, Sílvio Santos's STB television station, in Rio de Janeiro, broadcast more conservative and lachrymose novelas that were originally made in Mexico, while producing its own melodramatic soaps based on historical events. Both became successful with STB's working- and lower-middle-class audiences as well as with other viewers who had tired of the nudity and violence typical of TV series of the period.[15] In fact, Globo has often had difficulty exporting novelas to other Latin American countries and elsewhere because of nudity. In the meantime, Mexico has been producing novelas that are every bit as melodramatic as their golden-age" film predecessors, with evocative titles such as *Lágrimas amargas* (Bitter Tears, 1967), *Los ricos también lloran* (The Rich Cry, Too, 1979), and *Te amaré en silencio* (I'll Love You in Silence, 2002).

Although fewer in number and more expensive to produce, the miniseries is the preferred vehicle for aficionados of TV melodramas. In her essay Catherine L. Benamou discusses the broad reach of the telemelodrama industry in Spanish and examines its reception among Latinos in the United States. Among recent Globo productions, *Os Maias* (The Maia Family, 2002) was one of the best, although its slow-paced narrative did not appeal to all viewers. Based on Eça de Querioz's epic saga about three generations of an upper-class Portuguese family, the plot involves nefarious social and political alliances, doomed love affairs, incest, and suicide. The soundtrack by the Portuguese group Madredeus, with its moaning voices and crescendos, provides the perfect emotional accompaniment for the tale.

In 1998 Globo entered the feature film industry and to date has co-produced nearly one hundred movies, including the popular musical melodrama *Os dois filhos de Francisco* (The Two Sons of Francisco, 2005). Other projects included Jayme Monjardim's *Olga* (2004), a dramatization of the life of German-born Jew Olga Benário (Camila Morgado), who accompanied Brazil's left-wing "Cavalier of Hope," Luís Carlos Prestes (Caco Ciocler), back to Brazil from his visit to the Soviet Union. The plot concerns their tragic love affair prior to World War II, focusing on the couple's persecution and imprisonment by Vargas's right-wing regime and, despite Olga's pregnancy, her deportation to Germany, where she died in a concentration camp.

In 2007 Globo produced a film adaptation of Eça de Queiroz's *O primo Basílio* (My Cousin Basilio, 1878), a book sometimes referred to as the Portuguese version of *Madame Bovary*. Directed by Daniel Filho, the film takes place in São Paulo during the 1950s as opposed to nineteenth-century Lisbon, which was the setting of Eça's novel. It focuses on the adulterous relationship between Luísa (Débora Falabella), a bored housewife, and her visiting cousin Basílio (Fabiano Assunção). When the maid Juliana (Glória Pires) discovers their love letters to one another, she blackmails Luísa, who ultimately commits suicide. It is interesting that Filho had initially adapted the novel as a miniseries in 1988, and there are obvious similarities between that series and the film. In this case, the series was acclaimed by both the critics and the public, whereas the film's reception was lukewarm. The major criticism of the film was that it resembled a telenovela.

In adapting *O primo Basílio,* Filho was actually remaking a work that had been made in Mexico in 1934 starring Andrea Palma, who had just finished filming her famous role as a prostitute in *La mujer del puerto*. Mexican director Carlos Carrera's 2002 adaptation of Eça's novel *O crime do Padre Amaro* (The Crime of Padre Amaro, 1875) emphasizes the enduring success not only of Eça but also of melodrama as a cinematic (and televisual) commodity. At least one critic praised Carrera's film for unraveling like a "quintessential Mexican *telenovela*" (González n.p.), with emotional build-ups and steamy sex scenes involving Amaro, a village priest (Gael García Bernal), and his young parishioner Amelia (Ana Claudia Talancón). Had the film, like the novel, been set in nineteenth-century Portugal, perhaps the Catholic Church in Mexico would not have attacked it. (The film is actually a softer, more romantic version of the novel, in which Amaro is a predator-schemer and the one responsible for Amelia's death.) Thrust into the spotlight by the church's condemnation, the film became a box-office hit in Mexico—more successful than Alfonso Cuarón's impressive but unmelodramatic hit *Y tu mamá también* (2001).

Perhaps because we are living in an increasingly emotionally fraught world, melodramas continue to play well with audiences, whether on the large or the small screen. If not exactly an escape from the day-to-day, they provide succor in their representations of small personal triumphs in the midst of disappointments and suffering. As Mariana Baltar discusses in her article for this collection, even the documentary, which we tend to associate with objectivity and truth, is not immune from the melodramatic imagination. What was once described as a kind of movie for weeping in the dark is today a much larger phenomenon that includes not only film but also television series, broadcast news, and the tabloid press. Melodrama can still make us cry, but it is much less a domestic affair than a public gestalt.

The high modernists of the interwar years and the committed leftist filmmakers of the 1960s were understandably reluctant to accept the mass appeal of melodramatic art, which often makes the world seem more glamorous or more poetically sordid than it actually is, which creates simple distinctions between heroes and villains and which manipulates its audience into believing that social evils can be overcome through the overflow of individual passion, pathos, and good instincts. But the pleasures of melodrama are nonetheless real, and the form of melodrama is capable of more positive effects than certain puritanical critics of the Left or the Right have recognized. Although melodrama is the populist mode par excellence, and although the historical record shows that it can be used for bad or dubious ends, in some of its manifestations it also has the ability to bring women and other groups who have lacked social power into communities of emotional solidarity and strength. The history of the form is rich, and its complexity is evident in essays collected in this book, most which were written expressly for it. Taken together, they give us a sense of melodrama's range and variety and help us understand why it has been the most durable form of popular art in the Latin American cinema.

## Notes

1. *La mujer del puerto* was based on the story "Le port" by Guy de Maupassant, which concerns prostitution and incest. Cultural critic Carlos Monsiváis refers to the period spanning roughly from 1935 to 1955 as the golden age melodrama ("Mythologies" 117). He adds: "In fact, this was a 'golden age' not for the cinema, but for

the public, who, among other things, trusted that idols would explain how to survive in a bewildering age of modernization. . . . Devotees of comedies and melodramas were not seeking to 'dream,' but to learn skills, to lose inhibitions, to suffer and be consoled in style, painlessly to envy the elites, happily to be resigned to poverty, to laugh at stereotypes that ridiculed them, to understand how they belonged to the nation" (117–18). Unless stated otherwise, page numbers given in the text refer to the special issue of *Artes de México,* Winter 1990.

2. English translations appear in the publication.

3. The argument for melodrama as a displacement of social anxiety onto stylistic "excess" can be found in "Minnelli and Melodrama" by Geoffrey Nowel-Smith and "Tales of Sound and Fury" by Thomas Elsaesser. These essays and more specifically feminist arguments, such as "Notes on Sirk and Melodrama" by Laura Mulvey and "The 'Woman's Film'" by Mary Ann Doane, are collected in Christine Gledhill's *Home Is Where the Heart Is* (London: BFI, 1987). Marcia Landy's edited collection *Imitations of Life* (Detroit: Wayne State University Press, 1991), includes other studies, among them Raymond Durgnat's seminal 1951 essay "Ways of Melodrama." For an important study of how melodrama is constructed in a different discursive context, see Barbara Klinger, *Melodrama and Meaning: History, Culture, and the Films of Douglas Sirk* (Bloomington: Indiana University Press, 1994).

4. In her book *Mexican National Cinema,* Andrea Noble describes Mexican melodrama as a "ubiquitous film mode with transhistorical significance" (96). Julianne Burton-Carvajal's essay "Mexican Melodrama of Patriarchy" provides an insightful commentary on the different varieties or subgenres of melodrama in Mexico.

5. The period from 1908 to 1911, often called the golden age of Brazilian cinema, was hastened to a close by the merging interests of local cinemas with foreign companies, resulting in the prioritized distribution and exhibition of foreign films rather than Brazilian products and the rapid decline of the local industry. Despite this decline, *O guarani's* popularity as a "foundational fiction" about the cultural encounter between a European maiden and a Brazilian Indian warrior, not to mention Gomes's operatic version, which opened to raves at Milan's La Scala, made it an attractive and commercially viable project to remake in 1916, 1920, and 1926. The 1916 film has been lost. According to Capellaro's son, the 1926 version was funded in part by Paramount Pictures and was the first co-production made in Brazil (*Dicionário* 394). The popularity of *O guarani* has yet to abate, as suggested by the 1996 adaptation, which was the third version to appear since 1950.

6. An Italian immigrant, Pedro Sambarino, directed the first Bolivian picture, *Corazón Aymara* (Aymara Heart, 1925), which focuses on a woman's suspected marital infidelity and ends in her condemnation and death. In an essay about silent cinema, the critic Aurelio de los Reyes writes about the importance of early Italian art cinema to the development of melodrama in Mexico. He draws comparison between Piero Fosco's torrid love story *Il fuoco* (The Fire, 1916) and films such as Ezequiel

Carrasco's *La luz* (The Light, 1917) and Mimí Derba's *La tigresa* (The Tigress, 1917) (72–73).

7. In 1941, Mexico made twenty-two films to Argentina's thirty; in 1942, the ratio was forty-seven to fifty-six; in 1943, it was seventy to less than thirty (Pineda and Paranaguá 33–34). The U.S. denial of raw film stock to Argentina had a devastating effect on its film industry. For more information on this topic, see Falicov.

8. A famous tango singer, Libertad Lamarque made more than twenty films in Argentina, beginning with her breakout performance in *Ayúdame a vivir* (Help Me to Live, 1936), a melodrama that she herself wrote about a young woman who marries to get away from her family, falls ill, is falsely accused of killing her husband's lover, and narrowly escapes imprisonment. In 1946 she left Argentina to pursue a movie career in the more stable and prosperous Mexican industry, where she starred in melodramas such as *La mujer sin lágrimas* (Woman Without Tears, 1951), *Acuérdate de vivir* (Remember to Live, 1954) and *La Mujer X* (Madame X, 1955).

9. Another possible exception is *Gilda,* with its song-and-dance numbers by Rita Hayworth.

10. The existence of the Latin American musical melodrama tends to contradict Thomas Elsaesser's argument about the "sublimation" of musicals (and action films) in domestic and family melodramas ("Sound and Fury" 76).

11. Lamarque dons a long set of braids for many of her songs, often looking more like a brunette Brunnhilde than a María Candelaria–style peasant.

12. An image from the partly recovered film shows a character dressed as Uncle Sam reaching out and tipping the scales of justice. The U.S. State Department intervened in the film's initial distribution and exhibition, and it wasn't until the mid-1980s that footage was found and shown.

13. Fernández starred as an Indian peasant in Carlos Navarro's *Janitzio* (1934), a film that shaped his vision of Mexico as a director.

14. A widely cited example of the left-wing critique is Enrique Colina and Daniel Díaz Torres's "Ideology of Melodrama in Old Latin American Cinema," which was translated and reprinted in Zuzana Pick's *Latin American Filmmakers and the Third World* (Ottawa: Carleton University, 1978).

15. For further information about the Brazilian telenovela, see Hamburger, La Pastina, López, and Straubhaar.

## Works Cited

*Artes de México: Nueva época. Revisión del cine mexicano* 10 (Winter 1990).

Barnard, Timothy, and Peter Rist, eds. *South American Cinema: A Critical Filmography, 1915–1994*. Austin: University of Texas Press, 1996.

Brooks, Peter. *The Melodramatic Imagination: Balzac, Henry James, Melodrama and the Mode of Excess*. New York: Columbia University Press, 1985.

Burton-Carvajal, Julianne. "Mexican Melodramas of Patriarchy." In *Framing Latin*

*American Cinema: Contemporary Critical Perspectives.* Ed. Ann Marie Stock. Hispanic Issues, vol. 15. Minneapolis: University of Minnesota Press, 1997. 186–234.

*Dicionário de filmes brasileiros.* Ed. Antônio Leão da Silva Neto. São Paulo: Futuro Mundo Gráfica and Editora Ltda., 2000.

Elsaesser, Thomas. "Tales of Sound and Fury: Observations on the Family Melodrama." In *Home Is Where the Heart Is: Studies in Melodrama and the Woman's Film.* Ed. Christine Gledhill. London: British Film Institute, 1987. 43–69.

Falicov, Tamara. "Hollywood's Rogue Neighbor: The Argentine Film Industry During the Good Neighbor Policy." *The Americas* 63, no. 2 (October 2006): 245–60.

García, Gustavo. "Melodrama: The Passion Machine." In *Mexican Cinema.* Ed. Paulo Antonio Paranaguá. Trans. Ana M. López. London: British Film Institute; Mexico: IMCINE, 1995. 153–62.

González, Ed. "The Perfect Crime." www.slantmagazine.com/film/film_review .asp?ID=548.

Hamburger, Esther. *O Brasil antenado: A sociedade da novela.* Rio de Janeiro: Jorge Zahar Editor, 2005.

La Pastina, Antonio C. "The Sexual Other in Brazilian Television: Public and Institutional Reception of Sexual Difference." *International Journal of Cultural Studies* 5 (2002): 83–99.

López, Ana M. "The Melodrama in Latin America: Films, Telenovelas, and the Currency of a Popular Form." In *Imitations of Life: A Reader on Film and Television Melodrama.* Ed. Marsha Landy. Detroit: Wayne State University Press, 1991. 596–606.

Monsiváis, Carlos. "Mythologies." In *Mexican Cinema.* Ed. Paulo Antonio Paranaguá. Trans. Ana M. López. London: British Film Institute; Mexico: IMCINE, 1995. 117–27.

Mora, Carlos. *Mexican Cinema: Reflections of a Society, 1896–1988.* Rev. ed. Berkeley: University of California Press, 1989.

Noble, Andrea. *Mexican National Cinema.* London: Routledge, 2005.

Oroz, Silvia. *Melodrama: O cinema de lágrimas da América Latina.* Rio de Janeiro: Ministério de Cultura/FUNARTE, 1999.

Pineda, Alexandra, and Paulo Antonio Paranaguá. "Mexico and Its Cinema." In *Mexican Cinema.* Ed. Paulo Antonio Paranaguá. Trans. Ana M. López. London: British Film Institute; Mexico City: IMCINE, 1995. 15–62.

Reyes, Aurelio de los. "The Silent Cinema." In *Mexican Cinema.* Ed. Paulo Antonio Paranaguá. Trans. Ana M. López. London: British Film Institute; Mexico City: IMCINE, 1995. 63–78.

Straubhaar, Joseph. "The Development of Telenovelas as the Pre-eminent Form of Popular Culture in Brazil." *Studies in Latin American Popular Culture* 1 (1982): 138–50.

# 1

# Melodrama of the
# Spirited Woman
## *Aventurera*

**GILBERTO PEREZ**

Everybody speaks of melodrama, often disparagingly, but it's not easy to define it. The definition I heard as a kid was that melodrama makes the characters subordinate to the plot, but when I read the *Poetics* I saw that Aristotle prescribed the same thing for tragedy. Some would define melodrama by its play on our feelings, by the intensity of emotion that it elicits, but that again scarcely distinguishes it from tragedy. Looking to the audience, others would distinguish melodrama as popular art from tragedy as elite art, but then few tragedies would make the grade besides the courtly French ones, and Shakespeare's would be melodramas. Once I asked an older colleague at the school where I teach what the difference was between tragedy and melodrama, and he answered: "If you don't like it, it's melodrama." Still others would say that the crux of melodrama is a simplified moral scheme, an unqualified conflict between good and evil, virtue and villainy, but look, for example, at *Stella Dallas,* a melodrama if there ever was one, and you will find no villains.

If, like tragedy, melodrama tells a sad story, often enough, like comedy, it comes to a happy ending. It should be considered not only in relation to tragedy but also to comedy.[1] Comedy and tragedy are ancient, whereas melodrama, Peter Brooks maintains, "appears to be a peculiarly modern form" whose origins "can be accurately located within the context of the French Revolution and its aftermath" (14). But a form arising from a break with tradition may still have links to traditional forms. This is how John G. Cawelti describes the melodrama of the late eighteenth century:

> The central figure ... was usually a virtuous young lady of some lower or ambiguous status—village maiden, orphan, daughter of parents in reduced circumstances—who was pursued by a male character of higher status and dubious intentions, a figure of aristocratic, erotic, financial, and social power; in other words, some form of the stereotypical squire with curling mustaches. The sorely beset heroine commonly loved a more worthy and innocent young man, who was himself enmeshed in status difficulties, often because his true parentage was concealed for one reason or another. This primary triangle was the essence of melodrama and was capable of two major permutations, corresponding loosely to comic and tragic modes of action. In the first case, the heroine resisted the entreaties and threats of the villain and was ultimately united in marriage with the noble young man. ... In the tragic melodrama, the heroine succumbed to the villain's plots. ... The single most important outcome of any melodrama was the marriage of the virtuous heroine to the right man—or, in the tragic version of melodrama, the degradation and death of the fallen heroine. (33–34)

This largely remains, more than a century later, the plot of Griffith's *Way Down East*—except that the Lillian Gish heroine, even though she succumbs to the villain, nonetheless abides in her virtue, narrowly escapes death, and marries the noble hero. The tragic and comic modes of melodrama that Cawelti differentiates come together in this movie. They are not so far apart, after all: the desired outcome, marriage to the right partner, is in both cases the same. And that is also the desired outcome of comedy, what Aristotle might call the final cause of the plot. Whether comic or tragic, melodrama can be said to be in that way essentially comic.

The melodramatic plot that Cawelti outlines recalls the plot of New Comedy, in which young lovers meet with opposition to their union and, through developments as contrived as those in melodrama, get the better of the blocking figures in their way and reach the happy ending of marriage. There are differences, of course. Neither virtue nor villainy is as heightened in comedy as it is in melodrama. The heroine's virtue is not so crucial in comedy, the young woman herself usually not so central, the blocking figures not so sinister as the villain of melodrama. Marriage in comedy is not the matter of life and death that it is in melodrama. But it is a matter of life: comedy seems to have originated in rituals of fertility, and the concluding union of the young lovers celebrates procreation. And more than a personal affair, their marriage is a matter of life in society: like the melodramatic villain, the comedic blocking figures enjoy social prominence and power, and the young lovers' triumph represents a renewal of the social order. Tearful like tragedy, melodrama, even when it ends unhappily, shares with comedy a reaching toward a happy marriage implying a larger social happiness. *Way Down East* ends not just with a marriage but with three at once. After the awful winter storm that almost kills the heroine on an frozen river, in this communal happy ending spring triumphs over winter as in the ancient ritual at the root of comedy.

Comedy, as Northrop Frye says, is about incorporation into society, and tragedy about isolation from it. Melodrama unstably combines isolation and incorporation. Much of it takes place in privacy, within closed doors, and yet no form has been more social: what would be kept inside always reflects what's going on outside. A bourgeois form—whose original villain, in the days of bourgeois struggle with aristocratic rule, was a figure of the aristocracy—melodrama expresses the contradictions of bourgeois thinking, the individualist emphasis on privacy coming into continual tension with the public business, the capacity to determine social existence, of a once-rising and now-ruling class.

Like *Way Down East, Aventurera* is a melodrama whose heroine succumbs to the villain yet marries the hero, a fallen woman who bounces back. And bounce she does, Elena, a cabaret dancer of quick beat and fast ways, tough and loud and fiery, an angry tigress ready to pounce and take revenge on those who wronged her—a far cry from the demure and dignified Lillian Gish, who has her own strength but not this indomitable energy. Elena is portrayed by Ninón Sevilla, a Cuban dancer and actress who became a movie star in Mexico, where *Aventurera* was made in 1949, part of a cycle of melodramas called cabareteras, or cabaret pictures, and a very popular one. Alberto Gout directed; Alvaro Custodio, like Buñuel an exile from fascist Spain employed in the Mexican film industry at that flourishing time, wrote the story and co-wrote the screenplay; and several noted musicians participated: the composer and lyricist Agustín Lara, the crooner Pedro Vargas, Ana María González, Pérez Prado, and the Trio Los Panchos. So salient are the musical numbers that the movie has been called a compound of melodrama and musical, but better to call it a melodrama in the original sense of the word, a drama with music.

In the city of Chihuahua, Elena is the daughter of a respectable bourgeois family and such a good girl that when her dance class lets out early she goes straight home, where she finds her mother kissing Ramón, the chauffeur. Elena walks away appalled, thinking of her loving father and her betraying mother, who now runs off with Ramón. "I'll never forgive her," she says. "Ramón is a scoundrel. If some day I come across him I'm capable of killing him"—at which point the sound of a gunshot is heard, the sound of her father killing himself. All this happens as quickly and disconcertingly as in a dream. Melodrama, as Eric Bentley put it, is the naturalism of the dream life (Bentley 1964, 205).

Now we move to Ciudad Juárez, where Elena is on her own. Practically an orphan, certainly in reduced circumstances, she fits Cawelti's description of the melodramatic virtuous young lady. She has a succession of jobs, which she quits because men keep accosting her, and then she runs into Lucio (Tito Junco), a shady character, good-looking and mustachioed, not the aristocrat of old melodrama but a lowlife. He promises her a job with a woman named Rosaura (Andrea Palma) who needs a secretary, he says, but who actually owns a cabaret that doubles as a whorehouse and who by deceit and force enlists Elena into her dual establishment. "You won't get out of here," she tells her. "Whoever enters this business, hear me well, never leaves it." Much later we find out—it is the biggest surprise in a film full of twists, coincidences, and improbable turns of plot—that Rosaura has another life as an aristocrat, or the

Ninón Sevilla and Andrea Palma in *Aventurera*

latter-day equivalent, a figure of the high bourgeoisie. It is a person of higher social status, after all, who leads the virtuous young lady into perdition.

This film is crammed with incidents yet punctuated with pauses at musical numbers commenting on the action and opening it to reflection. Before he introduces her to Rosaura, Lucio has dinner with Elena—though we see no eating, just drinking—in the cabaret, where there is a show on a stage. First Ana María González sings "Adiós," which alludes to Elena's impending good-bye to her life of virtue. Then Pedro Vargas sings "Amor de Medianoche" (Midnight Love), Elena and Lucio get up to dance, and when Vargas intones the words "puerta de pecado" (door of sin), Rosaura, watching from her office above the dance floor, notices "Lucio the pretty boy. He brings a girl. Nobody can pick them better." We again see Elena and Lucio dancing, and from her perspective we get a blurred, intoxicated view of the singer on stage. By the time she's taken to see the woman who will employ her, Elena is quite drunk: "But, Lucio, I'm going to see two women instead of one." Beyond her drunken vision, this remark alludes to the two women who bring on Elena's ruin, her mother and Rosaura, and the two women Rosaura is, the whorehouse madam and the upper-class matron.

"It took me work to tame her," Rosaura tells Lucio after some time has passed, but now Elena "is a sensation as a dancer." Elena has not been tamed, though—she gets into fights so often that Rosaura fears that the police may close the cabaret—and Ninón Sevilla, who choreographed her own numbers, is not an accomplished dancer. But, in a way she might not have managed had she been a better dancer, she is a sensation all the same, precisely because she is untamed, appealingly unrefined. Some take her numbers to be camp, but the fun she had doing them is palpable on the screen, and rather than laughing at her expense we can have fun along with her. The musical is the genre of high spirits, and *Aventurera,* though terrible things happen to the heroine and she retaliates in kind, is a melodrama of the spirited woman.

Forcibly pulled away from one of her fights by the thug Rengo (Miguel Inclán, who played the blind man in Buñuel's *Los olvidados*) and dragged upstairs for a dressing-down by Rosaura, the chastised Elena returns to the cabaret. As she steps down to the floor, Pedro Vargas steps up to the stage, which begins a counterpoint of movements and gestures and glances enacted between Vargas and Elena as he sings and she listens. He sings the title song, written by Agustín Lara: "Vende caro tu amor, aventurera" (Sell your love dearly, adventuress). In this remarkable sequence the song not only comments on the action but also enters into it. The singer addresses the song directly to the heroine, and she assumes the position of the referent and recipient.

As Vargas intones the word "aventurera," a cut to a reverse angle shows Elena looking at him and responding with wrinkled brow to his singing about "el precio del dolor" (the price of pain). Cut back to him, returning her gaze, then back to her, who now starts moving toward him. The camera moves with her, bringing him into view just when he says "tu pecado" (your sin), and now that the two are framed together, he starts moving on the stage in a direction parallel to hers on the floor and to the camera movement. At the point when she, approaching the stage, lines up with him and he halts, there is a cut to a higher, wider view, the camera continuing to move with her as she walks across the floor to the other side. He starts moving again, looking at her, but now she moves away from him and seems to be avoiding his gaze; she hides behind a pillar as if ashamed of what the song is saying about her. Cut closer to her as he sings about "la infamia de tu cruel destino" (the infamy of your cruel destiny) and she starts moving again, away from the stage. But she turns to look at him, prompting a cut to a close-up of him singing "marchitó tu admirable primavera" (wilted your admirable springtime), followed by a cut to a deep-focus shot with her in front and him well in back, the two of them and the camera again moving in parallel paths, now in the opposite direction, leftward rather than rightward as before. When Vargas, a distant figure on the stage, comes to a halt, so does Elena, hiding behind another pillar, and the two of them again line up on the screen, so exactly that she obscures him from view. At this point, reasserting the parallel, the film cuts from the heroine's profile to the singer's, in close-up, as he reprises the line "Vende caro tu amor" and turns to look at her when he sings the word "aventurera." Cut to a reverse angle that shows her in close-up as, emerging from behind a curtain, she turns to look at him and faces the camera.

Judging from this film, the only one of his that I have seen, Alberto Gout is a very good director. Pedro Vargas is stiff, but Gout orchestrates the singer's movements together with Ninón Sevilla's and the camera's—and with the words of the song—in a way that brings the singer and the song into arresting rapport with the action and the heroine being addressed. This is true melodrama, music not merely as accompaniment, background, interlude, but as central to the drama. First the heroine recognizes herself in the song and moves toward the singer, but then—the shift marked by a cut when she and he line up—she moves away from the singer and seems upset, shamed by the song. And when—the shift again marked by a cut at a point of alignment—Elena, in frontal close-up, looks at the singer and at the camera and for an instant appears to break out of the world of the movie and look right at us in the audience, then back inside the movie looks at this and that and we're not sure what, Gout does something extraordinary with her gaze and its objects.

Bringing into the action a song commenting on the action is a self-conscious move declaring the film's artifice, a kind of Brechtian alienation effect. Doesn't melodrama do its utmost to involve us emotionally, the opposite of the calculated detachment, the curb on dramatic illusion and emotion, in Brecht's modernist theater? Most of his plays are in the original sense melodramas, though, dramas with music, and with songs in the manner of musical comedy or comic opera. Comedy has a long tradition of declaring its artifice, a practice of self-consciousness much older than modernism, and what Brecht did, as Eric Bentley has argued, was to apply to tragic situations comedic forms and techniques—not so different from melodrama (Bentley 1975, 158).[2] In addition to making us aware of the film's contrivance, the song that Vargas sings to Elena makes her aware of her own predicament. The gaze she turns to the camera is a gaze of self-consciousness, both the film's and hers.

Though we just saw her behind a pillar, it is from behind a curtain that she emerges into the close-up at the conclusion of the song. Few will notice this error in continuity, and the curtain suggests, more than the pillar would have, her emergence onto a stage, the stage that is the film, the stage that is her life. And there she is, front and center, no longer trying to hide, aware of the part she is to play, prepared to face her future without being held back by her past, to take command of her life without inhibiting shame. *Aventurera* has been called a shameless melodrama for the way it dispenses with plausibility in its convoluted plot, and it is also shameless in the way it dispenses with moralizing and embraces the shamelessness of its spirited heroine.

Who is she looking at when she faces the camera in close-up? At first it is Pedro Vargas as he finishes singing "Aventurera." Then, momentarily, she seems to glance at the viewer. Then a reverse angle shows Lucio as the object of her gaze. Sitting at a table, he has heard the song about the life of sin he led her into, and they exchange glances, she accusingly, he responding with a smirk. But now she looks past Lucio at something all the way across the floor, which is where she was when the song began and where she now resolutely returns. It's a return to the beginning not only of this sequence but also of the whole story of her fall from grace: the object of her gaze is none other than Ramón. Having spotted the scoundrel as soon as he arrives at the cabaret with a party of revelers, she briskly proceeds to break a bottle over his head and to kick him and hit him and kick him as he lies on the floor until Rengo carries her away. Spirited, indeed. The gaze of her self-consciousness, directed in turn at the singer telling her story, at the audience being told it, and one then another villain playing a part in it, lets loose her vengeful fury.

Plato distinguished three parts of the human soul: the part that reasons, the part that desires, and the part that gets angry, the spirited part. Anger is in rather low repute nowadays, an emotion often thought to call for therapy, "anger management," but Plato valued it almost as highly as reason: it is the emotion that makes warriors, and the rulers of the Republic are to be warriors as well as philosophers, outstanding not only for their love of wisdom but also for their spiritedness. Elena may not be a philosopher but she is certainly a warrior, and *Aventurera* celebrates her invincible spiritedness.

Another melodrama of the spirited woman is *Doña Bárbara* (Mexico, 1943, directed by Fernando de Fuentes from the novel and screenplay by Rómulo Gallegos and photographed by Alex Phillips, who also shot *Aventurera*). The heroine is played by María Félix, perhaps the greatest star of Mexican cinema's golden age, one of the most beautiful women ever to appear on the screen and one of the most powerful, regal rather than plebeian like Ninón Sevilla but no less feisty and fiery. Doña Bárbara is the fallen woman of melodrama risen to the top, destroyer of men, owner and virtually absolute ruler of vast expanses of land on the plains of the Orinoco basin. As recounted in an introductory flashback, six brutal men killed her boyfriend and raped her on a boat when she was very young. After this incident we see her in close-up staring penetratingly into the camera, fixing us with her angry, adamantine gaze. The gaze of self-consciousness, which Elena gains through the song addressed to her, Doña Bárbara has from the start. Like Elena's, this is a warrior's gaze, a gaze that does not simply look but means action, vengeance against the wrongdoers. Doña Bárbara avenges herself for what those men did to her by assuming power over all men as far as her commanding eyes can see. The dark, intense eyes of María Félix dominate the film right to the end, when Doña Barbara the witch loses to her good daughter the man she would put under her spell, and yet her spellbinding gaze, directed at the camera, seems to bring on that happy ending for her daughter, to will it into being.

Mexico, the country that gave us the notion of *machismo,* also gave us María Félix and these melodramas of the spirited woman and the dominant female gaze. True, melodrama often centers on women, and women in Hollywood melodramas, from Lillian Gish to Barbara Stanwyck and Bette Davis, are often stronger than people think. The theory of the male gaze may apply to some movies, but it fails with melodramas and the female perspective they frequently assume. In his study of the "melodrama of the unknown woman," Stanley Cavell has argued that the women portrayed in such films as *Stella Dallas, Now, Voyager,* and *Letter from an Unknown Woman* are not the submissive, self-sacrificing ninnies that they are sometimes taken to be. But neither are they the warriors that the heroines of *Doña Bárbara* and *Aventurera* are. In order to find in Hollywood movies women so powerful and so assertive of their power, one would have to go to the femmes fatales of film noir, and those women, unlike Doña Bárbara and Elena, are presented from a male point of view.

Stella Dallas and *Doña Bárbara* make an interesting comparison. Stella is the social climber who gives up her climbing and lets her daughter take over from her; Doña Bárbara, of even humbler origins than Stella, rises much higher, but rather like Stella, she withdraws in the end and passes on her power to her daughter, who inherits all her land and marries the rival landowner in the region. Like the young man Stella's daughter marries, this landowner represents not only wealth—Doña Bárbara has plenty of that already—but also the refinement of a higher class. Like Stella, Doña Bárbara may be perceived as the loser, which in both cases may have been what the authors intended: we are probably meant to see Stella as unworthy of the upper class and capable only of sacrificing herself for her daughter's sake and Doña Bárbara as the embodiment of a matriarchal barbarism defeated by patriarchal civilization. But in both cases our experience of the movie is at odds with that construction. If Stella and Doña Bárbara are losers, they come across as stronger than the winners. Barbara Stanwyck's Stella and María Félix's Doña Bárbara command the screen in such a way that everyone else pales beside them, and we take their side against the supposedly superior virtues of upper-class refinement and patriarchal civilization. That may be why Stella is an "unknown woman": we feel that there is much more to her than the movie seems to know. Doña Bárbara is similarly unknown, beyond the movie's knowledge. Not Elena, however: everything about her is loud and clear, and the movie takes her side as much as we do.

Scolded for making trouble at the cabaret, Elena listens to "Aventurera" and right away makes more trouble by assaulting Ramón. She couldn't help herself, she explains, this man brought ruin on her family, but Rosaura doesn't care and orders Rengo to teach the unruly young woman a lesson with a slash of his knife. Lucio bursts in and almost kills the thug, who is spared thanks to Elena and from then on is devotedly grateful to her. She and Lucio take off together with a wad of money that he forces the madam to hand over, but he lands in prison when he attempts to rob a jewelry store and a member of his gang, Pacomio, sells him out to Rosaura, who tips off the police. Elena goes on to become a successful dancer in Mexico City, where Mario

(Rubén Rojo), a well-bred young lawyer from an old Guadalajara family, falls in love with her (we hear the Trio Los Panchos singing a love song: "Your lips taught me to feel / What tenderness is / And I will not tire of blessing / Such sweetness") and proposes marriage. To get away from Pacomio, who has caught up with her and tries to blackmail her for her complicity in the robbery, Elena decides to marry the upstanding Mario and accompanies him to staid Guadalajara. There, in his family's mansion, she meets his mother, a paragon of respectability who turns out to be Rosaura.

Elena finds herself in a perfect position for vengeance. She is the love and the happiness of a son Rosaura loves and wishes to be happy. Rosaura sees herself as "a mother who has sacrificed everything for the benefit and happiness of her sons," and the last thing she wants as a mother is for her son to discover that she has been leading another life as a madam. Elena uses Mario to punish Rosaura—not a nice thing to do, we recognize, but we still take her side because we also recognize that Rosaura did worse things to her, and because we cheeringly identify with her defiance of a social order whose proprieties and hypocrisies she, and we along with her, see through.

Revenge is sweet for Elena in *Aventurera*.

She gets drunk at her wedding party and dances so outrageously in the eyes of Guadalajara society that all the guests leave. And she does it on purpose, flaunting the vulgarity that she knows the upper class looks down on, and flaunting it subversively. "Wasn't I up to the level of high society?" she asks mockingly. Melodrama here comes close to comedy and its deflation of pose and pretense. The society matron who doubles as the madam of a whorehouse can be seen as a satirical caricature, almost a figure of comedy.

Rosaura's posture as the sacrificial mother ("If my business dealings haven't been clean, at least I have fulfilled a mother's duty") can be taken as part of the comedy. It's like a parody of maternal pathos, and we smile when Elena shows no compassion: "You don't move me, Rosaura. I go on hating you with all my soul." Rosaura turned her into a whore, and now Elena turns that against her with poetic justice: she seeks revenge on the madam and mother by making a fool of her son and letting the world know he has married a whore. Her impudent behavior, the private brought out in public literally with a vengeance, strikes at Rosaura where she is most vulnerable. The mother withdraws from Guadalajara and goes off to Ciudad Juárez, where

Rosaura meets her match in *Aventurera*.

the madam can perhaps regain control. It just so happens that Elena's own mother is there, dying in a hospital, and Rosaura makes sure that Elena gets word. She wants Elena back in the city where the young woman first fell and can fall again into her hands; she tells Rengo to take care of Elena when she comes, and take care of her he does, but not in the way Rosaura had in mind. Elena does return to visit her mother, who asks for her daughter's forgiveness so that she can die in peace, but Elena remains stonily silent, though after her mother dies she softens and weeps. As for Rosaura's nefarious designs, the grateful Rengo puts Elena under his protection. Neither Pacomio, who threatens her again but plummets to his death while fleeing from Rengo, nor the wicked madam can do any harm to our heroine.

*Aventurera* is a melodrama that not only has a woman as the protagonist but also a woman as the villain. Ramón, Pacomio, even Lucio are minor villains in comparison to Rosaura. And if she is a doubled character, mother and madam, she is further doubled with another mother, Elena's. Rosaura represents the mother that Elena is fighting, the mother that is within her, a figure of the upper class and of the lower depths, standing both for repressive propriety and for dangerous sexuality. Mario and Lucio, who in an old melodrama would have been, respectively, the noble hero who offers the heroine a good marriage and the villain who puts her virtue in peril, are here lesser figures next to the mother, the respectable mother Mario reveres and her dirty other self, the madam Lucio pimps for. Here the central conflict is between daughter and mother. *Aventurera* is a melodrama of two spirited women.

Elena would have wanted the respectable mother, not the dirty one who ran off with Ramón and whom she does not forgive to the end. And yet it is the dirty Elena who fights the respectable Rosaura in Guadalajara, who exposes the falseness of bourgeois respectability, who wins because she fights dirty. Such are the contradictions of melodrama. Back in Ciudad Juárez, Elena goes back to her dirty dancing, and Mario arrives from Guadalajara and rebukes her, holding up his mother as a model of respectable womanhood. In retaliation, Elena takes him to the cabaret and whorehouse and introduces him to the dirty Rosaura. Her vengeance is complete. But as she comes down to the cabaret floor, she hears again the song "Aventurera," now sung in duet by Pedro Vargas and Ana María González, who stand side by side on the stage like a father and mother posed for a family picture as they sing to the daughter gone astray. This time Elena does not move but is moved to tears. The spirited woman has had her revenge, but these, in tightening close-up, are the tears of the good girl.

Her earlier tears were too late to assuage her mother's sad end; these tears prepare for a happy ending. They are tears of comedy—not the comedy that mocks, the social satire lending a sharp edge to the Guadalajara scenes, but the comedy that accepts and reconciles. And Elena is ready for reconciliation with her husband, who, after the shock of seeing his mother in her guise of madam, still wants Elena back. Mario regrets what his mother did to Elena— even if Rosaura sacrificed herself for him and his brother, he says, her conduct has no excuse—and Elena regrets what she did to Mario while settling scores with his mother. The noble hero meets the fallen yet once again virtuous heroine. But the villainous Lucio, who has escaped from prison and wants Elena for himself—all the men in the movie want Elena—has been listening in and before long breaks in on the reconciling couple. Elena is caught between two men who are associated with the mother's two sides, the respectable Mario and the dirty Lucio. The good girl chooses the good boy, but it takes Rengo to save the situation with his knife. The dirty mother's thug, won over by a good-girl gesture on Elena's part, kills Lucio in the nick of time and enables the reunited wife and husband to reach their happy ending to the strains of "Aventurera."

Isn't this finally the taming of the spirited woman? Isn't the good girl surrendering to the values of a society that the spirited woman defied? Elena is, after all, a daughter of the bourgeoisie, which betrays her and which she rebels against but in the end makes her peace with. It would not have been right for her to have rejected Mario and gone off with Lucio, which was what her mother did with her father and Ramón, leading to all the daughter's troubles. But the good girl reconciled with her husband at the end is not the same as the good girl shocked to find her mother with the chauffeur at the beginning. The mother who was the enemy, who personified the bourgeoisie through betrayal and rebellion, is by the end vanquished and gone and has left her place to the daughter. It is with herself that Elena makes her peace, and she surrenders but also triumphs. This is essentially the ending of New Comedy, the triumph of the young lovers that brings on a renewal of the social order—a renewal, not an overthrowing. Just like its heroine, *Aventurera* is daring but also conventional, subversive but also accepting. It reflects the divided values of the bourgeoisie. By dirty means Rosaura keeps up respectability, by dirty means Elena combats it, and all the while both of them, villain and heroine, believe in respectability, Rosaura sacrificing herself for it, Elena getting angry when she perceives it to be false and embracing it when persuaded it will come true. Such are the contradictions of the bourgeois world finding expression in melodrama.

## Notes

1. "To my mind," Bentley wrote, "Brecht's theory of theater *is* a theory of comedy" (158).

2. Stanley Cavell has looked discerningly into the relation between melodrama and comedy in the Hollywood genres that he calls the "melodrama of the unknown woman" (*Stella Dallas; Now, Voyager; Letter from an Unknown Woman*) and the "comedy of remarriage" (*It Happened One Night, The Awful Truth, His Girl Friday*). See his *Pursuits of Happiness* and *Contesting Tears*.

## Works Cited

Bentley, Eric. *The Life of the Drama.* New York: Atheneum, 1964.

———. "The Stagecraft of Brecht." In *In Search of the Theater.* New York: Atheneum, 1975.

Brooks, Peter. *The Melodramatic Imagination: Balzac, Henry James, Melodrama, and the Mode of Excess.* New Haven: Yale University Press, 1975.

Cavell, Stanley. *Contesting Tears: The Hollywood Melodrama of the Unknown Woman.* Chicago: University of Chicago Press, 1996.

———. *Pursuits of Happiness: The Hollywood Comedy of Remarriage.* Cambridge: Harvard University Press, 1981.

Cawelti, John G. "The Evolution of Social Melodrama." In *Imitations of Life: A Reader on Film and Television Melodrama,* ed. Marcia Landy. Detroit: Wayne State University Press, 1991.

# 2

# Melodrama and the Emergence of Venezuelan Cinema

### LUISELA ALVARAY

## Melodrama and National Identity

> In the presence of Hollywood's subjugation, the Latin American film
> industry vivaciously produces its versions of melodrama—unrestrained,
> tied to excess and to the genealogies of sorrow.
>
> —Carlos Monsiváis, "El melodrama," 2002

The melodramatic imagination in Venezuela as in other parts of Latin America has been described by many theorists as accompanying the experiences of modernity. It manifests itself through different media and acquires multiple formats—theatrical chronicles, the *feuilleton,* radionovelas, telenovelas, *rancheras,* tangos, boleros, and cinematic melodramas, among others. It also provides readers and audiences with an emotional education or tools for social behavior within particular ideological frameworks. Many times, melodramas are centered on female subjectivities in search of sentimental and sexual reaffirmation in a world that oscillates between independence and conformism or between liberation and submissiveness. Therefore, even though women might conform to particular moral codes, they might also show forms of transgression within that very social system.[1]

During the 1930s, there was a continent that was predisposed to and ready to welcome a genre that would model and fulfill particular modes of perception and subjectivities. Radio waves became instrumental for transmitting serial narratives such as radionovelas. First popularized in Cuba, radionovelas were promptly imported by Venezuela, and soon thereafter domestic adaptations with idiosyncratic singularities became popular nationwide.

As José Ignacio Cabrujas recounts, the remake of the famous *El derecho de nacer* (The Right To Be Born, a Cuban work by Félix B. Caignet) was a news item daily in Caracas in the 1940s, and it broke audience attendance records in several other nations (173). Somehow, melodramas in their oral and later audiovisual forms (film and television) became in Latin American countries a way to articulate commonalities, integrate regional feelings, and configure similar cultural identities. Referring to the impact of melodrama in Latin America, Jesús Martín-Barbero writes: "In the form of tango, telenovela, Mexican cinema or newspapers' crime pages, melodrama affects a deep vein in our collective imaginary, and there is no possible access to historic memory without that imaginary" (69).

By including the factor of "historic memory," Martín-Barbero alludes to a more transcendental function of the melodrama: that of connecting cultures to nations and their history or making their narrative part of the discourse of the national. Referring to cinematic melodrama, he remarks, "A nationalist and populist cinema par excellence, melodrama is vital for urban masses who through its images are able to reduce the impact of cultural shocks and for the first time *have an image* of the country *to their likeness*" (77, emphasis in original). In that sense, melodrama has tended to be connected to national and regional identities as much as to the modernization of Latin American societies. As Ana López has argued, Mexican cinematic melodramas have been connected to the nation-building project since the revolution of 1910–20 and, therefore, have had a place in the rearticulation of national identity (258).

## Mexican and Venezuelan Border Crossings

In 1936 the Mexican film *Allá en el rancho grande* (Over There at the Big Ranch, by Fernando de Fuentes) appeared in Venezuelan movie houses, and, according to one critic, "it beat every picture that ever played . . . by 100% and that include[d] even the biggest Hollywood-made product" (quoted in Usabel 129). Fascinated by Tito Guízar's songs and the romance between Martín (Lorenzo Barcelata) and Crucita (Esther Fernández), Venezuelan audiences flocked to the comedic melodrama, which was to open the way for the success of the Mexican film industry. By 1938, Hollywood features dropped to 45 percent of the Venezuelan market, which had been taken over by Mexican and Argentine productions (Roffé 250). Five years later, fifty-nine Mexican films were shown in Venezuela (Usabel 185). The esteem for Latin American stars among Spanish-speaking audiences was at its height, and Mexican literary adaptations, along with melodramas, musicals, and comedies, were ubiquitous. According to Rodolfo Izaguirre, the influence of Mexican cinema on the nascent Venezuelan film industry of the 1940s was significant both in formal terms and in the selection of subject matter. In particular, co-production agreements enabled Venezuelan performers to appear in Mexican productions (116). This was true of numerous melodramas, including José Benavides's *Tierra de pasiones* (Land of Passions, 1942), Miguel M. Delgado's *El secreto de la solterona* (The Spinster's Secret, 1944), and Aurelio Robles Castillo's *La ametralladora* (The Machine Gun, 1943). In the Castillo movie, Venezuelan actor Margarita Mora romances a little-known Pedro Infante.

In 1943 the golden age of Mexican cinema was at its peak. Emilio Fernández premiered his two rural melodramas, *María Candelaria* and *Flor Silvestre* (Wild Flower), to wide acclaim; Julio Bracho broke ground with his dark urban tale *Distinto Amanecer* (Different Dawn); and, especially important for my interests in this essay, Fernando de Fuentes boosted María Félix to iconic status by casting her as the beautiful "devourer of men" in his adaptation of Rómulo Gallegos's 1929 novel *Doña Bárbara*.

This novel was the first of many works by the Venezuelan author to be adapted by the Mexican film industry. The movie broke all box office records in Venezuela in a landmark year for great Latin American pictures, none of which were produced in Venezuela (Tirado n.d.: 112). The film's success in Venezuela, as elsewhere in Latin America, was in large part due to the enormous star power of María Félix and Julián Soler, but the adaptation of the novel also created unprecedented expectation among audiences there. No ordinary novel, *Doña Bárbara* was a canonical text about Venezuelan national identity and pride written by the country's most distinguished living author.

*Doña Bárbara* is only one example of a connection between Mexican melodrama and its Venezuelan counterpart—a connection that influenced the emergence of Venezuelan cinema. Mexico and Argentina, the countries that produced the largest number of Spanish-language films, had a major influence on the region's smaller film industries. They disseminated not only Spanish-language stories but also a structure of feeling connected to melodrama and to individual screen personalities.[2] Later, the direct input of talent from Mexico and Argentina would prove to be critical to the development of Venezuelan cinema.

The purpose of this essay is to describe in greater detail the migratory forces at work in the development of melodrama in Venezuela and to call attention to pioneering work of directors and stars from outside Venezuela who came to the country to make movies and helped define the direction of the national cinema.

*Doña Bárbara,* the ultimate example of the collaboration between Mexico and Venezuela, proved to be an exceptional model for future melodramatic adaptations of literary works. Set in the Venezuelan plains, the novel provides a realistic look at the ruthlessness and cruelty of rural life in the 1920s, when the dictator Juan Vicente Gómez ruled the country; in stark fashion, it portrays the confrontation between the forces of progress and rationality embodied in the character of Santos Luzardo (played by Julián Soler) and the primal and wild forces of nature personified by Doña Bárbara (played by María Félix). Pitting civilization against barbarism was Gallegos's way of emphasizing the necessity of modernizing Venezuela in order to put an end to a brutal despotism.[3] This opposition, however, is treated in relatively complex ways in the novel, which gives the characters mixed motives. The film is more Manichaean in its approach, in keeping with its melodramatic form. The psychological motivations of characters are simplified, and the moral division between good and evil is clear and unambiguous. Marisela (María Elena Marqués), a symbol of virtue, wears a white dress in the film, whereas her scheming mother, Doña Bárbara, is consistently attired in black. In the end, romance overcomes all obstacles and reinforces conventional female and male roles.

The widespread success of *Doña Bárbara* resulted in Mexican adaptations of other works by Gallegos. These included Gilberto Martínez Solares's *La trepadora* (The Social Climber, 1944), *La señora de enfrente* (The Woman Next Door, 1945), Julio Bracho's *Cantaclaro* (1946), and Miguel M. Delgado's *La doncella de piedra* (The Stone Maiden, 1956). With the exception of *La señora,* all of these films were co-produced with the Venezuelan company Salvador Cárcel C.A. Most of the films also featured Venezuelans in secondary roles, which resulted in sound tracks with mixed regional accents.

Beginning in the early 1940s, the movement of technical and creative personnel was no longer a one-way street. In 1941 Condor Films S.A., a Venezuelan production company, began to import actors of Mexican and Spanish descent to star in Venezuelan features. In that way, the "feel" of foreignness that characterized productions made outside the country could be reproduced locally and without difficulty. Stars who were imported for this purpose included Spanish actor Carmen Rodríguez and Mexican performers Elena D'Orgaz, José Baviera, and Miguel Arenas, who were cast together in René Borgia's *Noche inolvidable* (Unforgettable Night, 1941), a melodrama about a musician who twenty years earlier had killed his wife. In that year they also performed in José Fernández's

*¡Pobre hija mía!* (Poor Daughter of Mine!), a melodrama based on a popular radionovela of the time (Tirado n.d.: 7–89, 93). Venezuelan producers copied not only Mexico's mode of film production but also its narrative and formal patterns, which guaranteed some commercial success at the local box office.

Although profit was the main objective of entrepreneurs who attempted to industrialize cinematic production in Venezuela in the 1940s and 1950s, there was also a desire to connect with local audiences by "nationalizing" the topics of their movies and generating images that Venezuelans would recognize and embrace. Such desire was motivated not only by models from abroad but also by the relation between cinema and the state. During the dictatorship of Juan Vicente Gómez (1908–35), the cinema consisted of a few pioneer filmmakers who dreamed of making independent movies and who survived by selling propaganda-style documentaries and newsreels to the government. After Gómez's death in 1935 and until the 1950s, commercial advertising and official propaganda films were the main sources of profit for local film companies (Marrosu 1996: 56–58). Many works of the 1940s and 1950s (documentaries and features) used folkloric themes and songs, emphasized and exalted local landscapes, and were based on well-known stories with recognizable character types. These were also fundamental traits of the films imported from Mexico and Argentina, which provided models to follow.

The Mexican adaptation of Gallegos's works created in Venezuela an admiration for and pride regarding the nation and its values as depicted in the films. At the same time, local voices were critical of the trend, arguing that the Mexican industry was doing what Venezuelans ought to have done. This was especially true given the importance of Gallegos not only as a writer but also as a critic of the Gómez dictatorship and eventually as the president of the republic. One reviewer wrote: "In Caracas, [*Canaima*] has been exhibited for a month to full houses with three daily shows. . . . [The film] has been a mandatory motif in conversations and discussions at every social level. . . . [It] is a pity that only Mexican cinema is making good Venezuelan films" (quoted in Tirado n.d.: 132). In the meantime, other noteworthy Mexican melodramas, such as Miguel Contreras Torres's *Simón Bolívar* (1941), based on the life of the Caracas-born leader of South America's move to independence, and Joselito Rodriguez's *Angelitos negros* (Little Dark Angels, 1948), based on a poem by Venezuelan writer Andrés Eloy Blanco, were continuing to focus on key aspects of Venezuelan nationalism—in particular, issues of social equality and democratic values that were heavily debated in the twenty-two year period (1935 to 1958) between the end of the Gómez dictatorship and the coup by Marcos Pérez Jiménez that brought an end to the Gallegos presidency.[4] The idea of the national in these two films was conflated with that of the regional, creating a shared sense of community that had characterized the Latin American continent since the movements that brought independence from Europe.

## The Transnational Formula of Bolívar Films

In 1942, after several failed attempts by local entrepreneurs to establish a commercially successful film industry in Venezuela, Luis Guillermo Villegas created Bolívar Films. Initially allied with advertising companies to make commercials, the company produced official newsreels and soon became the most profitable film enterprise of the time. By the end of the 1940s, Villegas embarked on a project to make quality marketable features by means of co-production agreements with Argentina and Mexico. From 1948 to 1953, Bolívar Films made six melodramas, two comedies, and one musical, all of which were directed by foreign filmmakers.[5] Villegas responded to the public desire for movies that featured local color and themes, but he was distrustful of local people who had been unable to produce quality films that earned a profit (Caropreso 24; Marrosu 1996: 59). Among those contracted by Villegas were prominent Argentine director Carlos Hugo Christensen and celebrated actors Susana Freyre, Juan Carlos Thorry, Juana Sujo, and Horacio Peterson. The latter two ultimately settled in Caracas and contributed to the local theater scene. Other imported artists came from Cuba and Mexico. Among them were well-known Mexican performers Arturo de Córdova, Olga Zubarry, and Virginia Luque and director Victor Urruchúa. A few technical experts came as well, including Spanish cameraman José María Beltrán, who went on to win a prize at Cannes for cinematography in *La balandra Isabel llegó esta tarde* (Sailboat Isabel Arrived This Afternoon, 1949).

Carlos Hugo Christensen was already a celebrity by 1940, having directed more than twenty films during the previous "glorious" decade of Argentine cinema. He was an expert in both comedy and melodrama, and many of his features were based on literary works, successful theater plays, and radionovelas (which in Argentina were called *radioteatros*). After shooting *El demonio es un ángel* (The Devil Is an Angel, 1949), the first comedy he made in Venezuela, he led a crew of Argentineans, Venezuelans, and Spaniards in the making of the passionate and melodramatic *Balandra* in ten weeks. It was the most expensive feature made in the country up to that time.

A box-office hit, *Balandra* became a revered spectacle for Venezuelan audiences. It was also the first Venezuelan feature to win a prize at Cannes, which gave it international exposure. Many local critics credited Christensen with improving Venezuelan cinema. One reviewer for *Mi Film* wrote: "With continental—and maybe universal—repercussions, the name Carlos Hugo Christensen has been sufficient guarantee for our cinema to experience a radical change." A critic writing for *El nacional* was equally enthusiastic about Christensen: "Thanks to the mastery of his direction, all the characters perform with extraordinary sincerity and naturalness" (quoted in Tirado n.d.: 201).

*Balandra* is the story of a sailor named Segundo Mendoza (Arturo de Córdova) who oscillates between the love of his wife Isabel (América Barrios) at Margarita Island and the "sinful" love of Esperanza (Virginia Luque), a prostitute at the port of La Guaira, who is intimately linked to the sorcerer Bocú (Tomás Henríquez). Esperanza's use of black magic and Segundo's passion for her lead him on a path to ruin when he decides to leave his family and pursue the attractive prostitute. Christensen's adaptation of the Venezuelan writer Guillermo Meneses's 1934 short story becomes a morality tale in which

Tomás Henríquez and Virginia Luque in *La balandra Isabel llegó esta tarde*

the traditional archetypes of women from the golden-age melodramas are personified by two female protagonists, the saintly wife and mother and the femme fatale. Elements of folklore were incorporated by adding scenes of rituals carried out by the black population living along the Venezuelan coast.

Although many critics believe that the transnational project of Bolívar Films did not aspire to contribute to the configuration of a national identity, largely because of its reliance on foreign talent (Marrosu 1996: 61) and narrative techniques (Colmenares 135), sufficient local talent and autochthonous narrative elements were used in the film to enable one to conclude otherwise. *Balandra*'s screenplay was written by noted Venezuelan writers Guillermo Meneses and Aquiles Nazoa, whose participation suggests the company's desire to "indigenize" the film project. Nazoa, in particular, was well known and loved by Venezuelans for his literary works about the people, their customs, and their language, and he was permanently on staff at Bolívar Films to write dialogue that would reflect the Venezuelan milieu. Other important contributors were musician Eduardo Serrano and poet, essayist, and critic Juan Liscano, who became a folklore adviser for *Balandra*. They added elements of music and lore that gave the narrative a specific indigenous identity. Those elements were noted by a critic from *Mi Film* who wrote: "The excellent cinematography, sets and situational music stand out, as much as the central musical theme 'Esperanza' and the folkloric scenes, which, we believe, will be very attractive to audiences abroad" (quoted in Tirado n.d.: 201). Still another critic at *El nacional* was impressed by the fact that *Balandra* was based on a Venezuelan literary work: "In this way, the Venezuelan film industry not only adheres to its rich folklore, but also makes a film that connects with our own literature and thus makes the most of its works" (quoted in ibid.: 202). The critic for *El Universal* was equally impressed: "The mere initiative of filming our literature deserves applause. We had asked ourselves many times, why had Venezuela's autochthonous literature of quality never been used as the basis for our films?" (quoted in ibid.).

After producing nine features in four years, the attempt by Bolívar Films to become a commercially successful film enterprise was abandoned. It remained a successful production company, however, because of its work in advertising, which became even more profitable after the advent of television in 1952. Its incursion into the production of features in 1949 was, nonetheless, a legitimate attempt to consolidate a film industry in Venezuela that, although it did not prove profitable (a lack of vision concerning distribution and marketing of the products might have been the cause), left behind a consolidated infrastructure and a group of trained personnel who would continue producing and promoting films in the country. It also left a legacy of generic films, and melodramas in particular, whose production was useful for building transnational alliances with some of the major industries elsewhere on the continent. At the same time, Bolívar Films also naturalized the melodramatic narrative as the standard form for cinematic language—a situation that was challenged in the following decade by critics and theorists of the revolutionary New Cinema of Latin American.

## The Waning of Melodramatic Films

Throughout the 1940s and 1950s, smaller production companies in Venezuela—Civenca, Hispano Films, Salvador Cárcel C.A., Fílmica del Caribe (Fidelca), Vicente Blanco C.A., and Tropical Films C.A., among others—continued to invest in features (mostly melodramas) made in Mexico, Argentina, and even Brazil. A noteworthy example of transnational collaboration at the time involved the Mexican director Juan Orol. A veteran of comedy and melodrama, Orol arrived in Caracas in 1953 to promote his films and recoup his investments in Mexican film. There he was invited by producer Salvador Cárcel to shoot *El sindicato del crimen* (The Syndicate of Crime, 1953). Set in New York and Havana, the melodrama was not well received by the critics but was a success with Venezuelan audiences (Tirado n.d.: 281), for whom melodramatic stories continued to have great appeal.

By the end of the 1950s, serial melodramas in the form of telenovelas had captured audiences throughout the continent. Of the small number of locally produced films completed during the years of Jiménez's dictatorship in Venezuela (1948–58), a few were based on popular TV melodramas. This was the case with César Enríquez's *Tambores de la colina* (Drums of the Hill, 1956) and Antonio Gracciani's *Papalepe* (1957). With the rising popularity of television, the film industry suffered, and because of social changes the traditional melodrama was becoming obsolete for many. As film historian Silvia Oroz noted: "With the decline of the industry in the 1950s, the melodrama faced a crisis as its values were questioned. The traditional family was facing a crisis because of the contraceptive pill" (169). A symbol of women's liberation and of the transformation in social roles for men and women, the Pill was challenging the region's traditional values. But struggles for political power were also taking place in Latin American societies. Many countries had recently been or were still under authoritarian rule, and left-wing activists and movements appeared across the continent. The values of the melodrama, or what the young Marxist revolutionaries called the values of "bourgeois society," no longer corresponded to the aims of the ideal social order that they imagined. The Latin American intelligentsia, including many young filmmakers, turned to a political, avant-gardist discourse for articulating the struggle for political and ideological transformation. Nonetheless, melodramas continued to be featured, especially on television, and remained popular among a substantial portion of the population.

## Cinema of Auteurs

> I liked cinema so much that I had several albums of newspaper clippings, which I systematically collected—one of film critiques, another one of film photographs and a very special third one dedicated to María Félix. Since seeing her perform in *Doña Bárbara,* I was a slave to her beauty and her arrogance.
>
> —Román Chalbaud, "Apuntes de un Cineasta," 1979

While telenovelas dominated prime time in Venezuela through the 1960s and 1970s, cinematic melodramas and comedies became the standards of the waning trend of commercial co-production with Argentina, Mexico, and Brazil and later with Italy and Spain. These films served to launch several Venezuelan performers into the international arena, but, as stated above, these collaborations did not substantially contribute to the development of a national industry. At the same time, an auteurist cinema was struggling to come into existence in the newly democratic Venezuela. As a result of the failure of private entrepreneurs to commercialize Venezuelan films in the 1950s and of the total indifference of the governments to legislate in favor of national film production, individuals took the initiative to produce and direct national narratives. The two most significant works to be filmed at this time were Margot Benacerraf's *Araya* (1959) and Román Chalbaud's *Caín adolescente* (Adolescent Cain, 1959). A documentary about the life of salt miners in a remote Venezuelan town on the coast, *Araya* became internationally famous after winning two awards at the Cannes Film Festival.[6] Margot Benacerraf had been absent from the Venezuelan film scene since moving to Paris to study cinema, and that was where her work underwent postproduction. As a result, *Araya* was not shown in Venezuela until 1977. Thus, despite being one of the country's major cinematic works of the period, it did not contribute to any new filmmaking trend there (Marrosu 1997: 42). With its focus on poverty and migration, *Caín adolescente,* on the other hand, became a sort of paradigm of a new social cinema and was the work that propelled the unique career of the prolific Román Chalbaud.

A film lover and enthusiast of the Mexican golden age, Chalbaud participated in the attempt by Bolívar Films to industrialize Venezuelan filmmaking. At a young age, he became assistant director to Mexican director Victor Urruchúa for two features that he directed for the company. With the advent of television, Chalbaud gained more experience and became a director in the new medium. He initially directed television plays based on works of literature; later, he directed telenovelas. He was also heavily involved in the Caracas theatrical world, where he staged his first plays, including the very successful *Caín adolescente* (1955). Chalbaud's decision to adapt the play for the screen was understandable, but filming the movie was difficult. When the picture was finished, the military government censored it because of its representations of grinding poverty. It was shown only after the fall of the dictatorship in 1959.[7]

Although *Caín* has been praised for its content—it tries to grapple with the reality of slums and the misery of peasants who migrate to the city—it infuses this content with melodramatic elements. As Paulo Antonio Paranaguá noted: "[*Caín*] includes many elements of the golden age of Mexican films: melodramatic climaxes, bar and the cabaret locations, typical characters, gestures and forms, and, above all, the young girl, who is seduced, abandoned, and continuously rejected because of her loose morals" (165). The film also includes aspects of Venezuelan customs and folklore that represent local filmmakers' continued desire for an autochthonous cinema. Although *Caín* was criticized for its excessive theatricality (its sounds and images do seem rather dated now), it was also admired for its originality. Amy Courvoisier, a contemporary critic, was especially enthusiastic: "*Caín adolescente* is a clear vision of what our cinema should be—not a blind imitation of foreign productions. The author [Chalbaud] was inspired by different events that we have witnessed ourselves and, from those, has constructed a realistic and emotional film that is alive" (quoted in Tirado n.d.: 338).

*Caín* has been assessed as a transitional work that links tradition and innovation in the search for a national imagery. And, certainly, elements of melodrama had a strong presence in that effort, as in the rest of Chalbaud's oeuvre. As Ambretta Marrosu points out: "Even if the melodramatic commotion of Chalbaud's personal world is not characteristic of Venezuelan culture, it is very much his own as a variation [within the national film world] and, most of all, it contains [many] of the elements that gave life to the fiction films of the next decade" (1997: 42). Although her statement s that Venezuelan culture lacks a melodramatic vein is questionable, it is true that Chalbaud and his melodramatic style became influential in the country during the subsequent two decades.

During the 1960s and early 1970s, Chalbaud, like many other young film-makers, continued to make films, but not without difficulty and, regrettably, without official support. The first attempt to create a new law to protect the national film output by guaranteeing screen space for local productions occurred in 1967, but it was adamantly opposed by distributors and exhibitors, who contended that it would hurt the film business and reduce the number of films that played in the country (Tirado 1988: 123). But the persistence of the new generation finally gave way to new governmental support for film-making in Venezuela.

The media researcher Antonio Pasquali wrote in 1972: "The distributors' shortsightedness, the producers' lack of impetus and the state's indifference have resulted in thirty years in which two activities, the production and distribution of films, have increased without ever being in contact with one another" (quoted in Marrosu 1985: 29–30). He was stressing the lack of coordination between the "nuts and bolts" of the industrial machine and the need of institutional policies to create and consolidate a film industry in Venezuela. Mexico had already passed a film law in 1951, and Brazil did so in 1966. However, things were about to change for Venezuela.

## The State Supports a National Cinema

In 1974 Mauricio Walerstein, the son of Mexican producer Gregorio Walerstein, premiered his first Venezuelan film, *Cuando quiero llorar no lloro* (When I Want to Cry, I Don't). The ongoing collaboration between Mexico and Venezuela is perhaps best represented by this father-and-son creative team. Gregorio had produced a number of films since the golden age, among them the 1945 adaptation of Gallegos's novel *Canaima*. Thereafter, he maintained relationships with Venezuelan entrepreneurs and performers, some of whom he hired for his productions. A film producer as well, Mauricio came to Venezuela to help his father with a production and ended up working with Román Chalbaud in writing the script for what was to be his first film as a director in the country. *Cuando quiero llorar no lloro,* based on a Venezuelan best-seller by Miguel Otero Silva, became an immediate box-office hit. At a time of social upheaval and revolution around the world, its treatment of urban violence by the working poor, political guerrilla fighters, and young upper-class adults appealed to the new generation.

Chalbaud released *La quema de Judas* (The Burning of Judas), which was also a hit in Venezuela, in 1974. The critical and commercial success of Walerstein and Chalbaud's features spurred the state to initiate a policy that would support and promote a national cinema. Until that time, only the advertising industry had risked producing an individual film. One year later, in 1975, nine features were financed by the government, and there was talk in the industry and by critics of a New Venezuelan Cinema (Aguirre and Bisbal 21).

In 1980 critics Jesús Aguirre and Marcelino Bisbal identified ten thematic categories, three of which—marginality, guerrilla warfare, and passionate drama—were the most frequently revisited by filmmakers (141). Denunciation of social malaise and references to the political struggles of previous decades were typical themes. The manner of their depiction was usually (but not always) indebted to melodrama. As Carlos Rebolledo noted: "Venezuelan cinema, with few exceptions, has tried to emulate the telenovela—a sure way of securing the public—leaving aside the intensive and extensive complexity of the country in order to use schematic dramatic forms which would please a mass, paying public" (quoted in King 223). By this time, Chalbaud's influence in the cinematic world was even greater as a result of his success with three consecutive films: *La quema de Judas* (1974), *Sagrado y obsceno* (Sacred and Obscene, 1975), and *El pez que fuma* (The Smoking Fish, 1976). Each of them presented a critical view of Venezuelan society, focusing on such topics as corrupt economic and political practices, popular culture, the values of marginalized people as opposed to the values of the bourgeoisie, and the search for a national identity. All of his films had a strong melodramatic component, which became part of his signature style.

Chalbaud has stated several times that many of his features were made with the deliberate intention of paying tribute to Mexican films of the golden age, in which songs formed part of the melodramatic pulse. His own love for films as a teenager had caused him to admire many of the renowned works of the period. He wrote: "At that time . . . I felt overwhelmed by the naturalism of Mexican cinema—a cinema close to the *feuilleton*, to dialogue and to simplistic situations that were, nonetheless, a reflection of the Latino spirit" (1979: 4). The film that most successfully conveys Chalbaud's admiration for Mexican cinema probably is *El pez que fuma*—a critically acclaimed feature based on his 1968 play of the same title, which is evocative of melodramas made during the golden age. Like the Mexican cabaretera movies of the 1940s, the film is about a brothel called The Smoking Fish that comes alive during the late-night hours and transforms its daytime workers into brilliant performers. They work for the torch singer La Garza (Hilda Vera), the brothel's self-made owner. An independent, powerful character, La Garza is somewhat reminiscent of the Doña Bárbara archetype played by María Félix. But the combination of compassion, motherly feelings, and a strong will that overwhelms and then abandons men at her convenience makes La Garza a far more complex character. The Mexican composer and poet Agustín Lara, whose musical scores enriched numerous golden-age features, expressed sympathy for the prostitute in his songs, and that sympathy is manifested in the treatment of La Garza in *El pez que fuma*. As Ana López recalls, "Lara's songs idealized woman as a purchasable receptacle for man's physical needs—the ultimate commodity for modern Mexican society—but also invested her with the power of her sexuality: to sell at will, to name her price, to choose her victim" (266). Both strong and sensitive, La Garza embodies a new kind of empowered female subjectivity that, nonetheless, is nullified in the end when she is accidentally shot by one of her lovers.

But *El pez que fuma* is also a story of power struggles that has been interpreted as an allegory of the nation. Corruption, lies, and exploitative economic relationships determine how power changes hands in an inexorable cycle. In Chalbaud's words: "I painted a brothel . . . not because of the brothel in itself, but because I believe that there is a kind of magic and cruelty there, something terrible that seems very much like the society in which we live" (quoted in Naranjo 68). Several men struggle to become La Garza's *macho* and boss, but it is ultimately La Garza who controls and determines every-

Orlando Urdaneta and Hilda Vera in *El pez que fuma*

thing. Accompanying each turn of the plot are musical numbers. The lyrics of classic boleros, tangos, and salsa tunes complement major events while being reminiscent of and paying tribute to a certain era of cinematic history—not only of the continent but also of the country. The song "Taboga," which is played a couple of times on the soundtrack, was the basis for a short musical film in 1937 that was the first sound film made in Venezuela. With its popular characters, music, and settings, as well as with its irony and humor, the film expresses its maker's interest in an autochthonous culture and indigenous national character. Chalbaud's use of "Taboga" along with other popular songs was critical to the film's success and essential to what critic Alvaro Naranjo described as his "great melodramatic vision of national life" (71).[8]

From 1975 onward, Venezuelan cinema proved for the first time that it could be a profitable business. Its critical and box-office success convinced the government of the commercial potential of local filmmaking, and several official institutions responded by giving credits and loans to filmmakers, who, by then, had become their own producers. Names such as Román Chalbaud, Mauricio Walerstein, and Clemente de la Cerda were synonymous with profit and with Venezuelan subject matter. The nation's film industry finally seemed to be under way, and melodrama was one of its fundamental traits.[9] The prospects of a viable industry began to fade after the economic crisis of 1983, which affected industries throughout Latin America. But the roots of a melodramatic imagination had taken firm hold of cinematic and televisual images, and Venezuela, along with Mexico, Brazil, and Argentina, became a major exporter of telenovelas to the world. It is not surprising that Venezuela continues to be one of the major consumers of the melodramatic form.

## Notes

All translations from the Spanish are my own unless stated otherwise.

1. See Herlinghaus; Monsiváis.

2. The romantic excess of 1940s radionovelas, taken up by telenovelas in the 1950s, also contributed to the popularity of the genre.

3. Because of the novel's implicit critique of the dictatorship, Gallegos was forced into exile until 1935.

4. In 1948 a coup d'état overthrew the government of Rómulo Gallegos, who was Venezuela's democratically elected president at the time. From then on a military junta ruled the country. In 1952 Marcos Pérez Jiménez became dictator until 1958, when a democratic government was reinstated.

5. The melodramas were *Amanecer a la vida* (Dawn of Life, by Fernando Cortés, 1950), *La balandra Isabel llegó esta tarde* (Sailboat Isabel Arrived This Afternoon, by

Carlos Hugo Christensen, 1950), *Seis meses de vida* (Six Months of Life, by Víctor Urruchúa, 1951), *Territorio verde* (Green Territory, by Horacio Peterson and Ariel Severino, 1952), *Luz en el páramo* (Light in the High Plains, by Víctor Urruchúa, 1953), and *Noche de milagros* (Night of Miracles, by Renzo Russo, 1953). The comedies were *El demonio es un ángel* (The Demon Is an Angel, by Carlos Hugo Christensen, 1949) and *Yo quiero una mujer así* (That's the Woman I Want, by Juan Carlos Thorry, 1950). The sole musical was *Venezuela también canta* (Venezuela Also Sings, by Fernando Cortés, 1951).

6. It won the award of the International Federation of Film Critics and the prize for best cinematography.

7. For a more complete picture of the trajectory of Chalbaud's career, see Naranjo.

8. See King (220) for additional commentary on the film's score.

9. After making several political films, Walerstein went on to produce passionate stories with strong melodramatic components, as some of his film titles suggest: *Macho y hembra* (Male and Female, 1985), *De mujer a mujer* (Woman to Woman, 1986), *Con el corazón en la mano* (Heart in Hand, 1988), and *Movil pasional* (Passionate Cause, 1994).

## Works Cited

Aguirre, Jesús M., and Marcelino Bisbal. *El nuevo cine venezolano*. Caracas: Editorial Ateneo de Caracas, 1980.

Cabrujas, José Ignacio. *Y Latinoamérica inventó la telenovela*. Caracas: Alfadil Ediciones, 2002.

Caropreso Ponce, Luis. *Breve historia del cine nacional, 1909–1964*. Mimeograph. Cúa, Venezuela: Concejo Municipal del Distrito Urdaneta, 1964.

Chalbaud, Román. "Apuntes de un cineasta," *El nacional* (Caracas), August 12, 1979, 4.

———. "Apuntes de un cineasta," *El nacional* (Caracas), September 23, 1979, 12.

Colmenares, María Gabriela. "Industria e imitación: Los géneros cinematográficos en los largometrajes de ficción de Bolívar Films." *Archivos* 31 (Madrid) (February 1999): 123–35.

Herlinghaus, Hermann. "La imaginación melodramática: Rasgos intermediales y heterogéneos de una categoría precaria." In *Narraciones anacrónicas de la modernidad: Melodrama e intermedialidad en América Latina*. Ed. Hermann Herlinghaus. Santiago: Editorial Cuarto Propio, 2002. 21–59.

Izaguirre, Rodolfo. "Del infortunio recurrente al acto promisor: 1940–1958." In *Panorama histórico del cine venezolano, 1896–1993*. Caracas: Fundación Cinemateca Nacional, 1997. 115–28.

King, John. *Magical Reels: A History of Cinema in Latin America*. London: Verso, 1990.

López, Ana M. "Tears and Desire: Women and Melodrama in the 'Old' Mexican Cinema." In *Multiple Voices in Feminist Film Criticism*. Ed. Diane Carson, Linda

Dittmar, and Janice R.Welsh. Minneapolis: University of Minnesota Press, 1994. 254–70.

Marrosu, Ambretta. "Cine en Venezuela." *Encuadre* 59 (January-March 1996): 55–65.

———. *Exploraciones en la historiografía del cine en Venezuela: Campos, pistas e interrogantes.* Caracas: ININCO, 1985.

———. "Los modelos de la supervivencia." In *Panorama histórico del cine venezolano, 1896–1993.* Caracas: Fundación Cinemateca Nacional, 1997. 21–47.

Martín-Barbero, Jésus. "La telenovela desde el reconocimiento y la anacronía." In *Narraciones anacrónicas de la modernidad: Melodrama e intermedialidad en América Latina.* Ed. Hermann Herlinghaus. Santiago: Editorial Cuarto Propio, 2002. 61–77.

*Mauricio Walerstein (Cuadernos cineastas venezolanos).* Caracas: Fundación Cinemateca Nacional, 2001.

Monsiváis, Carlos. "El melodrama: 'No te vayas, mi amor, que es inmoral llorar a solas.'" In *Narraciones anacrónicas de la modernidad: Melodrama e intermedialidad en América Latina.* Ed. Hermann Herlinghaus. Santiago: Editorial Cuarto Propio, 2002. 105–23.

Naranjo, Alvaro. *Román Chalbaud: Un cine de autor.* Caracas: Fondo Editorial Cinemateca Nacional, 1984.

Oroz, Silvia. *Melodrama: O cine de lágrimas da América Latina.* Mexico City: UNAM, 1995.

Paranaguá, Paulo Antonio. "Román Chalbaud: The 'National' Melodrama on an Air of Bolero." In *Framing Latin American Cinema: Contemporary Critical Perspectives.* Ed. Ann Marie Stock. Minneapolis: University of Minnesota Press, 1997. 162–73.

Roffé, Alfredo. "Políticas y espectáculo cinematográfico en Venezuela." In *Panorama histórico del cine venezolano, 1896–1993.* Caracas: Fundación Cinemateca Nacional, 1997. 245–67.

Ruffinelli, Jorge. "Bajo cinco banderas: El cine multinacional de Carlos Hugo Christensen." In *Revisioning Film in the Fifties.* Stanford: Nuevo Texto Crítico, 1999. 277–325.

Tirado, Ricardo. *Memoria y notas del cine venezolano, 1897–1959.* Caracas: Fundación Neumann, n.d.

———. *Memoria y notas del cine venezolano, 1968–1988.* Caracas: Fundación Neumann, 1988.

Usabel, Gaizka S. de. *The High Noon of American Films in Latin America.* Ann Arbor: UMI Research Press, 1982.

# 3

# The Building of a Nation

## La guerra gaucha *as Historical Melodrama*

### PAULA FÉLIX-DIDIER
### AND ANDRÉS LEVINSON

> There is nothing remarkable in the fact that periodically a country reexamines events from its past and describes them anew in order to know what can be done with them. These are and should be regular procedures of valuation.
>
> Roland Barthes, *Cinema et verité*, 1966

In every review of, tribute to, or celebration of the history of Argentine cinema there is invariably a reference or allusion to *La guerra gaucha* (The Gaucho War, 1942). Directed by Lucas Demare, the film became one of Argentina's most revered pictures. Its public and critical success owes much to the prestige of its cast and crew and its quality as a big-budget production. Adapted from a 1904 volume of short stories titled *La guerra gaucha* by the Argentine writer Leopoldo Lugones, the film takes place in the northern province of Salta in 1818 during the War of Independence (1810–20).[1] Waged by General Martín Miguel Güemes and his gauchos against the Spanish Empire, the War of Independence initiated the long and conflicted process of constructing the Argentine nation-state. Defending what is now the northwestern part of Argentina, Güemes and his gaucho militiamen embodied the heroic struggle of the larger populace in the battle for liberation.

Despite its position in Argentine cinema, *La guerra gaucha* has been the subject of relatively few in-depth critical studies, none of which have approached it from a historical point of view. By approaching the movie from this perspective, we can trace some of the paths that converged in the formation and consolidation of Argentine national and cultural identity as well as some of the different narratives that constitute that identity. The period of the nation's symbolic construction is contemporary with the publication of Lugones's book. Between that period and the making of the film, the image of the nation's construction was reworked, transformed, or reaffirmed by different means. The film offers a popular reading of history at a specific point in time. Moreover, as the French sociologist Pierre Sorlin has argued in *The Film in History*, historical films offer privileged access to the ways in which a society relates to its own history and to the role that historical understanding plays in everyday life. The present essay contends that *La guerra gaucha* offers a specific portrait of Argentina that, like late-nineteenth-century writings about the nation, uses melodrama to say certain things about its war of independence—an event that had renewed significance for the country at the end of the 1930s and the beginning of the 1940s.

*La guerra gaucha* was the most important film produced by Artistas Argentinos Asociados (Associated Argentine Artists, AAA), a company founded in 1941 by several of the most prominent figures in Argentine cinema, including director Lucas Demare, producer Enrique Faustín, actors Enrique Muiño, Elías Alippi, Angel Magaña, and Francisco Petrone, and screenwriters Ulises Petit de Murat and Hómero Manzi. The company benefited greatly from its financial partner, San Miguel Studios, which was Argentina's largest film company and the property of the Machinandiarena family.[2] The group's objective was to produce high-quality films with a *national* focus for mass consumption. The emphasis on "national" was a way of distinguishing their movies from what they regarded as the weak products of an impoverished Argentine cinema. For AAA, that impoverishment stemmed from an "internationalist" strategy adopted by large studios to consolidate their position within the Spanish-speaking marketplace. Argentine films increasingly sought to conceal their national character by reducing or removing regional references, by replacing Argentine words and expressions with more neutral language (for example, using the pronoun *tú* instead of the more characteristically Argentine *vos*), and by adapting world as opposed to national literary classics. The interest of AAA in developing a different kind of film project that would call attention to and defend Argentine cultural identity led them to Lugones's book, which they selected for their first production.[3]

According to surveys conducted by the Buenos Aires Film Museum in 1977,

1984, and 2000, *La guerra gaucha* has been constantly ranked among the most beloved films ever made in Argentina, a ranking that confirms its place in the national conscience. For this reason, it is generally assumed that a considerable amount has been written about the film over the years, and in fact much was written for newspapers and film magazines. For the most part, however, these articles and reviews merely repeated the commentary of Domingo Di Núbila in his seminal *Historia del cine argentino* (1959) or what those who reviewed Di Núbila's book had written. Released in 1942, *La guerra gaucha* was recognized early on as comparable to the best international productions. As the years passed, however, its place within the local canon was increasingly questioned. Influenced by the revolutionary ideas that resulted in the left-wing political films associated with the New Latin American Cinema, critics writing in the 1960s felt that the film's narrative structure was simply an imitation of Hollywood's formula. Regardless of the position for or against the film, critics tended to repeat the same generalized notions: *La guerra gaucha* was an epic that exalted patriotic feelings, it followed the Hollywood western formula, and it subscribed to various kinds of nationalism, some conservative, others popular. Whereas more conservative critics of the earlier period praised the actors' performances, the younger left-wing community criticized them for being exaggerated and unrealistic. Everyone agreed that the film was lyrical and grandiloquent, but there was basic disagreement between the generations about the value of those qualities, which appealed only to the film's conservative supporters. José Agustín Mahieu, a film historian writing in the 1960s, was especially critical of the movie's "facile patriotism" and "almost didactic" style (quoted in Barnard 21).

Among the few academic studies written about *La guerra gaucha,* two works merit special attention. Ana Laura Lusnich's essay "Artistas Argentinos Asociados" discusses the film in the context of AAA's history, and her later article "Los relatos de la frontera en el cine argentino: Estrategias narrativas y textuales" views it in the context of narratives about the frontier in Argentine cinema (following in the footsteps of Eduardo Romano, who began a series on this topic in the 1990s). According to Lusnich, *La guerra gaucha* is part of a body of narratives dedicated to the "exaltation of military figures, the exposition of combat strategies, the use of force, the submission of the Indian and of the gaucho to State norms, the close relationship between man and the landscape . . . interests [that] are translated into the glorification of past military heroism and a privileged historic subject, [the military hero]" ("Relatos" 37). Lusnich argues that this strategy could have served the new (barely democratic) political project of the 1930s but that the film ultimately strays from "republican values and language" (38). Lusnich's commentary on the close relation between man and landscape in the film is convincing, but her other observations are difficult to support. Problems arise when attempts are made to establish close or direct ties between a political moment in the country's history and cultural production—as if it were possible to establish from a political perspective a cultural hegemony free of all contradictions. As we discuss in more detail below, those who adapted the film were close to the democratic cause: Manzi belonged to the Fuerza de Orientación Radical de la Joven Argentina (FORJA), one of the political groups that most adamantly denounced the fraudulent practices of the government, and Ulises Petit de Murat was an intellectual well known for his social-democratic ideals.[4] Lusnich's notion that AAA made a film that was contrary to the political ideas that its members openly defended is curious and questionable.

The critic Elina Tranchini also considers *La guerra gaucha* within a broader body of work, pointing out that the films produced by AAA were to a great extent "historical films considered emblematic because of their popularity [and] their cinematic quality" (15). In her analysis, she emphasizes the ways in which cinema can influence ideas of nation, memory, and history and argues that in serving these ends, *La guerra gaucha* appropriated themes and rhetoric of melodrama—an observation with which we strongly agree—while formally modeling itself after the 1930s Hollywood western. Following this line of thinking, the epic-historic Argentine cinema not only narrated the origins of the Argentine nation in this manner but also "incorporated the forms of a U.S. cowboy sociability, giving them a *creole* turn" (16).

But let us examine these ideas from a different perspective. Clearly one of AAA's objectives was to forge a truly national cinema with its own style, which it pitted against the "internationalist" tendency of the time. Moreover, long before the existence of a U.S. cowboy cinema, late-nineteenth-century Argentine creole literature, such as José Hernández's celebrated poem *Martín Fierro* (1872), frequently described forms of gaucho sociability—forms that were easily adapted for the screen. Tranchini's comparative approach provides rich insights, but it overlooks AAA's mission to forge a "new" cinema and completely overlooks the importance of history as well as the gaucho tradition in Argentine literature that was central to *La guerra gaucha*.

## Historical Melodrama

At the end of the nineteenth century, Argentina's ruling class set out to build a modern democratic state. A crucial aspect of this task was to provide a narrative about a common history that would help define and construct a national identity. The War of Independence was foundational for the narrative. Marking the beginning of Argentine history, the confrontation with Spain is represented by a series of bloody battles with heroes and villains in a long struggle over the nation's freedom. In Latin America, foundational discourses about the nation were well suited to the narrative matrix of nineteenth-century melodrama, which emphasized the protagonists' spirit and love for their country. Melodrama's baroque excess complemented the hypernational nature of foundational narrative far better than did the positivist discourse that characterized most writings about history. Nonetheless, a curious overlapping was usually the result. The great national histories that appeared at the end of the nineteenth century appealed both to the scientific discourse of the period and to the discourse of highly dramatized epics. Argentine writers such as Bartolomé Mitre, a historian who was president of the nation from 1862 to 1868, and Vicente Fidel López, also a historian, are the genre's most important writers, and between them they launched the trend toward a historical nationalism.[5] Like realistic novels, their works contain moral instruction that provides important lessons for the citizens. Operating between dramatic narration and rigorous history, their writing stirred in readers a sense of duty as citizens of a nation whose forging, according to their narratives, demanded exceptional efforts and sublime actions.

According to cultural critic Carlos Monsiváis, melodrama is the mold upon which the consciousness of Latin America is imprinted. "History—the scholarly approach to History that still reigns—is one of the greatest matrices of melodrama. Heroes give their lives for others and walk with a steady pace toward the scaffold or the firing squad because they know that they will be reborn in the gratitude of their compatriots" (45). No precise point of origin exists for the nation, which is submerged in the depths of time yet somehow also legitimate and everlasting. A sort of essence of the nation, or "nation-ness," continues for years or decades without change, to the point at which the nation, which becomes its basic explicative principle, is beyond history. The idea of a national community emerges from the combination of different elements, the most important of which are the action of the state through its educational programs and civic festivities and narratives that circulate outside the state apparatus in literature, music, theater, and cinema. As Monsiváis has stated: "[By] watching Mexican, Argentine, and Brazilian films, the respective audiences learn to be national, an imprecise and even fantastic category; and if popular history is a selective mirror of heroes as gods and of tragedies as previews or summaries of personal life, cinema is a permanent mirror" (48).

Unlike other national stories that follow a romantic line, the foundation of Argentine history is basically territorial. Given the great heterogeneity of its inhabitants and the difficulty of finding a common past, language, or tradition, national narratives tend to assert the existence of the country on the basis of its legal territory. Throughout the twentieth century, the idea of a territorial nation is affirmed and expanded. A good example of this is the geopolitical analysis made in the 1940s during Perón's administration (1946–55). The different international conflicts that Argentina faced, generally against neighboring countries such as Chile, Paraguay, and Bolivia, had their origins in territorial concerns; in these cases, the state appealed consistently to the aforementioned narratives, thus feeding the binomial nation-territory. Land becomes the foundation of the nation and guarantees its unity; it becomes the object of patriotic respect, producing heroes who give their lives to liberate invaded territories—as is the case in *La guerra gaucha*.

Narratives of the state's formative period are based on stories in which patriotic heroes find their first expression. Lugones's *La guerra gaucha*, however, deserves special attention for having elevated "the people" to the level of the heroic. In the book as well as the film, the populace plays a fundamental role in the construction of the nation, but it is always under the guidance, first spiritual and then material, of its most famous leaders, José de San Martín and Manuel Belgrano, and, secondarily, of General Martín Miguel de Güemes. A community of men, women, and children is part of a destiny greater than its members. As Captain Del Carril, one of the film's main characters, remarks: "Somos pasto de la gloria grande" (We [the people's army] are the substance for the greater glory").

## Literature, Film, Politics, and History

If the popular imaginary of national identity is built from stories that organize a narrative matrix for Argentine history and give symbolic content to the nation, *La guerra gaucha*, in its literary and its filmic versions, has special importance. Like every case of literary adaptation, it is a particular reading of a precursor text. The politically committed reading that took place in 1942 of a text published in 1904 is the one that interests us.

Lugones's *La guerra gaucha* consists of twenty-two stories and is part of a series of books that were written prior to the centennial of the 1810 May Revolution. The period preceding the centennial celebration was an appropriate time to assess what had been achieved in the country and to plan for the future. A great deal of writing turned on the question of what the true national culture was and how to define the nation's being. The countryside and the gaucho were immediately offered in response to these questions; in effect, they formed the basis of a "lettered" construction and were turned into bastions of Argentine essence. This image of the nation was later called into question by the transformation of Buenos Aires as a result of the arrival of thousands of European immigrants.[6] Lugones, like other intellectuals and politicians working at the beginning of the century, was concerned with giving content and meaning to Argentina's cultural identity through the figure of the gaucho, and in this context he wrote *La guerra gaucha*, which concerned the gaucho-soldiers' struggle against Spanish forces. His stated intention was to provide Argentina with its first national text along the lines provided by *The Odyssey* and *The Iliad* for Greece or *The Divine Comedy* for Italy.[7]

The desire to produce the great Argentine epic implicitly involved special consideration of the type and form of language to be used. The language had to be foundational; the book had to show people speaking their own way, a national tongue, as opposed to one transformed by the different languages and dialects heard in Buenos Aires. Lugones faced a formidable and paradoxical task: creating a modern-day epic about the Argentine past in a cultivated language that would be accessible and adopted by the people as the tale of nationality. As critic María Teresa Gramuglio has argued, there were actually two Lugones: the *poet maldite*, who renovated literary forms, and the civic poet, who was committed to political reality. It is the latter—or perhaps a combination of both—who wrote *La guerra gaucha* in a grandiloquent and hypernationalistic style.[8]

In the 1930s the state and a large number of intellectuals again faced problems associated with national identity. Discussions and debates took up new problems and new ways of looking at the country. Beginning in 1930 with the Great Depression, the crisis of the agrarian export model, the effects of a substitute import industry, and the social and cultural transformation of the popular classes forced intellectuals to rethink the past. The national question reemerged in relation to the formulation of an anti-imperialist discourse that, from the extremes of the country's ideological spectrum, saw the presence of foreign capital as a threat to the nation's freedom. The concepts of imperialism, colonization, and economic dependence gained new importance.

In the years just prior to the 1910 centennial, extreme economic growth subdued any critique of nationality. The country's economic situation in the 1930s was a very different one, and a discourse about a colonized Argentina was widely disseminated. Different groups no longer hesitated to denounce the economic relations formed with Great Britain and maintained by the conservative government of General Agustín P. Justo—relations described as a new kind of colonialism that benefited the British capital and the major local landholders.[9] It is within this context that the movement called *yrigoyenismo* established FORJA, whose founders included Homero Manzi, author of the screenplay for *La guerra gaucha*. The explicit purpose of this group was to "infuse emancipation into the social conscience" (Scenna 76), and its statute of June 29, 1935, left no room for doubt as to its larger aim: "We are a Colonial Argentina, we want to be a Free Argentina" (quoted in Scenna 76). Meanwhile, conflicting opinions about nationalism on the part of conservatives, revisionists, and populists strove to conquer public opinion, while the state continued to define the attributes of nationality.

The versions of patriotism that existed within this bidding for a dominant popular nationalist discourse differed, but they also coincided in their belief that the teaching of history would strengthen patriotic feeling among the populace. Education became a fundamental tool, and, as in the beginning of the century, when the educational projects of Ricardo Rojas and Ezequiel Ramos Mejía emphasized the importance of teaching history in order to consolidate nationality, history played a major role in the formation of Argentine identity. The dissemination of history rose to record levels through the publication and widespread circulation of texts, some of which were specialized, such as the National History Academy's *Historia de la nación Argentina* and Ricardo Rojas's less rigorous *El santo de la espada* (The Sword-Wielding Saint). As historian Alejandro Cattaruzza has noted: "The historians, the State, the political parties, and the intellectuals who pondered the nation's situation seemed to understand in the 1930s—although this wasn't an understanding exclusive to the period—that the past could have some practical use in the present" (433). State-sponsored "patriotic education" gained additional force from the creation of such new national holidays as Rosette Day and National Flag Day, as well as monuments erected to the memory of heroes of the state such as Juan Bautista Alberdi. In the years prior to the centennial, intellectual discourse presented the gaucho as the true representative of the nation, an idea that by the end of the 1930s had become part of the social conscience. As a result, in 1939, the state proclaimed November 10, the birthday of José Hernández (author of *Martin Fierro,* the epic poem about the gaucho), to be part of its patriotic calendar in celebration of the gaucho as the authentic inhabitant of the Argentine countryside.

Appearing three years later, *La guerra gaucha* brought to the fore nationalistic ideology and popular themes that were widely circulated in the 1930s, in particular, the symbolic figure of the gaucho. The film allows for different kinds of readings, among them the already mentioned denunciation of imperialism that takes form in the film's portrayal of the land and the battle for independence. In its depiction of the nation, the film also refers to widely accepted ideas about the Argentine past that were constructed by liberal historiographies and to a large extent supported by FORJA. For example, there is no discussion of whether the country actually existed before the 1810 revolution—a topic impossible to address in those years.[10] The film basically follows established versions of history, although instead of emphasizing the nation's individual heroes, it shines a light on the heroic efforts of the people. This was a very different approach from that taken in most movies, which preferred to focus on individual protagonists. San Martín and Belgrano are referred to in the film, but they are never seen on screen, and Güemes appears only at the end.

As it celebrates the people, *La Guerra gaucha* effectively appropriates the country's patriotic heroes, whose images were deeply ingrained in the popular imagination. It provides considerable information about San Martín and Belgrano and shows the degree to which the conversion of the creole lieutenant Villareal (Ángel Magaña) from the Spanish side to the patriotic cause was a result of his reading Belgrano's letters. Throughout the film, San Martín serves as a spiritual guide for Güemes and his gauchos. The structuring absence of these historical figures merely reaffirms their images as popular heroes. The film's decision to tell another story that focuses on the people is possible only because it also includes the undisputable heroes of the war whose stories are well known. The story of the people's struggle for independence in the 1800s is therefore an allegory of the country's situation in 1942, and it calls implicitly for the Argentine people to rise up and free themselves from British economic colonization.

## Keys to a Cinematic Success

Lugones's hyperbolic style of writing was respected by Demare, Manzi, and Petit de Murat. The aesthetics of excess that characterized the book's language was actually well suited to the film's melodramatic portrait of a nation's liberation struggle. If the film in any way resembles classic texts about independence, it is in this melodramatic atmosphere. Although both the film and the book were interested in reviving and renewing their respective art forms, the film succeeded where the book failed. As the first large production to portray the War of Independence, *La guerra gaucha* provided Argentine cinema with a strong model and incentive for future high-quality films about the nation. On the other hand, the difficulties of reading *La guerra gaucha* are well known.[11]

Lugones's complex and ornate language did not appeal to the vast majority of Argentine readers at the time. Nonetheless, it is interesting that Manzi and Petit de Murat's adaptation does not stray far from the source text, and whole sentences were barely modified or simply used in their original form. Of course, audiences had changed since the book was first published, but it was the film-makers' choice to shape the book into a melodrama that was crucial to its overwhelmingly positive reception.

One of the main tasks of Manzi and Petit de Murat was to find a way to weave together the book's numerous independent stories into a single narrative. In Lugones's work, the characters have no names, but the script gave them first and last names and even nicknames to provide a sense of recognition and a stronger bond with the audience. Despite this consolidation, however, the film remained true to Lugones's exalted descriptions of patriotism, his identification of a people with their land, his portrait of the people as the protagonist, and his vision of the epic struggle for independence—ideas that were equally important to AAA's mission to construct a new national cinema.

At the same time, the film adheres to formulas of "classical cinema." Although it is best described as a historical melodrama, its collective protagonist and secondary emphasis on romance depart slightly from the norms of the genre. As mentioned above, *La guerra gaucha* has often been compared to the western in terms of its structure, characters, and theme. Although this may be an appropriate description of AAA's film *Pampa bárbara* (Savage Pampa), it is not adequate or appropriate for *La guerra gaucha,* and it has resulted in repeated misconceptions about the film.[12] The Hollywood western is often about the conquest of Indians and hostile nature by Europeans, whereas *La guerra gaucha* is about a romantic identification of man, nature, and the land. It makes numerous references to blood as the "seed" of a new nation, and it treats the countryside as the natural home of the gaucho. Moreover, contrary to the conventional Argentine practices of shooting on sets and indoors, AAA shot on location to capture the grandeur of Argentina's natural vistas as well as to emphasize the "mixing of blood and land" in the various battle sequences. In this respect, the film leaves no room for doubt: "Scruffy captains, mutilated, begging around the fields, hungry children, gauchos without glory, bleeding for the land they love more than their own lives. Think, lieutenant, think. Your blood mixed with the land continues to live," remarks Asunción Colombres (Amelia Bence), the female farmer and patriot who helps Villarreal. He has been wounded while fighting alongside the Spaniards, and Asunción intends to hand him over to the local army.

Whereas the western emphasizes the conquest of new territory and hostile savages to build the nation, *La guerra gaucha* puts forward an image of a people fighting to liberate their homeland from outsiders. Nature plays a prominent role in the gaucho's struggle; he is familiar with it and uses it against the Spanish. As critic Susana Cella has noted in the introduction to Lugones's book: "The [gauchos'] struggle is then legitimized by nature and the attempt of the Spanish becomes contrary to its eternal laws" (29). Lieutenant Villarreal ultimately converts to the local cause because he is American, born on Argentine soil, and his conversion is clearly patriotic. He ultimately leads the gauchos in battle against his former soldiers.

The U.S. western is also the genre of the individual hero par excellence, the man who builds his own destiny, who owes nothing to anyone, and who defends personal causes that have an indirect effect on the nation. In the Argentine film, an entire population fights in defense of a subjugated country. The staging and the use of cinematographic resources such as shot scale, montage, and a soundtrack reinforce the epic-heroic portrait of a people. *La guerra gaucha* therefore has much more in common with the historic melodrama than with the western: the visual excess, the cluttered images, the overacting of characters, the hyperbolic language, and speeches that often border on the unrealistic foster an estrangement that works toward the epic-mythic dimension of the history to be told. The melodramatic style is in keeping with the grandiloquent, emphatic, baroque, and excessive nature of Lugones's prose. In fact, the film has few or no pretensions of being realist. Its objective is to provoke emotions in relation to the Argentine homeland. The expressionistic musical scoring by Lucio Demare, brother of the director, reinforces the film's emotional atmosphere and emphasizes the pathos of events as they unfold.

A good example of the film's melodramatic character can be found in the scene in which Asunción tries to convert Lieutenant Villarreal to the patriotic cause. As she talks to the convalescing soldier, a storm rages outside, symbolizing the fierceness of Asunción's patriotism and the tumult of Villareal's thoughts about the war. The entire scene is shot in a series of dramatically lit close-ups and is accompanied by a musical score that emphasizes the intensity of what is happening both within and outside the house. Before the calm that follows the storm, the feverish lieutenant has made his decision to become a patriot. The consummation of Asunción and Villareal's mutual love is now possible thanks to their common nationalist cause, whose story is never subordinated to any other story in the film. This includes the budding

Amelia Bence as Asunción
in *La guerra gaucha*

romance and mounting sexual desire between Asunción and Villareal, which is forestalled, if not totally displaced, by their love for the nation. Recuperated, Villarreal leaves to rejoin the battle as Asunción awaits his return.

In the style of other widely circulated historical narratives, *La guerra gaucha* appeals to the public's emotions by means of a melodramatically charged format. It stirs emotions not only about the wartime past but also about the present day and the need for Venezuela to liberate itself from the constraints placed upon it by outside forces. In this sense the film seems much closer to popular nationalism and FORJA than to conservative nationalism—despite the importance it gives to the military. At the same time, the military represented in the film is not the professional soldier preferred by the conservatives but rather the gaucho militiaman who represents the people. The film makes this point very clearly in a line that serves as the movie's epilogue and statement of its overall nationalistic and melodramatically charged purpose: "This is how they lived and this is how they died, those without names who waged the gaucho war."

## Notes

1. Leopoldo Lugones (1874–1938), poet, essayist, and prose writer, was one of Argentina's most distinguished intellectuals at the turn of the century.

2. According to Timothy Barnard, San Miguel Studios tried to diversify its huge production base by using smaller, more efficient production teams. Its owner was impressed with AAA's innovative potential, and he gave them full access to his finest technicians and equipment (20).

3. The death of Elias Alippi, who was to star in *La guerra gaucha,* caused another film, *El Viejo Hucha* (Old Man Hucha), to become AAA's first release.

4. Fuerza de Orientación Radical de la Joven Argentina was a group composed of young intellectuals and politicians from the Radical Party who supported Hipólito Yrigoyen. A popular leader and defender of democratic values, Irigoyen was deposed in 1930.

5. See Mitre's *Historia de San Martín y de la emancipación sudamericana,* 3 vols. (Buenos Aires: Imprenta de "La nación" [1888]); Fidel López, *Historia de la república Argentina,* 10 vols. (Buenos Aires: Imprenta de Mayo, 1883–1893).

6. Between 1869 and 1914, the population grew from two million to eight million. By the end of the period, almost half of Argentina's population was of immigrant origin.

7. Lugones wrote: "The country needs its own *Iliad,* it needs a text that establishes its language and its lineage." See his *Obras completas* 143.

8. On this subject, Gramuglio notes: "The strangeness of the text says something about the conflict within its author. The fabulous lesson of Argentine history imparted by an expert philologist who displays his etymological knowledge resists any etymological manipulation. Far from contributing to the configuration of a linguistic community in search of national identity, the language segregates [its readers] and leads to dispersion. Lugones' early nationalism is curious in the sense that patriotic history becomes a hardly discernible epic" (21–22).

9. Justo won the presidential election in 1932, two years after the military coup that removed Hipólito Irigoyen from office. Justo's corrupt conservative administration was in power until a military coup removed him in 1943. Three years later, Perón was elected.

10. As we have indicated, for both traditional historiography and for the "revisionist" histories that appeared in the 1930s, the Argentine nation began with the May 1810 revolution. Later histories move that date to 1860, following the greater consolidation of the state.

11. Jorge Luis Borges wrote: "[T]he syntax is sometimes inextricable and the abuse of demonstrative pronouns which frequently forces the reader to turn back is an obstacle to further reading. The theme disappears under the luxuriance of the style." He added: "[B]ecause of its cinematic adaptation and its patriotic argument, not for its reading, *La guerra gaucha* has enjoyed widespread attention" (73).

12. The film was shown in Paris in 1947, and the reviews described it as a bad South American western. The French director Pierre Chenal collected these reviews, which subsequently influenced the writings of many Argentine critics.

## Works Cited

Barnard, Timothy. *South American Cinema: A Critical Filmography, 1915–1994.* Ed. Timothy Barnes and Peter Rist. Austin: University of Texas Press, 1996.

Borges, Jorge Luis. Introduction to *Leopoldo Lugones.* Buenos Aires: Troquel, 1955.

Cattaruzza, Alejandro, ed. *Nueva historia argentina,* vol. 3, *Crisis económica, avance del estado e incertidumbre política (1930–1945).* Buenos Aires: Sudamericana, 2001.

Di Núblia, Domingos. *Historia del cine argentino.* Buenos Aires: Ediciones Cruz de Malta, 1959.

Gramuglio, María Teresa. "Literatura y nacionalismo: Leopoldo Lugones y la construcción de imágenes del escritor." *Hispamérica* 22 (1993): 5–22.

Lugones, Leopoldo. *La guerra gaucha.* Preliminary study and notes by Susana B. Cella. Buenos Aires: Losada, 1992.

———. *Obras completas.* Buenos Aires: Ediciones Pasco, 1999.

Lusnich, Ana Laura. "Artistas Argentinos Asociados." In *Cine argentino, industria y clasicismo.* Ed. Claudio España. Buenos Aires: Fondo Nacional de las Artes, 2000. 346–99.

———. "Los relatos de la frontera en el cine argentino: Estrategias narrativas y textuales." In *Civilización y barbarie en el cine argentino y latinoamericano.* Ed. A. L. Lusnich. Buenos Aires: Biblos, 2004. 35–42.

Monsiváis, Carlos. "Se sufre porque se aprende (de las variedades del melodrama en América Latina)." In *Educar la mirada: Políticas y pedagogías de la imagen.* Ed. Inés Dussel and Daniela Gutiérrez. Buenos Aires: FLASCO, 2006. 23–57.

Romano, Eduardo. *Literatura/Cine argentinos sobre la(s) frontera(s).* Buenos Aires: Catálogos, 1991.

Scenna, Miguel Ángel. *FORJA: Una aventura argentina (De Irigoyen a Perón).* Buenos Aires: Ed. de Belgrano, 1983.

Sorlin, Pierre. *The Film in History: Restaging the Past.* Oxford: Blackwell, 1980.

Tranchini, Elina. "Cordilleras y exilios." In *La imagen como vehículo de la identidad nacional.* Ed. Clara Kriger. Cuadernos de Cine Argentino 5. Buenos Aires: INCAA, 2005. 11–29.

# 4

# Women as Civilizers in
# 1940s Brazilian Cinema
## *Between Passion and the Nation*

### CID VASCONCELOS

The growing interest of the Brazilian state in cinema from the 1930s onward took place within a very broad context. Under the Estado Novo (New State) dictatorship of Getúlio Vargas (1937–45), there was an attempt to achieve greater political and cultural centralization of local oligarchies that had controlled the First Republic (1889–1930). The nation was increasingly viewed through the filter of the state, which believed itself to be its most faithful representative. In films to be discussed in this essay, there was a definite and far from coincidental parallel between values associated with the nation's identity and those authenticated by intellectuals linked with the state—whether in the form of Marajó artwork in Humberto Mauro's *Argila* (Clay, 1940), in the image of First Lady Darcy Vargas in the hypernationalistic finale to Raul Roulien's *Aves sem ninho* (Birds without a Nest, 1939), or in the Brazilian-style ballet scored by Alberto Nepomuceno for Adhemar Gonzaga's *Romance proibido* (Forbidden Romance, 1944).

The selection of melodrama as the framework for nationalistic themes and values was not simply by chance, nor was it predicated on the Brazilian public's long fascination with the genre in the form of books, plays, radio broadcasts (which included the first radio soap in 1941) and the cinema itself. In the case of cinema, the use of melodrama for propagandistic purposes during World War II is well documented, especially with regard to German and Italian films.[1] Despite the popularity of the wartime melodrama formula in *Ships with Wings* (1941), England was one of the few countries with government guidelines that discouraged the use of sensationalism, melodrama, and heroic attitudes in favor of more realistic productions based on "ordinary people's" daily lives

(Enticknap 212). It is impossible not to compare Brazilian films of the period with Italian or German productions, given their shared interest in idealized heroes and other exalted characters associated with altruistic sacrifice for the nation. The similarities are far from coincidental. The idea of the nation-state formulated by the ideologues of the Estado Novo was directly influenced by the German romantic model and its idea of community rather than by the less cultural and more political French model, which was primarily based on the concept of the social contract. Yet there was a notable difference between Brazilian and German films, and it relates to their representations of women. Whereas German heroines (often peasants) are traditionally feminine and submissive, women in Brazilian melodramas are not.

In the culturally and politically heady period characterized by the rise of the New Man, *Argila, Aves sem ninho,* and *Romance proibido* portray the New Woman as a small-scale version of the great leader, the head of state, who is the most symbolically charged representative of the nation's values (Pereira 2003).[2] Traditionally such alter egos were male characters. A case in point is a Portuguese production by António Lopes Ribeiro, *A revolução de maio* (The May Revolution, 1937), in which the protagonist César Valente (António Martínez) represents the conservative values associated with the Portuguese dictator António de Oliveira Salazar. In the case of Brazil, all but one of the major protagonists in the three surviving films associated with the Estado Novo are women—a fact that is generally attributed to the films' being melodramas. Vitória (Déa Selva) in *Aves sem ninho* is in some ways like First Lady Darcy Vargas, who was known for her work with social organizations and whose photograph appears at the end of the movie. Luciana (Carmen Santos) in *Argila* and Gracia (Lúcia Lamar) in *Romance proibido* are more problematic characters; activists who fail to achieve their respective goals, they compromise the image of a powerful and successful political leadership.

At the time these films were being made, the situation of women in Brazilian society was undergoing considerable change. Historian Ana Pessoa comments on the period:

> In February 1932, Getúlio Vargas decreed a new electoral law that called for elections of a Constituent Assembly. This law introduced important innovations, such as the secret ballot, Electoral Justice, and the granting of the vote to women.
>
> Long demanded by the feminist movement, the right to vote recognized the social and political space that women were gradually entering. There were notable women in letters and the arts, such as Gilka Machado and Tarsila do Amaral. In the sciences, ethnographer Heloísa Alberto Torres and engineer

Carmen Portinho were noteworthy. New ideas for the inclusion of women in the political arena were being offered, as exemplified by the works of Maria Lacerda de Moura, who questioned the bourgeois concepts of sex and love.

Women broke through social barriers and into public spaces. Traditional high schools, such as the Pedro II, opened their doors to young women. Elsewhere women began going to nightclubs and showing more of their bodies on the beaches. (158)

The present essay is interested in the representation of this "modern" woman in the three aforementioned films and, more specifically, the image of women as civilizers who challenge the established moral and social order and advance new ideas about work, education, and social relationships. Although these films supported and disseminated the prevailing values of the Estado Novo, they also constructed an image of women that was much more similar to that of the liberated female in certain Hollywood movies than to the regime's overall notion of womanhood as obedient and submissive.[3] For example, in *Argila,* Luciana combines her active support for an authentically national art with her concern for the welfare of pottery workers, and she strives to improve the quality of their lives while promoting the cause of an indigenous Brazilian art. In *Aves sem ninho,* Vitória works to transform orphanages for girls into professional education centers that will facilitate their (re)entry into society. In *Romance proibido,* Gracia takes a community without a school and transforms it into the municipality with the largest decrease of illiteracy in the state. It is not by chance that two of the three women characters are teachers, but they are also social activists who orchestrate pedagogical proposals to bring about change; the third character, Luciana, makes plans for the workers that include providing a school for their children.

Added to this representation of the modern, socially active woman are two characteristics that are much more common to melodrama: self-sacrifice and impossible passion. Not surprisingly, tensions build when the emancipated woman is also endowed with typically female attributes derived from Judeo-Christian tradition that show her to be nurturing or emotionally vulnerable. That women must pay a price in melodrama for their civilizing crusade is an idea that dates back to biblical times. One of the best examples (repeatedly portrayed in the movies) is Joan of Arc, the prototype of female self-sacrifice, who is burned at the stake. In his discussion of melodrama, critic Pablo Pérez Rubío comments on this theme: "[I]t always implies a self-annulment of desire, almost exclusively the female's, and therefore constitutes—besides the evidence of the patriarchal order—a kind of dilettantish masochism, a complacent self-destruction prior to the final reward that signifies a generalized recognition of its good faith" (40).

To a lesser or greater degree, the self-sacrifice of the three protagonists in the Brazilian films results in their being cut off from their upper-class social environment, which is generally represented as frivolous and uninterested in the poor and the working class, feeling no responsibility to support the less fortunate. Thus, Luciana's interest in Marajora art is ridiculed by her friends, Vitória's work with the orphanage is treated derisively, and Gracia suffers romantic disillusionment within her elite social circle as she attempts to found a school.[4] The protagonists' conflicts with the moneyed class draw them even closer to the less privileged, creating an interclass bonding that was encouraged by the Vargas administration. But as the following discussion will show, the theme of self-sacrifice is only one of the melodramatic elements that helped shape the three films' nationalistic ideology.

*Argila*'s Luciana is a young, rich widow who is attracted to a humble yet talented potter named Gilberto (Celso Guimarães). Luciana's interest in Gilberto causes his fiancée, Marina (Lídia Mattos), to become jealous, which, in turn, upsets her brother Pedrinho, who is witness to his sister's growing unhappiness. In one scene, Gilberto gives Luciana a rare indigenous Marajora artifact, which is his way of thanking her for nursing him while he recovered from a fall when working in her house. Shortly afterward, Luciana buys the factory that produces the pottery used in the region and decides to transform it into an enterprise for the selling of the pottery as local art objects. On the night of a lavish party to celebrate Luciana's new venture, to be called the Salão Marajora, Pedrinho steals the artifact that Gilberto gave to Luciana. When Pedrinho's father discovers what his son has done, he tells Luciana. He also informs her that Marina and Gilberto are in a precarious situation because of rumors that Gilberto is attracted to Luciana. Later, when Gilberto returns the artifact to Luciana, she pretends that her attraction to him was merely a rich woman's whim and reminds him that she is his employer.

Luciana sacrifices her feelings of desire for Gilberto so that the engaged couple and the larger community are not adversely affected. What is uncertain is whether the community will experience any significant improvement as a result of her act because the film ends with her farewell to Gilberto. Nor is it clear whether Luciana's decision to abandon her leisured life to promote the region's potters has actually changed her worldview; her decision, after all,

Luciana seduces Gilberto in *Argila.*

was motivated by her attraction to Gilberto. We also learn from one of the film's secondary characters that Luciana had an earlier relationship with a local musician named Mário, whose career was destroyed when she abandoned him. The film's ending leaves open the possibility that something similar might happen to Gilberto, and it is not clear whether Luciana's interest in Marajora art will continue or be abandoned.

*Argila*'s ideological flaw has to do with its particular approach to romance as an expression of national cohesion and internal unity. More specifically, the film associates the valorization of the genuinely national with Luciana, a sexually aggressive woman whose eroticism problematizes her role as a potential symbol of the nation. In this regard, the film differs from well-known nationalistic works by Brazilian as well as Spanish American nineteenth-century writers. To borrow an insight from Anthony Smith, who writes about nationalism in literature and film, although *Argila* articulates the same myth as the one found in nineteenth-century romantic literature about a glorious, though not problem-free, ethnic past, it fails to offer an equally promising national future (47). As such, its narrative is closer to what critic Doris Sommer calls the "atypical novel" *Maria* (1867), by the Colombian writer Jorge Isaacs, a narrative in which the "impossible love between historically antagonistic lovers (sectors) underlines the urgency for a national project that would reconcile the antagonisms [but] doesn't point to a solution" (174). Note that *Argila* employs strategies that are similar to but not identical to those often found in romantic literature. Whereas romantic literature usually points to impossible love as an indicator of potential national conciliation, *Argila* starts with a much more explicit proposal for conciliation that wears itself down during the course of the narrative.

The film's failure to achieve conciliation in the end reflects the difficulty of forging an interclass pact in Brazil at the time—a pact undoubtedly aspired to by the director, Humberto Mauro, but problematized by the melodramatic plot. Unlike contemporary Latin American melodramas, Mauro's film failed to adapt its ideological message to a story about productive love. Luciana and Gilberto's sexual attraction threatens the limits of social common sense and seals the failure of the project's nationalist potential. The film's decision to support Gilberto and Marina's continued relationship reaffirms the values of the society at large, or, as Silvia Oroz has noted: "[I]n order to be productive, love should walk 'with smooth steps' and 'down the road of goodness'"(63).[5] Where it fails is in its decision to associate nationalist ideals with Luciana rather than with Marina. Doing the latter would have undermined the theme of an interclass pact, one of the film's major objectives. Moreover, by identifying the nationalist cause with the least privileged class, the film would have resulted in a less favorable image of the bourgeoisie as a whole.

In the end, *Argila* was both a public and a critical failure. Despite being one of Brazil's best-known makers of silent film and the director of the celebrated *Ganga Bruta* (1932), Mauro was criticized for abandoning his "spontaneous" style of moviemaking and adopting production values that seemed artificial and forced. Some critics blamed the failure of the film on the actress and producer, Carmen Santos, who was one of the most influential names in Brazilian cinema at the time. In fact, the character Luciana more closely resembles Santos, a daring and exceptionally independent woman than any of Mauro's earlier popular heroines, who were slightly more malicious and sensual than the typical Hollywood women played by Lillian Gish, Florence Lawrence, and Mary Pickford.

A love triangle can also be found at the center of *Romance proibido*, directed by Adhemar Gonzaga, a filmmaker known for "photogenic" melodramas featuring beautiful young actors and luxurious postcard settings—trademarks established long before he founded the magazine *Cinearte* (1926), which promoted Hollywood-style moviemaking, and the movie studio Cinédia (1930), which was modeled after Hollywood. In *Romance proibido,* the upper-class heroine, Gracia Rangel, becomes involved with Carlos Modesto (Milton Marinho), a handsome businessman from the interior who visits Rio de Janeiro to make professional contacts and enjoy nightlife in the capital. While they carry on a passionate affair, Tamar (Nilza Magrassi), Carlos's fiancée and a former friend of Gracia from boarding school, loses her father in an automobile accident. As a result, Carlos leaves Gracia and returns to the grieving Tamar. Disillusioned with love, Gracia decides to dedicate her life to teaching.

After studying and receiving a diploma, she travels to a town without a school in the interior of the state, where she plans to introduce an innovative literacy project. This also happens to be the town where Carlos and Tamar live and where they are about to be married. The innocent Tamar tries to rekindle their schoolgirl friendship, but Gracia avoids her because of Carlos, who still loves her and wants to run away with her. When her work in the town results in public recognition of the state's lowest municipal illiteracy rate, Gracia refuses Carlos's impassioned plea for her to flee with him. Instead, she leaves to work in another town without a school, where she will try to forget Carlos once and for all and no longer stand in the way of Tamar's happiness.

The heroine's self-sacrificial posture is double-faceted: Gracia not only refuses to leave town with the man she loves but also gives up her social standing and withdraws from her elite social circle to become a public school teacher. Gracia's final refusal of Carlos is reminiscent of Luciana's rejection of Gilberto in the end of *Argila*, but there are important differences. *Argila*'s long farewell scene has strong emotional impact because of the attention given throughout the film to Luciana and Gilberto's intense yet problematic romance. In comparison, the breakup in *Romance proibido* seems void of

The romantic triangle in *Romance proibido*

emotion, although Gracia appears to cry in the film's final shot. Gonzaga's film fails to create melodramatic tension because Tamar never once suspects the affair between Gracia and Carlos but simply wonders whether Carlos really loves her.

A ballet performed in the Rio nightclub that Carlos visits at the beginning of the film deserves special attention because it attempts to infuse the film with additional nationalistic elements. Choreographed by the celebrated Brazilian dancer Eros Volúsia (daughter of the poet Gilka Machado), the ballet was based on a score by Alberto Nepomuceno, who was one of Vargas's favorite composers.[6] The dance provided an alternative to the "cheeky sambas" that appeared in films at the time and were disliked by conservative sectors of the public and the press. Criticism of samba was largely racist in character, as when one reader of the June 10, 1943, issue of *A scena muda* (The Silent Scene), the most influential film magazine of the period, derided the samba's origins and character by referring to its "thick Sudanese lips" (25).

The weight of "national authenticity" in the person of Eros Volúsia is considerable, and contrasting her with Carmen Miranda makes this aspect of her image even clearer. Comparisons between the two were fairly frequent in the 1940s, when the press played a major role in shaping public opinion. Unlike Carmen, Eros Volúsia was celebrated and defended as being authentically Brazilian in the sense that she didn't sell out to Hollywood or work in productions that caricatured the Brazilian nation. As the August 3, 1943, issue of *A scena muda* observed, Volúsia "wasn't seduced by gold. And she continues to be our increasingly great and applauded artist . . . who can return to work in Hollywood whenever she pleases. She has a permanent offer from Metro" (13). A comment in the April 27 issue is more ironic: "I don't agree with the fan who wrote that 'we only appreciate what is foreign.' If that were the case, why do we rebel against performances by Carmen Miranda (who is Portuguese) and unanimously applaud Eros Volúsia (a Brazilian)?" (6).

The ballet in *Romance proibido* also makes several references to black Brazilian culture: the dancers wear Baiana-style costumes, and Eros Volúsia pretends to smoke a pipe like the Preto Velho (Old Black), a figure in African candomblé. The combination of a classical style and black folk culture suggests miscegenation, a practice valorized by Gilberto Freyre's classic sociological study *Casa grande e senzala* (Masters and the Slaves, 1933) and by the Vargas dictatorship, which led to what Robert Stam calls the "lightly mulatto" movies of the 1940s (80). The mixing of classical and African, like the coming together of the indigenous with the upper-class in *Argila,* points in that direction. At no time, however, does the black or indigenous influence ever supersede the white in this exalted mix.

By avoiding the "impossible passion" approach, Raul Roulien's *Aves sem ninho* gets much closer to providing the national catharsis that other films hoped but failed to achieve. The film's protagonist, Vitória, is one of several girls who suffer traumas in a rigidly run home for orphans. Placed in solitary confinement after trying to help a companion, she manages to flee the orphanage and is later adopted by a well-known and beloved teacher, Professor Miranda (Darcy Cazarré), who raises her along with his spinster sister Luiza (Cora Costa). After considerable study and hard work, she graduates. But unlike Léo (Celso Guimarães), her suitor, and his friends, who prefer to invest in their personal careers, Vitória accepts an invitation to become the director of the orphanage where she once lived and whose structure she intends to change. The downtrodden young girls come alive and are full of expectations when they learn of Vitória's appointment. Prior to her arrival, however, a girl named Dora (Rosina Pagã) runs away from the orphanage and is raped by upper-class youths. After Vitória arrives, she learns of Dora's situation and takes her into her home. In the midst of implementing changes to the orphanage, Vitória is criticized by the home's principal financier (Mayda Maria), who is informed by one of the staff that the girls enjoy excessive liberties and that Dora is pregnant. Without consultation, the financier promptly fires Vitória from her position. In response, the girls riot and demand Vitória's reinstatement. In the midst of the rioting, Rapadura (Elsa Mendes), one of the girls, accidentally dies, and the orphanage is closed. Depressed and disappointed, Vitória learns sometime later that her proposal for modernizing the orphanage has not only been approved and will be funded by the government but will also serve as a model for the nation. With public recognition of her initiative, she finally agrees to marry Léo.

The final scene of *Aves sem ninho* shows the newlyweds being observed from a distance by Professor Miranda and Luiza. Whether or not it was the film's intent, the scene calls attention to the distance between the two women, who never once appear in the same shot. The camera seems to be emphasizing the distance between two generations of women and their roles in society. A kind and generous woman, Luiza has built her life around the home and has supported her brother in raising Vitória. Equally good-hearted, Vitória is a successful professional whose importance in the community surpasses that of Léo. In other words, her "feminine talents" as a compassionate woman and modern professional serve the nation as a whole. It is precisely her nurturing

Vitória's return as orphanage director in *Aves sem ninho*

quality, frequently associated in melodrama with unfilled desire and even resentment, that motivates Vitória to achieve her professional goals.

Vitória and Léo's betrothal contrasts sharply with the separations of lovers that occur in the other two films and with the destabilizing passions that characterize melodrama in general. In fact, instead of giving her husband a long, passionate kiss, Vitória simply presses her face alongside Léo's as they finalize their vows. Nor is there the slightest evidence of a love triangle in the film. Vitória simply waits to marry Léo until she achieves her professional goal and succeeds in her mission. The film's melodramatic devices are centered exclusively on power relationships in the orphanage. But though the melodrama emphasizes civic duty and pride, it was somewhat problematic for the government censors, who initially banned the film (Bernadet 1979). According to the censors, the depiction of a violent and dirty orphanage was not in the nation's best interests. But references added at the end of the film to First Lady Darcy Vargas and the government's support of Vitória's project provided sufficient counterweight to enable the film's ultimate release. This momentary run-in with the Estado Novo censors is an interesting aspect of the film's history because Roulien was regarded as a symbol of patriotic pride largely because of his work as a leading man in Hollywood. In 1936, after appearing in fifteen Hollywood movies, Roulien returned to Brazil, where he tried to capitalize on the wave of "civic pride" associated with his persona. His first job as a director was the film *O grito da mocidade* (Youths' Cry, 1936), based on a screenplay by Henrique Pongetti, who became head of the Vargas's Press and Propaganda Department in 1941. The film was so emphatically nationalistic that it was criticized even by a tabloid press that was notorious for its populist zeal.

On the whole, *Aves sem ninho*'s most markedly nationalistic moments do not derive from any melodramatic formula, nor do they have an organic relationship with the overall plot. This is also true of an indigenous dance sequence that takes place in *Argila* during the launching of Salão Marajora and of the scene from that film in which Luciana and Gilberto attend a lecture at the National Museum on Marajora art. The same is true of Eros Volúsia's nightclub dance scene in *Romance proibido*. In fact, in neither *Argila* nor *Romance proibido* do the main characters actually watch the performances. In *Aves sem ninho*, a strange and unexpected patriotic reference in Vitória's final speech is accompanied by shots of patriotic postage stamps and a flock of birds flying close to a Brazilian flag. Ironically, the cameraman barely gets the flag in frame as he follows the birds' flight. Here the inclusion of propaganda seems especially artificial and forced. The almost desperate effort to frame the two images in the same shot is a good analogy for the no less problematic effort to link melodrama and nationalist propaganda.

The fact that the three films most closely associated with the Estado Novo were melodramas is perhaps an indication that this was the genre that was best suited to making nationalistic movies. The opposite conclusion could also be reached, however, because, in two of the three, the theme of an impossible love hinders rather than helps the portrayal of a cohesive nation. Although such representations of an imagined community are rendered unconvincing by certain melodramatic elements, other elements can effectively support ideological objectives—especially the extreme self-sacrifice demonstrated by Vitória and Gracia, both of whom cut ties with their social circles to dedicate themselves to the cause of the less fortunate.

The interdiction of passion is given different shape in each of the films. Whereas in *Argila* it blocks a union between social classes that has been suggested throughout the narrative, in *Aves sem ninho* and *Romance proibido* it provides the starting point from which the heroines build their roles as civilizers to include the dispossessed. In the case of *Romance proibido*, however, Gracia's success in fighting illiteracy in the backlands (a metaphor for "Deep Brazil," which at the time had an illiteracy rate of 61.6 percent)[7] is less sweet because of her bitterness over an unfulfilled love. Only Vitória unites her personal love with her civic passion for the sick, orphans and workers, and she manages this because her feelings for Léo are not the passionate kind experienced by Gracia and Luciana. After giving up Carlos, Gracia is left only with her passion for teaching, which is hardly emphasized in the film. In the case of *Argila,* Luciana tries to unite both passions, that for Marajó art and that for the potter, but she is under pressure to give up one, which may have consequences for the other.

Resentment can be a driving force for self-sacrifice—whether it is the source of a character's actions as in the case of Vitória, who states that the orphanage "will be in my blood like poison for the rest of my life," or the result of a love denied because of another, as in the case of Gracia. Resentment alone does not motivate Gracia and Vitória's self-sacrifice; however, it is fundamental in the formation and success of their pedagogical projects. The relation between personal life and professional goals is hardly ever easy. In their different ways, these three films demonstrate the women's difficult journey between the public and the private, the individual and society, but also the difficult problem of bridging racial and class divisions.

## Notes

1. See, e.g., G. P. Brunetta, *Cinema italiano tra le due guerre: Fascismo e politica cinematografica* (Milan: Mursia, 1975); David Welch, *Propaganda and the German Cinema, 1933–1945* (New York: Oxford University Press, 1983).

2. Fascist regimes as well as democratically elected governments in the period from 1930 to 1945 idealized, above all, the "New Man" in political systems that were less dependent on parliamentary rule or were opposed to it. These New Men were "common men" from the masses who would purportedly carry out tasks of great moral and ethical value.

3. The woman's role was to be centered on the interests of the home, as indicated in the political writings of Gustavo Capanema, who worked in the Vargas administration and founded the country's Institute for Pedagogical Studies. See Schwarzman.

4. Originating on Marajó Island in the north of Brazil, Marajora art was practiced by pre-Columbian people. Vargas's dictatorship showcased the artwork and treated it as a national treasure. During the Estado Novo it appeared as decoration on government buildings and in magazine layouts. It was also used in the stories performed by samba schools and is central to *Argila's* plot. Young left-liberal directors of 1960s Cinema Novo made films in which middle-class characters approach and engage the less privileged. Notice also that *Romance proibido* is much more daring than many of the Argentine and Mexican melodramas of the period, which have an obvious Christian influence. As Sílvia Oroz stated: "The Holy Family is a fundamental iconographic reference point in this love in which the woman is asexual but procreates and the man is the provider" (64). David Welch has observed that a similar image

of the fecund, docile woman is found in German films of the period (66). Although *Argila's* Marina fits that profile to near-perfection, Luciana elides the equally melodramatic stereotype of the prostitute that was popularized by Latin American films at the time.

5. Luciana's self-sacrifice is even more strongly emphasized in the 1936 source text, *Nuestra Natacha* (Our Natasha), by the Spaniard Alejandro Casona. In the play, the protagonist decides that it is not the moment to marry her suitor because she believes her mission is still unfinished.

6. Alberto Nepomuceno (1865–1920) was a much-admired composer during the Estado Novo mainly because of his appropriation of motifs specific to black and northeastern culture. Unfortunately, the racial and regional aspects of his work continued to be stressed after the Estado Novo to the detriment of his overall talent and musical erudition—as can be seen in a 1950 speech by Humberto Mauro at the National Institute of Educational Movies.

7. The data are from the 1940 Demographic Census reprinted in the *Revista USP* 28 (December 1995–February 1996): 110–21.

## Works Cited

Bernadet, Jean-Claude. *Cinema brasileiro: Propostas para uma história.* Rio de Janeiro: Paz e Terra, 1979.

Enticknap, Leo. "This Modern Age and the British Non-fiction Film." In *British Cinema, Past and Present.* Ed. Justine Ashby and Andrew Highson. London: Routledge, 2000. 207–20.

Oroz, Sílvia. *Melodrama: O cinema de lágrimas da América Latina.* Rio de Janeiro: Funarte, 1999.

Pereira, Wagner Pinheiro. Guerra das imagens: Cinema e política nos governos de Adolf Hitler e Franklin Delano Roosevelt, 1933–1945. M.A. thesis, Universidade de São Paulo, 2003.

Pessoa, Ana. *Carmen Santos: O cinema dos anos 20.* Rio de Janeiro: Aeroplano, 2002.

Rubío, Pablo Pérez. *El cine melodramático.* Barcelona: Paidós, 2004.

Schwarzman, Simon. *Tempos de Capanema.* São Paulo: Edusp, 1984.

Smith, Anthony. "Images of the Nation: Cinema, Art and National Identity." In *Cinema and Nation.* Ed. Mette Hjort and Scott Mackenzie. London: Routledge, 2002. 21–47.

Sommer, Doris. *Foundational Fictions: The National Romances of Latin America.* Berkeley: University of California Press, 1991.

Stam, Robert. *Tropical Multiculturalism: A Comparative History of Race in Brazilian Cinema and Culture.* Durham: Duke University Press, 1997.

Welch, David. *Propaganda and the German Cinema, 1933–1945.* New York: Oxford University Press, 1983.

# 5

# The Humiliation of the Father

## Melodrama and Cinema Novo's
## Critique of Conservative Modernization

### ISMAIL XAVIER

During the late 1960s, a significant shift in focus toward the representation of private life and family dramas occurred in Brazilian cinema. This change took place after a decade in which the national cinema had primarily concerned itself with the public sphere and with labor exploitation, social movements, political history, and allegories of national identity. Some Cinema Novo and post-Cinema Novo films provide compelling evidence of this change of emphasis. For example, *Copacabana me engana* (Copacabana Deceives Me, Antônio Carlos Fontoura, 1969) and *Brasil ano 2000* (Walter Lima Junior, 1969) focus on moral conflicts deriving from the generation gaps dividing petit-bourgeois characters; *Matou a família e foi ao cinema* (Killed the Family and Went to the Movies, Júlio Bressane, 1969) displays a series of criminal acts committed by passionate people who, despite belonging to different social classes, present similar patterns of frustration and resentment, developed within the private space of the family. The degeneration of traditional households is depicted in films about the close connection between social changes and family decadence, as in *Os herdeiros* (The Inheritors, Carlos Diegues, 1969), *A casa assassinada* (The Murdered House, Paulo César Saraceni, 1971), *Os deuses e os mortos* (The Gods and the Dead, Ruy Guerra, 1970), and *Os monstros de Babaloo* (The Babaloo Monsters, Eliseu Visconti, 1970). It is significant that psychoanalysis comes into the foreground as an overt guiding principle in the composition of many of these dramas, to such an extent that such a film as *Culpa* (Guilt, Domingos de Oliveira, 1971) begins with a quotation from Freud that performs the same explanatory function that, in early 1960s Cinema Novo films, was fulfilled by social commentary and historical information.

From the late 1960s onward the experiences of the new generations, influenced by phenomena such as sexual liberation and other new codes of behavior fostered by the development of mass media, provided an impulse for films in which the concern with private life and sexual morality became a valid means of tackling political debates that, at that time, were made difficult by the military regime. The military, which assumed its task to be a contribution to Western civilization in the context of the cold war, was strongly anti-Communist and wanted to accelerate the country's economic growth. On the symbolic level, it undertook a strong defense of the archaic moral codes, including the traditional family structure, that were in fact threatened by capitalist development and by the consolidation of a consumer society in Brazil. Aware of this contradiction, artists searched for new cinematic forms in which to express their ironic stance toward the Brazilian conservative modernization. To this end, some Cinema Novo filmmakers moved toward capturing this patriarchal ethos in its most modest and petit-bourgeois form, observing its own household at the moment of its decline.

In composing their domestic tragedies, some filmmakers entered into a dialogue with playwrights, a process that involved two different trends in modern Brazilian drama. One group of filmmakers reworked the tradition of the politicized group Arena Theatre, which had developed a realistic aesthetic from the late 1950s onward. Two good examples of this trend are *Em família* (Inside the Family, Paulo Porto, 1971), with a screenplay by Oduvaldo Vianna Filho and Ferreira Gullar, and *Eles não usam black-tie* (They Don't Wear Black Ties, Leon Hirszman, 1980), based on a play written in 1958 by Francesco Guarnieri. Both films emphasize the relations between private dramas and class conditions, family affairs and economic crisis. Other filmmakers stress the realm of passion and desire, developing an interesting dialogue with a melodramatic tradition that in modern Brazilian literature is best represented by the plays and novels of Nelson Rodrigues, a playwright whose work offers a rich stock of characters and dramatic situations for a cinema engaged in a harsh critique of family life.

The film director Arnaldo Jabor played a key role in this dialogue between cinema and literature.[1] He made two films based on Rodrigues' texts: *Toda nudez será castigada* (All Nudity Shall Be Punished, 1972) and *O casamento* (The Wedding, 1975). In both films he creates an ironic style of representation in order to posit bad taste, hysteria, and family problems as historical symptoms of the decline of patriarchy in Brazil. Jabor's aim is to explore the intimate link between the conservative thought and the melodramatic imagination at this specific juncture. Melodrama is incorporated in his work in order to expose the contradictions of Brazilian modernization during the most severe period of the authoritarian regime (1969–74). I approach Jabor's two films in chronological order so as to highlight the gradual process of dramatic amplification within his strategy: *Toda nudez* deals with the family drama as an almost closed system; *O casamento,* with its more complex cast of characters, is centered once more on family dramas but connects the way the middle-class males handle their private traumas to specific historical moments of Brazilian political life.

In the opening shot of *Toda nudez será castigada,* Jabor signals the change in the strategies of Cinema Novo in the late 1960s and early 1970s, when it became clear that the military dictatorship, which had come to power in 1964 and was consolidated by stronger repressive measures in December 1968, was to last longer than had at first seemed likely. In this shot, we follow the film's protagonist, Herculano (Paulo Porto) as he drives his car along the Flamengo Beach road in Rio de Janeiro, with the sky and street-front buildings on the background. This image recalls a nightmarish shot from Glauber Rocha's seminal work *Terra em transe* (Land in Anguish, 1967), a major allegory of the 1964 coup d'état. In Rocha's film, the tracking shot along the Flamengo Beach avenue, surrounded by Burle Marx gardens, becomes a kind of emblem for the rise of the conservative forces. There the protagonist, Porfirio Diaz (Paulo Autran), is seen from the same viewpoint and crosses the same space as Herculano does in Jabor's opening sequence, in what is suggested as a triumphal parade.[2] Diaz presents himself as a fixed mask, exhibiting his proud chin in profile, holding a dark banner in one hand and a crucifix in the other. The whole composition connotes the idea of an angel of darkness who is arriving to begin a new era in Eldorado.[3] Herculano's ride in *Toda nudez* is a more prosaic, everyday event, pointing to the protagonist's self-assurance and enjoyment. The soundtrack sets a tone that is radically opposed to that of Diaz's parade. The ceremonial sounds of the Afro-Brazilian religion *Candomblé* in the Rocha film's sequence, with their associations with myth, are replaced in the Jabor film by a concert piece by the modern tango composer Astor Piazzola that will accompany Herculano's entire story. Passionate, modern, and "cool," from the start the music anticipates the kind of sensibility privileged by Jabor's narration. It helps set up the contrast between this mode of representation and that of *Terra em transe* while the visual structure of the shot indicates a continuity of concerns, linking Jabor's view of Herculano with Rocha's view of Diaz. With this opening acknowledgment of the classic Cinema Novo film and the self-conscious way in which it is consistently followed in the rest of the film, Jabor is able to translate his basic assumption: that family affairs constitute a hybrid domain, a point of conjunction in which public and private spheres meet and in which the confrontation between sexual drives and moral codes acquires a clear political content.[4]

Unlike Diaz, Jabor's protagonist Herculano is not parading toward a government palace to give an inaugural speech. He is going to his secluded mansion, the private domain in which he has seemingly confined Geni (Darlene Glória), his wife, achieving in this way a happy bourgeois marriage. He is in good humor when he arrives at home, looking for Geni in order to give her the flowers he brought, but he receives no answer when he calls out her name. Instead, his attention is distracted by the noise of a tape recorder. The tape discloses his wife's last message, recorded just before she committed suicide. This message takes us back in time, and Geni's narrative, which is addressed to her husband, dominates the entire film until the last sequence, when the scene switches back to the moment of Herculano's arrival at the mansion. Geni's revelations function as a final gesture of desperate revenge, performed to denounce loudly the way in which Herculano's whole life has always been based on illusions: illusions about her, about the character of his young son, and about the very meaning of their marriage.

The flashback follows the pattern of a three-act play full of intense conflicts and spectacular twists and turns in the opposition that the film creates between Herculano's desire and a varied set of moral constraints. As a spectacle, the film takes advantage of Nelson Rodrigues's dramatic machinery, which, by effectively and competently mixing different traditions (from Strindberg and O'Neill to popular melodrama), has had a powerful effect on Brazilian audiences since the 1940s. When the earlier reception of Rodrigues's plays is considered, it becomes clear that what Jabor did was to inaugurate a radically new reading. He enacts the play as a farce in which the victimization of the main characters acquires a tragicomic effect owing to the gap between the way they see their dramas and the way the narrative presents them.

In its early stages, Herculano and Geni's love story obeys a series of stratagems devised by Herculano's brother Patrício (Paulo César Peréio), who lives at Herculano's expense. First Patrício uses Geni, introduced as a prostitute-friend, to save his brother from a state of mourning and melancholy caused by the death of his first wife. Taken to the brothel, a drunken Herculano undergoes an auspicious rebirth of his sexual life that brings mutual passion. To soothe his troubled conscience after having slept with a prostitute, however, Herculano masks this desire under the appearance of charity (he wants to redeem Geni). Meanwhile, for her part, Geni lives out her own rescue fantasies by falling in love with the distressed widower. After this stage, Patrício instructs Geni in how to overcome his brother's remaining moral resistance by proposing marriage as a precondition for continuing their sex life. This, though, merely displaces the conflict from the widower's conscience onto his open and comic struggle with the rest of the members of his family, who are not disposed to accept Geni. Central to this struggle is the uncompromising demand of Herculano's son Serginho (Paulo Sacks) that his father continue to be faithful to his late mother. Serginho enters the drama, then, as the agent of castration, switching roles with his father as he becomes the family authority figure whose permission Herculano must solicit in order to marry Geni.

A central opposition between death—embodied in Herculano's family—and life—embodied in Geni's "sunny" figure—is clearly established throughout Rodrigues's original. Jabor's film version translates this visually in the contrast between the restraint of the lugubrious family houses and the freedom, energy, and sound of the colorful brothel. What is clearly symbolized using space and light is the traditional duality of Brazilian patriarchal life: the family household and the brothel as the two complementary poles of an old social order, ones that were supposed to be kept apart, connected only by the comings and goings of men. Given the archaic nature of his family, Herculano's mistake lies in his desire to connect these two worlds by integrating Geni, the prostitute, into the space of the family. Even before he is granted permission to marry, he secretly confines Geni to the second of the two family homes, the old secluded mansion that had been abandoned after the death of his wife. Moved by jealousy of her life in the brothel, he places Geni within his own domain, starting a ridiculous game of seduction (fueled by his desire) and restraint (caused by her strategic chastity) that seems completely out of place in that house, haunted as it is by his first wife's death. Geni's first contact with that space, her future tomb, prefigures her ultimate misfortune.

So that the couple can be freed from the uncomfortable deadlock, a sudden and melodramatic turn precipitates Serginho's change of heart about granting permission for them to marry. Disturbed by his father's continued affair, Serginho becomes drunk, is involved in a fight, and goes to jail, where he is raped by a cellmate, the "Bolivian bandit" (Orazir Pereira). When Herculano finds out, he blames Geni, and their whole affair seems ruined. But her rescue fantasy is displaced onto the victimized Serginho and coincides

A distraught Darlene Glória in *Toda nudez será castigada*

with the young man's own plan of revenge against his father. They start a secret love affair, and he grants Herculano permission to marry Geni. Their wedding finally takes place, and thus begins a bizarre version of the love triangle in which Serginho assures his revenge via the incestuous love affair with his stepmother. For her part, Geni prefers Serginho, and Herculano is thus condemned to play a dual victim role as the deceived husband and as the father outwitted by his son. But Serginho's hatred for his father turns out not to exclude Geni. Pretending to go away on a trip to "forget all his recent traumas," he makes Geni take him to the airport only to witness the scene that reveals the true meaning of her life as a wife and stepmother: she has to watch Serginho get on the plane with his homosexual lover, the Bolivian bandit. After returning home she kills herself, but first she tapes a message for Herculano in which she reveals all the stratagems that had turned him into the puppet of both Patrício and Serginho. Before she dies, she curses Herculano's entire family and also curses her own breast, a symbol of the vanity that in her view, helped the family lead her to her death.

With the curse addressed to her breast, the character of Geni gives resonance to an internalization of Christian morality that has already been signaled in the film by her taste for premonitions ("I will die of breast cancer"). Feelings of guilt are at the root of her motherly rescue fantasies concerning seemingly fragile men. They are also at the root of the romantic masochism

Geni records her final message in *Toda nudez será castigada*.

evident in her affair with Serginho (the one who seemed the weakest only to reveal himself to be the strongest). Geni, the character who is most akin to a vital force, becomes the principal victim of Herculano's family's decadence. She allows her role as a substitute mother, replacing the "other" in the home, to go too far. She ends up in a tropical version of the gothic scenario in which the woman imprisoned in a morbid household becomes the victim of forces attached to the past. At the same time, her sad story ends in a bitter parody of a more optimistic scenario in conventional melodrama, that of the redemption of a "pretty woman," the prostitute with a heart of gold. Either way, Geni loses; the death forces embedded in the archaic moral code give proof of their fatal power. Nonetheless, she attracts our sympathy and exits the narrative with dignity.

The same, however, cannot be said of Herculano. His penchant for temporization and self-deception places him halfway between an archaic morality that he has neither the force nor the legitimate authority to sustain and a modern sexual life that he is afraid to assume. Under pressure, he chooses to mask his contradictions in a game of appearances that is perversely manipulated by his own son and that ends with the unexpected revelation of all the lies that had sustained his good fortune. After a hard struggle and the apparent removal of all barriers, the self-assured father and ruler of the domestic sphere has to face his blatant fall and humiliation at the very moment when he might achieve happiness. The deceptions revealed by the taped message are not dwelt on by the film. Instead, the entire final sequence concentrates on and profits from the dramatic force of Geni's traumatic last day; the film ends with a close-up of her dead face near the room where Herculano finds the tape recorder. He has not been able to reconcile patriarchal law with his transgressive passion, but this unsolved contradiction does not make him a tragic hero. The major concern of the narrative has been to expose the internal family workings that ruin his life and kill Geni, all to the sound of Piazzola's tango.

In order to see the paterfamilias taking a further step beyond collapse and humiliation we have to wait for Jabor's *O casamento* (1975), a film in which another "fallen" paternal protagonist, Sabino (Paulo Porto), is given time at the end to display his radical choice of the Christian path of repentance and purification. Afflicted in a way similar to Herculano's by the contradiction between his sexual drives and his moral values, Sabino is a mirror image of the protagonist of *Toda nudez,* no stronger than he, no less ridiculous in his difficult moments, despite his final radical step. Sabino's difference lies in his readiness for action, clearly demonstrated by his profession: he became wealthy through speculation in real estate, the corrupt business sector that was most heavily involved in the disastrous and chaotic urban growth in modern Brazil.

In *O casamento,* Jabor adapts a Rodrigues novel written in 1966 that once again displays the vicissitudes of a conservative father obsessed by a passionate and transgressive love, this time involving his own daughter Glória (Adriana Prieto). The father has already faced up to the truth when we meet him. The reversal of fortune occurred on the previous day in a hectic chain of events involving many characters, this time from different social milieux. The plot of the film, like that of the original novel, seems much less structured than that of *Toda nudez,* its dramatic condensation leading the mise-en-scène to the edges of hysteria. Intensive subplotting creates narrative parallels with the protagonist's story, and though he will survive at the climax, a working-class character will, in contrast, find his solution to suffering and frustration in crime and suicide. At the center of the narrative is the mind of a bourgeois man in crisis: Sabino, a nervous father ill at ease with his daughter's marriage. The wedding ceremony must be performed perfectly, however, because it is one of the stratagems for gaining social visibility that he has arranged in order to seduce men in power—a government minister is expected to attend. On the other hand, deep inside, Sabino knows that the idea of giving his daughter Glória to another man has become quite unbearable.

The narrative begins on the morning of the wedding. Sabino is still lying in bed, assailed by nightmares. A carefully chosen opening sequence has already connected the public and the private spheres, providing a social framework for the family affair. Before showing Sabino in bed, the film displays a long credit sequence with a series of images taken from one of Rio de Janeiro's summer floods, annual instances of social tragedy and death that are not unrelated to the real estate business, private profits, and political corruption. The opening sequence sets the tone for the entire film and, with its images of mud, dirt, rats, pestilence, and human suffering, establishes the central metaphor of overflowing, which will permeate both the narrative and the unbounded behavior of the characters. Among the images that make up Sabino's nightmare is the memory of the last words his father said to him on the day he died: "Be a man of honor." Sabino wakes up and starts walking around in his huge apartment. Looking at a mirror, he repeats the words "man of honor" while his face suggests a clear awareness of the unfulfilled promise. He goes to his daughter's bedroom and looks at her exposed body while she feigns sleep. In the living room, the white bridal gown reveals the source of Sabino's crisis and, leaving the image of this disturbed man, the film takes us back in time to the events that have led to his present state. The action portrays the previous day, and the film alternates Sabino's experiences and Glória's recollections until, at sunset, they get together for a revealing scene on a deserted beach.

Sabino's crisis of identity in *O casamento*

The flashback starts with Sabino seated in the back of his chauffeur-driven car, hurrying his driver and complaining about the slowness of their journey, while a mob encircles the car and looks at Sabino (and at the camera, which is also inside the car). The tension caused by the crowd connotes once more the social context—in this case, the extreme economic gap that separates Sabino from the people on the street—and creates a feeling of claustrophobia akin to the opening sequence of Fellini's $8\frac{1}{2}$. Sabino's arrival at his office brings temporary relief, but very soon his secretary Noêmia (Camila Amado) announces a visitor, Doctor Camarinha (Ambrósio Fregolente), the family gynecologist, and the calamities of the day begin in earnest. Camarinha has come to tell Sabino that he has witnessed scenes involving his own assistant and Glória's fiancé that make him suspect that the latter is homosexual. The doctor insists that Sabino cancel his daughter's wedding ceremony, which is due to take place the next day. Divided between his social duties and unconfessed jealousy, Sabino does not receive the seemingly terrible revelation in the way one might expect. Instead of canceling the wedding, he spends the whole day trying unsuccessfully to deal with both the compulsive sexual anxiety caused by his own desire for Glória and his uncontrollable urge to disclose his secrets. His first confession takes place in the church, where he becomes hysterical and vomits. Among vague references to humanity's corruption, he narrates to the priest a shameful episode from his childhood: his mother masturbating grotesquely while lying on the bed beside him. His second confession is made to Noêmia, with whom he arranges, for the first time, a sexual liaison in a filthy apartment that he keeps for such occasions. Once again he becomes hysterical, treating the secretary very badly, and he narrates another childhood episode in which he was raped by a stronger and older boy. Obsessed with virility and, like Camarinha, troubled by the "flood" of homosexuality, he plays out this act of self-flagellation in front of a woman who means nothing to him. This grotesque scene culminates with his shouting out Glória's name when sexually excited. Back in the office late in the afternoon, he vows to kill Noêmia, but his daughter calls him, interrupting this latest hysterical attack. He leaves the office to meet her.

Meanwhile, in the parallel flashback to the events involving Sabino's daughter on the day before the wedding, Glória first pays a visit to her father's office, where she is received as a goddess, with her father playing the role of the high priest. Flirtatious yet ambivalent, she is completely at ease with this worship. Her manner suggests some complicity with Sabino's secret desire for her, though not without a sadistic edge, as when she announces that she will shortly visit Camarinha, saying, "The doctor wants to tell me something special. I am curious." Throughout the flashback, while Sabino discloses his own stories concerning sex and penetration, Glória's mind returns to her first sexual experience. She will go to Camarinha to confess her own secret—to tell him that his late son was the man to whom she had lost her virginity. At the doctor's office, she enacts a parody of confession, undressing herself and defying the doctor to "attest to her chastity," a guilt-free variation on her father's humiliating impulse to blend confession and sexuality. Later in the film, her memories reach back to her sadistic affair with Camarinha's strange son Antônio Carlos (Érico Vidal). On the only occasion when they had sexual intercourse, they had visited Doctor Camarinha's homosexual assistant. The latter, for his part, had chosen that day to take revenge on his homophobic father, who had been paralyzed by a brain hemorrhage. Camarinha's assistant's plan was to be penetrated by his male lover right in front of his father. Although the plan did not proceed as far as this step, it was enough to excite Antônio Carlos and Glória, who went off to another room to have sex. And it was also enough to cause the death of the wheelchair-bound father. Later that day, Antônio Carlos called Glória to declare his feelings for her, but she coldly rejected him. Shocked and frustrated, he committed suicide.

Glória's recollections underline her competence in the erotic games of aggression. On the beach, at sunset, she outwits her father, who makes a fool of himself, betrayed by his own illusory assumptions as to the extent of his power and of her innocence. She provokes him, saying that he probably

The forbidden kiss in *O casamento*

never loved her mother, and adds that she has never liked her mother herself, nor she does she love her fiancé, but only "the man I am forbidden to love." Encouraged by her confession, Sabino imagines that things are ready for his own crucial revelation of desire for her, and he cannot stop himself from kissing her passionately. Stepping backwards and seeming extremely shocked, Glória runs away, followed by her humiliated father, who tries to explain himself.

This pathetic scene finds resonance in the cathartic sequence that closes the intricate story involving Sabino's principal "mirror image" in the film: Xavier (Nelson Dantas), a sentimental working-class man. The lover of Sabino's secretary Noêmia, Xavier is married to a woman (Gianna Singulani) who is deformed and blinded by leprosy. While Sabino is having his traumatic experience on the beach, Xavier, already upset by Noêmia's constant lack of enthusiasm in their affair, overreacts to her rejection of him, which is caused by overblown expectations after her earlier liaison with Sabino. When Xavier comes to see her at the office, she orders him to leave. This he does, but then he returns and stabs her numerous times, creating a blood bath in Sabino's deserted office. Xavier does not stop there; returning home, he kills his wife and commits suicide.

The following day, Sabino calmly takes his daughter to the church in spite of everything, including Noêmia's death. "It is the wedding that matters, above all," he keeps saying. At the end of the ceremony, induced by the eloquent sermon of the priest (Carlos Kroeber)—"we all have to acknowledge our leprosy"—Sabino quietly leaves the church to go to police headquarters. As he comes upon the press waiting there for the news of the murder, he performs a final, public act of confession, claiming that, in his office on the previous night, he had killed his lover Noêmia. He holds out his hands to be cuffed and allows himself to be arrested, with a smile on his face and his eyes turned to heaven, as if leaving all human bonds behind him. The sound of the "Wedding March" plays over this final image of joy, reminding viewers of the priest's ridiculous speech and creating a gap between Sabino's spiritual intentions and the farcical scene of his arrest. Behaving like a character who has stepped from a Dostoyevsky novel, he does not find the appropriate context for a metaphysical leap. Moreover, there is a considerable ironic distance between Sabino's view of his "saintly" illumination and the dominant point of view in the film's narration. Failing to inspire empathy, he remains the pathetic, defeated bourgeois father, a man who finds a different imaginary resolution but is stricken by the same impotence as a whole set of other paternal characters in the film. Doctor Camarinha is a ruined man after his son's suicide, his assistant's father died in his wheelchair, and Xavier turned to unbridled aggression and suicide. The similarity in the predicaments of these characters strongly suggests some kind of narrative orchestration, one that demands the display of misery and male impotence. I have already referred to the crisis in Brazilian patriarchal morality that took place in the late 1960s and early 1970s but, beyond this ironic treatment of conservative fathers and archaic family values, one question remains. It concerns the particular point of view behind Jabor's depiction of the younger generation, the sons and daughters: On whose behalf and on whose terms is Jabor's irony addressed to the paterfamilias?

Until this point, something remained implicit in my discussion of *Toda nudez* and *O casamento:* the tone of both narratives and their presumed tragicomic effect. Although they follow the fathers quite closely, the narratives do not propose a moral identification with them. The protagonists are subjected to a kind of ironic anatomical investigation that reveals their weaknesses and deep contradictions. Neither villains nor enemies, the two patriarchs Herculano and Sabino are shown as victims of their own system of values. Their sad stories are offered up as parables that through exaggeration and the melodramatic rule of transparency, expose their deepest impulses and their effect on the social dynamics of the family. Social types at odds with the ways of the world, they find an imaginary resolution in the fabric of suffering, which is, in melodrama, the most frequently represented kind of response to reality. In both films, a kitsch melodrama is lived out by the conservative figures who take themselves seriously as virtuous victims. Yet the narrative, always keeping them at a distance, seems to frame this self-deception in a modern satirical melodrama or tragicomedy, which discloses the illusory nature of their redemption. On this level, their defeat is taken somewhat as if it were a matter for laughter, not for tears. It is not difficult, of course, to find the victors in these stories. The children, Serginho and Glória, contribute enormously to their fathers' falls. Their final move into the arms of gay men (this is what Sabino assumes on the basis of Dr. Camarinha's report) brings into the family a taste of that "flood" of homosexuality that feeds the paterfamilias's paranoia. For the young, the final act of both dramas is an occasion for revenge; in this sense, theirs is the final laugh. But we are far from that optimistic comedy that celebrates the joyous victory of the son or daughter over the authority of the father, the kind where marriage always means a happy ending.

Serginho and the Bolivian bandit do look at the camera before getting into the airplane. But the latter's sarcastic smile is directed not at Serginho's father

Herculano but at Geni, Serginho's lover. It is she who is seen as the victim of the aggression, a detail that connotes Serginho's gesture as a last perverse stroke from the morbid family that he, despite his escape, still represents. If there is a figure to whom we feel closest in *Toda nudez* it is Geni, a character who signifies life, pleasure, and giving, however clumsy her conduct may be. In the end, such feeling is only reinforced by the concentration on her drama and despair, which culminate in the powerful scene of her curse on Herculano's family. Throughout the film, Serginho's behavior, in contrast with Geni's, is shown as egotistical. The revelation of his plot to destroy her prevents any identification with his point of view. The final impact comes from the shot of Geni's dead face: it condenses the moral effect of the whole story, which was completely mediated by the sound of her recorded voice.

At the end of *O casamento*, Glória's wedding does not represent a liberation from the past, from the perverse game she shared with her father in which her effectiveness in aggression gave her the advantage. From the outset, her sexual life, like that of her father, is connected to death and to sadomasochistic scenarios that she is easily capable of manipulating for her own ends, regardless of the consequences. Self-centered, she is the embodiment of seduction with all its ambivalence. She is the strong woman who, within the perspective of the film, does not come to the foreground as the source of another point of view but instead remains simply the object of an exterior view. Her figure and manners display a narcissistic touch that is gradually associated with the codes of the femme fatale as visually represented by the film's quotation of fin de siècle iconography of decadence. This reference indicates very clearly that she is conceived of as a symptom, as a charming flower of decadence symbiotically attached to a whole set of fragile figures— Antônio Carlos, Doctor Camarinha's assistant, and her absent fiancé.

Ineffective as the locus of legitimate point of view, the younger generation, as represented in both films, exhibits a behavior that can be described as symptomatic, for it derives overwhelmingly from the status quo. There is something vicious in the son's and daughter's schemes of revenge and the stratagems they use to liberate themselves from the patriarchal order. Despite their effectiveness in humiliating the fathers, we are not encouraged to see Herculano's and Sabino's falls through the younger generation's victorious gaze. There is no hope in either of these films, which prefer, instead, to stress that the young people's strategies are mechanisms of reproduction rather than of overcoming, an on-going force of sameness with all its social and individual costs. At the end of *Toda nudez,* Jabor seems to side with the vibrant young woman who is completely destroyed by the archaic family game. Meanwhile,

*O casamento* enacts the patriarch's illusory redemption such that the film appears aware that it is an entire style that wins out when Sabino makes his public stand surrounded by the "masses" at the police headquarters and is merged into the messianic. The moment of delirium in which he encounters the people, finding partners among them for his theater of salvation, frames Jabor's allegory of Brazilian political life. Sabino's pragmatism and economic success might have caused his initial isolation from the collectivity as represented in the opening sequence of the film, where he is shown alone in the car surrounded by the mob. In contrast, Sabino's hieratic trance, seen when he is handcuffed by the police, becomes an instance of social communion, almost an occasion for a political rally similar to those shown in Rocha's *Terra em transe* and whose atmosphere Jabor recalls again at the cathartic moment of his film. Jabor's style of representation stresses an ironic view of this communion: it is the great apotheosis of illusion, which is followed at the very end of the film by the return of the same urban flood seen in the overture, a flood that, with its biblical overtones and promises of plague, closes the circle of representation. This acute metaphor for the Brazilian misery provides the final framework for the humiliation of the father, inscribing Jabor's film within the Cinema Novo trend of presenting totalizing views of society.

It could be said, then, that in Brazil there exists a polarity between the modern, which isolates, and the archaic, which congregates. It is easy to understand why the military regime exploited this patriarchal tradition, on an ideological level at least, in order to maintain cohesion, to seduce the middle classes, and to create a source of authority that could discipline society though its own most effective social bases were of a more technocratic sort and were engaged in a very modern capitalism. Note, however, that, once this polarity has been detected, it would be a mistake to attribute to the archaic-modern binary a mutually exclusive opposition. Brazil has clearly shown how the dialectical association of these two poles has repeated itself throughout history, the strength of each of these terms and their manner of interaction altering itself according to specific historical conjunctures. This is one of the reasons why the allegory of the military coup d'état in *Terra em transe* had such a big impact on the culture of the 1960s, for it placed the patriarch, a figure from the most archaic reaches of national symbolism, at the center of the scheming behind the coup. Positing recent history as a drama of palace intrigues, obsessions, and melancholia, and in keeping with Walter Benjamin's concept of baroque theatre, Rocha's film found a brilliant way of condensing a specifically Brazilian tradition of political "solutions" that have marked the nation's history ever since independence, solutions in which the contrivances of social, economic, and political elites have frequently masqueraded as revolutions. For the left-wingers, *Terra em transe* crystallized an imagery that was capable of connoting, at the very heart of the conservative triumph of 1964, the return of a violence whose decisive agent was the section of the dominant class that formerly was comprised of slave owners. These heirs of the Portuguese colonizers gave birth to a rural patriarchy of Iberian descent, considered still to be actively influential in Brazil during the 1960s despite industrialization, the rise of the new middle classes, intense urbanization, and the increasing entry of women into different spheres of work including high public administration. Although present in the plot of *Terra em transe,* the military and the modernizing bourgeoisie with its material interests are far from undertaking the leadership of the coup d'état. Instead, it is Porfirio Diaz who monopolizes this role in the film. As the father figure who represents tradition and the Christian family, he is shown as orchestrating the conservative victory, displaying in his triumphal parade the grotesque physiognomy of a fascinating fascism under the critical eye of Cinema Novo.

After the appearance of *Terra em transe,* the trend toward the production of dramas of bourgeois decadence—one reflected in the opening tracking shot in *Toda nudez*—corresponds to a desire to undermine the ideological tenets of the military regime. This goal is achieved by means of a curious operation that requires the constant representation in these dramas of impotent and self-pitying father figures in decline in order to sabotage the values associated with these figures. Such ironic "trials of the family" appeared not only in Brazilian cinema but also throughout the cultural production, involving theater and popular music in a movement called Tropicalism, whose greatest impact appeared in 1968.[5] Patriarchy became a basic target for Tropicalism owing to its central role in the legitimization of censorship and in other repressive measures adopted by the military regime. Filmmakers were thus seen to be engaged in a left-wing critical program aimed at revealing the backward, provincial nature of the regime's ideological enterprise, all the time pointing at what they saw as the continuum of patriarchal power, from the public, political sphere to the private, domestic sphere.

I have singled out Jabor because, among other reasons, I argue that this approach achieved its greatest success when filmmakers drew attention to social sectors and experiences in society in which it was still possible to detect the survival of the archaic amid the modern, as in the films examined above.[6] Perhaps nobody has ever articulated this pessimism with such a total dismissal not only of the patriarchs but also of the potential for change embodied by younger generations as Jabor does in *Toda nudez* and *O casamento*.[7] One might say that this irony contains some sort of wise realism, but I question this conclusion by suggesting certain affinities between Jabor's wide-ranging pessimism and older forms of disenchantment whose origins, themselves being of a moral character, involve frustration and resentment. In fact, in this presupposition of a general and inevitable corruption, one might discern a peculiar convergence involving the common sense of a culture that felt the impact of psychoanalysis as well as of an age-old moralist tradition whose formulas have been condensed in a saying by La Rochefoucauld: "Vice is the moving principle of all actions." This last convergence of the old and the new provides yet another instance of the dialectic of the archaic and the modern. But it might also prove to be rather controversial when discussing the work of a filmmaker whose extremely pessimistic portrayal of patriarchal decadence may, depending on the tone and style of representation, slip into a conservative attitude as it articulates these earlier traditions of issuing moral diatribes.

I do not postulate the presence of such a convergence in Jabor's films as a general hypothesis. Instead, I suggest it as a provocation based on evidence that, I feel, indicates that the cinematic criticism of patriarchal values gained in dramatic strength precisely when filmmakers such as Jabor adapted the work of the playwright Nelson Rodrigues for the screen. This was, after all, a writer who paradoxically was devoted to the defense of the coup d'état, one who was ironic in calling himself a reactionary and zealous in publicly avowing his Catholicism. Rodrigues's resistance to modernization, before and after 1964, manifested itself in works that depict a world of vanities and resentments, of individual subjects who are unhappy because they are set apart from a state of purity that no historical experience can really offer. They are solitary figures who unite for mutual destruction because they find themselves, in Rodrigues's words, in the "most cynical age." Before the release of films that borrowed his stories and dramas, Rodrigues was the most insistent artist in Brazil when it came to dissecting the masculine failure, displaying the figure of the guilty father and feeble husband, the head of household who partakes in the dissolution of values that prove him incapable of fulfilling the role tradition had in store for him. There is an interesting debate to be had concerning the specific purport of Rodrigues's plays, because their agility, powers of observation, and modern language define the space of ambiguity that is particular to works whose ideas exceed the capacity of a single author to articulate. Filmmakers associated with Cinema Novo, including Jabor, consciously worked out this ambiguity in their interpretations of his dramas. They assumed Rodrigues's acute criticism of the present, no doubt made in the name of a purity that is, after all, abstract. But they transformed these elements into a tool for ideological unmasking, carried out in the same manner as their original, forceful and sarcastic appropriation of melodrama as a genre.

The dialectic of the archaic and the modern becomes, then, a facet of this cinema, which could so easily recognize it as a distinctive sign of the very Brazilian modernity from which this same cinema felt itself symbolically exiled. In this reading, films such as *Toda nudez* and *O casamento* result in aggressive transfigurations of the critical distance adopted by the young filmmakers in face of the process of modernization, because of the direction it took when the technical-economic development of Brazil came to be administered by the military.

## Notes

1. Since the late 1960s, Arnaldo Jabor has been one of leading figures of Cinema Novo. His first feature film, *Public Opinion* (1967), is one of the best examples of the Cinéma Vérité school in the Brazilian documentary tradition. Anticipating some of the issues raised by the fiction films that Jabor would make in the 1970s, *Public Opinion* presents a bitter diagnosis of the middle-class conservatism of Rio de Janeiro just after the 1964 military coup.

2. In *Terra em transe*, Porfirio Diaz embodies the ascetic Christian tradition. Positing himself as father figure for an entire country, he dedicates his life to the preservation of tradition and purity, deploying a rhetoric that is permeated by racial prejudice in overt defense of the privileges of the most aristocratic sector of the ruling class. As Robert Stam summarizes it: "Porfirio Diaz, named after the Mexican dictator, embodies the Latin American version of Iberic despotism" (161 n.1). See his essay "Land in Anguish." For discussion of *Terra em Transe,* see Xavier, *Allegories* 57–93.

3. This is the name of the imaginary state in which the film is set.

4. This notion of a "hybrid sphere" comes from a work of Jacques Donzelot titled *La police des familles* (translated into Portuguese by Edições Graal, 1980).

5. Tropicalism emerged at the end of 1967, first in popular music and theater and then in film, partly as a response to *Terra em transe*. Its overall strategy produced a significant shift in the articulation of basic questions concerning cultural nationalism, political art, the avant-garde, and underdevelopment. It directed a radical critique at the "dualist view" of Brazil and eliminated the distinction between pure national folklore and "corrupt" urban culture. Tropicalism blended modern and archaic techniques, assuming with good humor or bitter irony the syncretic nature of the Brazilian experience.

6. Another interesting example of this approach is Joaquim Pedro de Andrade's ad-

aptation of Dalton Trevisan's short stories in his bitter comedy *Guerra conjugal* (Conjugal War, 1975). Once more, the parodic incursion into domestic drama, with the brothel acting as a counterpoint, is guided by a gradual deconstruction of male sexual power throughout a series of episodes that subvert the so-called *pornochanchada,* a kind of erotic comedy that was very popular in Brazil during the 1970s.

7. There is no space here to analyze in detail Jabor's *Tudo bem* (It's All Right, 1978), with its humiliated protagonist Juarez, an even more fragile father figure than Herculano or Sabino, and its transgressive figures from the younger generation who, like Serginho and Glória, encourage neither spectatorial identification nor optimism for the future.

## Works Cited

Stam, Robert. "Land in Anguish." In *Brazilian Cinema,* ed. Randal Johnson and Robert Stam. New York: Columbia University Press, 1995. 149–61.

Xavier, Ismail. *Allegories of Underdevelopment: Aesthetics and Politics in Modern Brazilian Cinema.* Minneapolis: University of Minnesota Press, 1997. 57–93.

# 6

# Nelson Pereira dos Santos's
## *Cinema de lágrimas*

### DARLENE J. SADLIER

Wherever there is a woman, there is purity of life . . .
But wherever there is a mother, ah, there is God!

*Las abandonadas,* 1945

In 1994 the distinguished Brazilian director Nelson Pereira dos Santos, who is widely regarded as the founder of the radical Cinema Novo movement of the 1960s and 1970s, began work on a project for the British Film Institute (BFI) to commemorate the centenary of cinema. The BFI had commissioned nearly twenty directors worldwide to make movies that would portray the history of cinema in their respective countries. The idea was perhaps excessively nationalistic, and it was inconsistently applied.[1] Instead of recognizing Latin America as a large and culturally diverse geographic region where different languages are spoken, the BFI chose to regard South America, Central America, the Spanish-speaking Caribbean, and Mexico as comprising a homogeneous entity that could be surveyed in a single film. As Pereira dos Santos pointed out in an 1999 interview, a history of Latin American cinema as a whole would have required at least a four- or five-hour film (quoted in Amâncio 81). Although the BFI gave him complete freedom to take any approach he wanted, a documentary of this length was out of the question. On the other hand, the impossibility of representing all of Latin American cinema forced Pereira dos Santos to think creatively about the project. Instead of filming a documentary, which was how Martin Scorsese and others approached the assignment, he decided to make a dramatic film about the golden age of Latin American melodrama—a genre that had thrived in Mexico from the 1930s into the 1950s and had been produced in other countries in the region to great popular appeal.

Pereira dos Santos was inspired by the book *Melodrama: O cinema de lágrimas da América Latina* (Melodrama: Latin America's Cinema of Tears, 1992) by Silvia Oroz, which surveys the history of what were often referred to in Portuguese as "filmes para chorar" (films to cry at). Using a revisionist approach, Oroz's book focuses on the social implications of melodrama's emblematic themes of love, passion, and sacrifice and its allegorical treatment of history to comment on contemporary issues. The book also discusses the star system in Mexico, which was fundamental to the evolution and success of the genre, resulting in indelible associations of certain actors with certain roles. In Mexico these associations included Sara García as the suffering mother, Dolores del Río as the vulnerable beauty, and María Félix as the awe-inspiring "devourer of men." The stories of such women pervaded films of every kind, but especially films about domestic issues, and they often served repressive, socially conservative ends. As the critic Jésus Martín-Barbero notes:

> The melodrama was the dramatic backbone of all the plots, bringing together social impotency and heroic aspirations, appealing to the popular world from a "familiar understanding of reality." The melodrama made it possible for film to weave together national epics and intimate drama, display eroticism under the pretext of condemning incest, and dissolve tragedy in a pool of tears, depoliticizing the social contradictions of daily life. The stars—María Félix, Dolores del Río, Pedro Armendáriz, Jorge Negrete, Ninón Sevilla—provided the faces, bodies, voices and tones of expression for a people to see and hear themselves. Above and beyond the make-up and the commercial star industry, the movie stars who were truly stars for the people gathered their force from a secret pact that bonded their faces with the desires and obsessions of their publics. (365)

Pereira dos Santos used Oroz's book as a guide to the cinematic archive, in the service of a fiction film that also was titled *Cinema de lágrimas*. The film tells the story of an aging homosexual Brazilian film actor–playwright of the present day named Rodrigo (Raul Cortez), who is obsessed with a recurring dream about a childhood trauma—the suicide of his mother. In the dream, Rodrigo's mother enters his bedroom at night, sits on his bed, lovingly and tearfully takes her leave, and then walks out the door to her death. In order to understand his mother's act, Rodrigo decides to locate a movie that she had seen shortly before killing herself, which she referred to as "that film you cannot see." Prior to this search, he meets Yves (Andrés Barros), an attractive young man who asks to interview him for his graduate film thesis. Rodrigo ends up employing Yves as his research assistant, and they travel from Rio de Janeiro to Mexico City, where they spend several days viewing clips of Mexican melodramas in the cinematheque at the Universidad Nacional Autónoma de México (UNAM). These sessions in the cinematheque motivate a kind of survey of a historical genre.

Perhaps as a result of the melodramatic romance and passion that he sees on the screen, Rodrigo ends up falling in love with his young assistant. But Yves does not return Rodrigo's affection; in fact, he often shows up late for work, he repeatedly asks Rodrigo for money, and he harbors a mysterious secret. As the older man sits in the front of the theater, captivated by the projected drama and romance, the assistant sits in the back, and, to Rodrigo's slight irritation, he reads aloud from his notes about the melodramas, in which he theorizes about the female protagonists and the ideological effect of their various manifestations of love.

Like the characters in the films they watch, the actor and his assistant are caught up in a story of unrequited love, loss, and tragedy. After rebuffing Rodrigo's tentative amorous advances, Yves leaves him in Mexico City. Later, Yves writes from a hospital deathbed, explaining to Rodrigo that he is terminally ill, that he is a fugitive from drug traffickers and the police, and that by the time his letter arrives he will likely be dead. He also writes that he has finally located the melodrama for which they had been searching and will be sending a video copy. The sought-after film, titled *Armiño negro*

Yves and Rodrigo in *Cinema de lágrimas*

(Black Ermine, 1953), by the Argentine Carlos Hugo Christensen, is a tragic tale about an adolescent boy who kills himself after having learned that his mother is a prostitute. After viewing the video, Rodrigo realizes that his own mother may have decided to avoid the possibility of a similar discovery by ending her own life.

In *Cinema de lágrimas,* Pereira dos Santos returns us to the popular theme of the mother-son relationship in Latin American melodramas, which almost always involved suffering and self-sacrifice. Although usually not as extreme in their depiction of suffering as *Armiño negro,* typical films of the sort, such as *Puerta Cerrada* (Closed Door, Luis Saslavsky, Argentina, 1939) and *Las abandonadas* (Abandoned Women, Emilio Fernández, Mexico, 1945), portray financially destitute mothers who give up their children in the hopes that they can have a better life. The formula was also popular in Hollywood, where one of the most famous of its variations, *Stella Dallas,* was adapted in 1925, 1937, and 1990. It is interesting that the mother-son relationship also appears as a subplot in Pereira dos Santos's first film, *Rio, 40 graus* (Rio, 100 Degrees, 1956), which is often discussed as the first example of Brazil's Cinema Novo. *Rio, 40 graus* is a left-wing film that combines agit-prop montage with a neorealist treatment of characters in a Rio slum. In most ways it is the very opposite of the Mexican melodramas, but it uses what might be regarded as melodramatic emotion (in the broadest sense of the term) to criticize an oppressive class structure and to create sympathy for a large population of poor people. Dona Elvira (Arlinda Serafim), the maternal figure in the film, is a model of strength and virtue whose love and support for her son are unconditional. Although there are certain affinities between her character and the suffering mother figure made famous by Sara García and Libertad Lamarque, she is portrayed as neither martyr nor victim. Despite her poverty and bedridden condition, she is a conscientious mother and community member who accepts the kind acts of neighbors with grace and stands up to the authorities in order to keep an orphaned child out of the clutches of a dubious justice system.

On the other hand, *Cinema de lágrimas* uses middle-class characters to explore the sexual psychology of the mother-son relationship and the mother's enduring presence in her homosexual son's life. The film begins with the actor's dream about his mother, and this dream prepares us for an Oedipal quest into the "maternal" element of cinema itself. In some ways, the dream sequence in *Cinema de lágrimas* resembles the one in Luis Buñuel's *Los olvidados* (The Young and the Damned, 1950), in the sense that both movies feature sons who have unresolved or conflicted relationships with their mother and who dream about the mother approaching their beds. Buñuel, however, is explicit in his portrayal of Oedipal desire and much more unsettling in his use of a piece of glistening raw meat to suggest the mother's sexuality; his dream sequence creates a strangeness and deep unease that inhibits any feeling of pathos. Pereira dos Santos, by contrast, remains closer to the nexus of conventional melodramatic emotions, juxtaposing the son's dream of his mother's tearful bedside farewell with his adult fascination for movies featuring women and mothers in distress. Rodrigo's search through the cinematic archive is the very stuff of melodrama, replete with a family secret, a suicide, a case of unrequited love, a fateful letter that contains the answer to a riddle, and the death of a love interest. What is particularly interesting about this last aspect of the film, however, is that Pereira dos Santos has changed the classic melodramatic formula about heterosexual relationships into a drama about homosexual love. Although Rodrigo repeatedly asserts that women like "[his] aunts" were the primary audience for the old melodramas, we see him enjoying the old movies and becoming emotional and teary-eyed as he watches them.

Here we might pause to recall that, like their Hollywood counterparts, the Latin American melodramas of love and domesticity were produced, written, and directed almost exclusively by men, but the films were aimed primarily at women, who were thought to be their major consumers. In contrast, Brazilian Cinema Novo, which was also made by men, was probably conceived in unconscious ways for a kind of young man's gaze. It implicitly defined itself in opposition to the slick commercialism and melodramatic formulas and was a rejection not only of capitalist myths but also certain "feminine" elements of the capitalist culture—the posh bourgeois settings and stylish couture, the cult of glamour and entertainment, and above all the tendency to substitute pathos, tears, and masochistic suffering for rigorous political analysis and angry calls to social action. One of the most interesting qualities of Pereira dos Santo's *Cinema de lágrimas,* however, is the way it complicates or blurs this binary opposition between melodrama and Cinema Novo.

The use of the Rodrigo character does not exactly subvert the conventions of melodrama, which, as he himself declares, were largely intended for female audiences. But as a gay man and a theatrical type, Rodrigo has no problem identifying with the tearful women on the screen. Pereira dos Santos makes that point repeatedly by showing close-ups of Rodrigo's captivation with the women's dramas of suffering and their vivid display of emotional extremes. Pereira dos Santos could perhaps have made the character a heterosexual who derives the same pleasure and who experiences the same inner turmoil as does Rodrigo. That particular scenario might have been the more radical and more risky approach, especially given the fact that there are still social pressures and limits as to what the heterosexual male can openly feel and express, even in a darkened theater. Displays of emotion, especially volatile ones, have always been characterized as an attribute of the "weaker" feminine sensibility. Golden-age melodramas repeatedly depicted that sensibility as the exclusive province of women. But Pereira dos Santos's choice of a gay male protagonist who is treated sympathetically and without condescension is consistent with his attempt to blend melodrama and Cinema Novo, making them seem less far apart. He creates a realistic framing story about a mature male of the Cinema Novo generation who looks back at the old cinema and begins to feel a sort of kinship with a bygone period.

Rodrigo's search through the archive is also, of course, a fictional device that allows Pereira dos Santos to show clips, most of them in pristine condition, of more than a dozen wonderfully evocative black-and-white films of the studio era. By this means he pays tribute to a generation of directors, cinematographers, and stars who became internationally famous largely because of their work in melodramas. Although these films were critiqued in the 1960s—especially in the period of Cinema Novo—for having little to do with the social reality of the movie-going public, the Mexican and Argentine melodramas in particular were genuinely popular. Among the highest quality films ever made in Latin America, they were exported to other countries in the region in much the same way as the contemporary telenovelas. In effect, Pereira dos Santos, who began his career as a neorealist and a symbol of the Latin American new wave, revises his previous attitude toward a genre that, like the Brazilian *chanchada* (musical comedy), was often criticized by the Left because of its association with Hollywood. He is particularly adept at showing how melodramas can continue to enthrall intelligent viewers such as Rodrigo.

The Mexican and Argentine melodramas that Pereira dos Santos shows in *Cinema de lágrimas* include such early examples as *Santa* (Saint, 1931) by Antonio Moreno, which is the first feature-length sound film made in Mexico, and *La mujer del puerto* (Woman of the Port, 1933) by Arcady Boytler. Despite their forerunner status, the portraits of women under duress in these two films are among the most controversial in the history of the genre. Abandoned, young, innocent protagonists turn to prostitution as a way to survive. After a life of hard knocks, the title character in *Santa* (Lupita Tovar) succumbs to cancer and dies while on the operating table. Rosario (Andrea Palma), the leading character in *La mujer del puerto,* unknowingly has sex with a sailor (Domingos Soler) who turns out to be the brother she hasn't seen since early childhood; her realization of this incestuous act drives her

Rosa about to
discard her child in
*Víctimas del pecado*

to take her life by plunging into the sea. Later melodramas shown in the film include Fernández's *Las abandonadas,* starring Pedro Armendáriz and Dolores del Río (both of whom were also under contract in Hollywood), Roberto Gavaldón's *La diosa arrodillada* (The Kneeling Goddess, 1947) and *Camelia* (Camille, 1954), which starred Mexican diva María Félix, Tito Davidson's *Doña diabla* (The Devil Is a Woman, 1949), which also featured María Félix, Alberto Gout's *Aventurera* (Aventuress, 1949) and Gavaldón's *Víctimas del pecado* (Victims of Sin, 1950), both of which starred the Cuban-born rumbera Ninón Sevilla, and Luis Buñuel's surrealistic rendition of Emily Brontë's *Wuthering Heights, Abismos de pasión* (Abysms of Passion, 1953).

Like Rodrigo's dream, in which the father is totally absent, the film clips tend to be exclusively about women who have had sexual encounters of one kind or another and who are now left on their own with a child. A variation on this pattern occurs in *Víctimas del pecado.* Rosa (Margarita Ceballos), a young prostitute, runs after Rodolfo (Rodolfo Acosta), her pimp-lover, who works in the cabaret-brothel and who makes her choose between him and their baby. The clip shows the anguished mother gently placing her swaddled newborn in a roadside trash can and then racing to join her lover. The mother's "unnatural" act is immediately countered by Violeta, a dancer and Rosa's co-worker in the cabaret (Ninón Sevilla), who rescues the child and struggles for years to support it—despite her observation early in the movie that "We don't have any right to have children!"

The chief father figures shown in the various clips are usually aging and frightening family patriarchs who go to great lengths to protect their daughter's honor and overrule any unwanted suitors. Julio Bracho's *Historia de un gran amor* (Story of a Great Love, 1942) is perhaps the most extreme case of an overly protective father. Unable to bear the sight of his daughter in the arms of another, he kills her by throwing a knife from across the room into her back. The one clip that shows an exception to the violent patriarch is the character played by Arturo de Córdova in Gilberto Martínez's *Cinco rostos de mujer* (Five Faces of a Woman, 1947), who is reunited with a grown daughter, the product of a past love affair. But his delight seems less about finding the daughter than in discovering her strong resemblance to her mother, who, he says, will now be with him forever.

Although the figure of the child is vital to the emotional trauma that is played out in melodrama, the son or daughter is rarely, if ever, the central protagonist. Marisela (María Elena Marqués), the teenage daughter in Fernando de Fuentes's *Doña Bárbara* (1944), has a larger role than most because the plot is about the rivalry between an estranged mother (María Félix) and her daughter for the affections of the landowner Santos Luzardo (Juan Soler). In *Armiño negro,* the son (Néstor Zavarce) has a larger-than-usual role in order to establish the singularly loving relationship between him and his mother (Laura Hidalgo). Two scenes in the clip are worth noting: first, during his mother's visit to his private school, the boy takes her photograph on a stairway in front of a building. As he readies the camera, he looks up at his mother on her step-pedestal, and, like an adoring suitor, tells her how beautiful she is. In the second scene, he stares wide-eyed through a staircase banister as he observes his mother entering the house with one of her paramours, who passionately embraces and kisses her. These scenes with their Oedipal inspiration are crucial to the film's tragic denouement, in which the son kills himself in his bedroom.

In the framing story of *Cinema de lágrimas,* the mother is the motivation for a cinematic search in which the protagonist regresses to the condition of a child. As the camera pans across the bedroom in Rodrigo's dream, we see the comforts of a middle-class childhood that includes toys, stuffed animals, books, and, perhaps most important, a beautifully framed photograph of himself and his mother displayed on a bedside stand. The film emphasizes the relationship between Rodrigo and his younger dreamed self by showing him as he awakens in what could very well be the same room with the same comfortable-looking bed; although the toys and stuffed animals are no longer in evidence, the room is tastefully decorated with the same photograph of his mother at the side of his bed. But unlike the powerful mother figures featured in most melodramas, Rodrigo's mother is present only in dreams, although she obviously determines all the clips that Rodrigo views, and these clips respond in different ways to his obsession with the maternal. When he finally sees *Armiño negro,* it is as if he and the boy in the film have merged as they watch in silence and increasing dismay the transformation of the mother into a whore. That image contradicts not only the image of the fairy princess–mother whom the boy praises and photographs but also the maternal image that Rodrigo cherishes beside his bed. The boy's horror at the spectacle of the erotic mother prompts his suicide; Rodrigo, a grown man, is more sanguine, although he is moved to tears by the revelation. His mother's suicide is the essence of the melodramatic moment in which the mother makes the ultimate sacrifice to protect her child from a life of pain.

The emotional drama being played out between Rodrigo and Yves in the framing story involves the popular melodramatic motif of the incurable illness. In one of his theorizing moments, Yves alludes to his own situation by commenting on the complications created by diseases such as tuberculosis and cancer in love affairs, but Rodrigo misunderstands his remark. Thinking that Yves is alluding to him, Rodrigo says that he has no illness but offers to be tested for AIDS. Here as elsewhere, there is an interesting relation between the small personal drama played out in realist fashion in the framing narrative and the larger dramas being played out on the screen of the cinematheque. For example, while the beautiful but tubercular Camille (María Félix) gives up her younger lover to spare him the pain of her physical decline and death, the terminally ill Yves, who grows paler and thinner as the film progresses, keeps Rodrigo's growing and plaintive passion in check. In fact, although he knows something is wrong, Rodrigo is completely unaware of Yves's condition until he receives the death-bed letter in Rio.

Unlike roughly equivalent films made in the United States, Latin American melodramas often involved musical numbers that sometimes were directly connected to the plot and other times simply provided dramatic relief from the tense build-up of emotion. One of the most frequently cited instances of the first approach appears in *Aventurera,* at a reception for the newlyweds Elena (Ninón Sevilla) and Mario (Rubén Rojo). As Gilberto Perez notes in his essay about the film in Chapter 1 of this volume, in order to take revenge on her new mother-in-law Rosaura (Andrea Palma), who is a society matron but also, unknown to Rosaura's son, the owner of a brothel where Elena worked, Elena flaunts her sexuality, performing a steamy rumba that shocks the high-society gathering. Sevilla performs a much longer and more flamboyant dance number in *Víctimas del pecado,* but it is far less pivotal to the plot than the one in *Aventurera* and mainly provides a titillating reprieve from equally exploitative but more sordid aspects of cabaret life.

To maintain a link with this convention in *Cinema de lágrimas,* Pereira dos Santos includes a musical performance, but this one is of a different type. On two separate occasions, the camera focuses on a group of young men dressed in pre-Columbian costumes, their bodies on display, who are performing an ancient tribal dance in the outdoors. The scene has no apparent relation to the plot and at first glance seems to be an attempt to show a bit of local color as Rodrigo and Yves cross a large public square and enter the university. Eschewing the rumba of the melodrama, which originated in Cuba and was imported by Mexico, Pereira dos Santos opts for an indigenous music and dance, but the same performers reappear later in the film as Rodrigo exits the theater, and in this case they function less as an example of realist local color than as an "attraction" along the lines of the rumba. In this case the dance of partly clad male performers has nothing to do with women and heterosexual desire, but neither, of course, does the film's story of a relationship between Rodrigo and Yves. By using male as opposed to female performers, Pereira dos Santos keeps the focus on Rodrigo's homosexual gaze, through which most of the movie is viewed.

Because they occur within the context of a modern cityscape, the indigenous dance sequences also suggest the various ways in which the past is forever merging with the present to create a new sense of the past. *Cinema de lágrimas* makes this idea more explicit with its many references to New Latin American Cinema, which it often juxtaposes with the melodramas. Throughout the film, Pereira dos Santos points in various ways to the archival coexistence of the two forms: he incorporates bits and pieces from different classroom lectures by UNAM professors about Glauber Rocha and Cuban "imperfect cinema"; he slowly pans down hallways decorated with publicity posters of early melodramas and New Cinema productions; he focuses on banners outside the UNAM cinematheque that refer to the New Cinema; and back in Rio, he visits the cinematheque, whose hallways are decorated with Brazilian Cinema Novo posters and where, with Pereira dos Santos's typical ironic touch, a festival celebrating "100 years of cinema" is well under way.[2]

One might say that Rodrigo and Yves personify the still uneasy relationship between the old and the new cinema. As the author of a play called *Amor* and a man given to romance, Rodrigo is clearly moved by the emotional plots that feature women in danger and dangerous women. There is a resemblance between the close-ups of his adoring and impassioned face illuminated by the screen's refracted glow and the studio-crafted close-ups of melodrama's female stars, whose carefully lit faces often register a similar sort of gaze. On the other hand, Yves, at his small work table, maintains an analytic distance as he jots down notes about the films and occasionally pontificates about their motivations and meanings. He represents a "soft" version of the increasingly theoretical critique that was aimed at melodrama when the movement for a new Latin American cinema got under way. Unlike Rodrigo, he is not emotionally caught up by what he sees on the screen, and when we see him in close-up, the only illumination on his face is from a study lamp on the table.

In the movie's final scene, Rodrigo wanders from the screening of *Armiño negro,* the film associated with his mother, into a screening of Glauber Rocha's *Deus e o diabo na terra do sol* (Black God, White Devil, 1964), which he views along with students and others in a large auditorium. The chief theoretician of Brazilian Cinema Novo, Rocha made films in the 1960s and 1970s that brought together highly theatrical performances and sometimes Brechtian social criticism in an attempt to create a politically radical Third World cinema. According to his famous 1965 manifesto, the aesthetic premise for this new cinema was the hunger that exists throughout the developing world and the violence that massive hunger ultimately begets.[3] *Deus e o diabo na terra do sol,* along with Pereira dos Santos' *Vidas Secas* (Barren Lives, 1963), brought to the screen in unrivaled ways the full measure and impact of this hunger and violence, chiefly through stories about the poor in the interior of northeastern Brazil. Hunger and violence returned as central themes in Rocha's "sequel" to *Deus e o diabo, O dragão da maldade contra o santo guerreiro* (The Dragon of Evil Against the Holy Warrior, 1969), more commonly known as *Antônio das Mortes.* Pereira dos Santos also reworked these themes in his satiric and allegorical paean to cannibalism titled *Como era gostoso o meu francês* (How Tasty Was My Little Frenchman, 1972).

In *Cinema de lágrimas,* this radical cinema of the 1960s and 1970s serves as a counterpoint to the various melodramas. In effect, this film is an attempt to understand Latin American cinema in terms of a dialectic between two different moments in film history and two very different kinds of movies, one of which (the melodrama) was highly successful with audiences at home, and the other of which (Cinema Novo) was more popular with art cinema audiences and festival goers abroad. He does not appear to privilege one over the other, and he even suggests that there are affinities between the two forms.

Pereira dos Santos's homage to Rocha in the final scene of the film is especially interesting in this regard. The clip he selects is from the end of *Deus e o diabo na terra do sol,* when Corisco, the *cangaceiro,* or bandit (Othon Bastos) and Rosa (Yoná Magalhães), the farmhand's wife, are caught in a long and movingly tender embrace. An unusually long close-up that is beautifully photographed by Waldemar Lima, it allows the camera to revolve slowly around the couple. The highly emotional nondiegetic music by Sérgio Ricardo that underlies the close-up is quite similar to the music one hears in the older melodramas. The next clip shows the hired gun, Antônio das Mortes (Maurício do Valle), shooting the messianic Corisco while Rosa and her husband Manuel (Geraldo del Rey), race across the *sertão* (interior) to reach the sea. As in all of Rocha's work, the action is glamorously stylized, even if it does not have the slick, artificial look of the older studio productions. By choosing these scenes, Pereira dos Santos invites us to ask exactly how Rocha's shot of the couple's embrace or Corisco's death at the hands of Antônio das Mortes differs in kind from the close-ups of passionate lovers in *Camelia* or the dramatic death scene in Buñuel's *Abismos de Pasión,* in which the lovesick and crazed Alejandro (Jorge Mistral) is shot in the eye as he leans against his beloved's open coffin. The couple's race away from the villainous Antônio das Mortes and across the sertão is as melodramatic as any escape scene from the older movies. The soundtrack that fuels the eroticism of the prolonged kiss in Rocha's film is as stirringly sensual as Richard Wagner's *Tristan und Isolde,* which in the Buñuel film accompanies Alejandro's kissing of his beloved's decomposing corpse.

Rocha's film not only builds up emotion but also provides relief or catharsis with its last scene, in which the couple races to the sea. As in melodrama, the catharsis depends heavily on the soundtrack, which, in this case, is a joyful, fast-paced, and vigorously sung ballad that further animates the

Passion in the backlands in
*Deus e o diabo na terra do sol*

couple's race. The points of contact between melodrama and Cinema Novo seem even clearer as we watch Rodrigo looking at the Rocha film and come to realize that his tearful yet pleasurable reaction to *Deus e o diablo na terra do sol* is partly nostalgic and is not unlike his response to the melodrama. The fusion of the two forms takes hold in the auditorium scene. Rodrigo's unrequited love for his young assistant builds as he watches Corisco and Rosa kiss; overtaken by emotion, he taps a young man on the shoulder in the row in front of him. When he realizes that the young man is not Yves, he masks his disappointment and embarrassment by gently smiling as tears stream down his face.

*Cinema de lágrimas* offers viewers the opportunity to see a collection of remarkable clips from the golden age of melodrama (as well as a couple from the Cinema Novo) and with its own melodramatic plot offers a partial reassessment of a genre that fell out of critical favor in the late 1950s and 1960s. The film also provides a new reading of Latin American New Cinema in the light of the older films, showing us that the dramatization of emotion, the sentimental treatment of romance, and the interest in visual and musical

Raul Cortez in *Cinema de lágrimas*

excess were never completely absent from the radical cinema. Ultimately *Cinema de lágrimas* is about the pleasure of watching both types of films, each of which evokes a kind of historical nostalgia and pride.

## Notes

1. For a commentary on the BFI series, see Rosenbaum.

2. Another juxtaposition of a transnational sort appears in the UNAM film projection's room. There a large poster with a close-up of Marilyn Monroe in a revealing low-cut dress is positioned alongside another with a close-up of Pedro Armendáriz in revolutionary attire replete with sombrero, gun and bandoliers. Although Marilyn is a well-known object of male heterosexual desire, she was also one of the "heavenly bodies" whose sexuality was closely examined by the film critic Richard Dyer. Armendáriz is as sexy as Marilyn, and I would suspect that his dark-haired beauty, draped with hardware, was as desirable to gay men as it was to heterosexual women.

3. See Rocha, "An Esthetic of Hunger."

## Works Cited

Amâncio, Tunico. *Nelson Pereira dos Santos: Catálogo (mostra de filmes e vídeos)*. Rio de Janeiro: Centro Cultural Banco do Brasil, 1999.

Martín-Barbero, Jésus. "The Processes: From Nationalism to Transnationalisms." In *Media and Cultural Studies: Keyworks*. Ed. Meenakshi Gigi Durham and Douglas Kellner. Oxford: Blackwell, 2001. 351–81.

Oroz, Silvia. *Melodrama: O cinema de lágrimas da América Latina*. 2d rev. ed. Rio de Janeiro: Ministério de Cultura/Funarte, 1999.

Rocha, Glauber. "An Esthetic of Hunger." Trans. Randal Johnson and Burnes Hollyman. In *Brazilian Cinema*. Ed. Randal Johnson and Robert Stam. Expanded ed. New York: Columbia University Press, 1995. 69–71.

Rosenbaum, Jonathan. "International Harvest: National Film Histories on Video." In *Essential Cinema: On the Necessity of Film Canons*. Baltimore: Johns Hopkins University Press, 2004. 210–15.

# 7

## Luis Alcoriza; or, A Certain Antimelodramatic Tendency in Mexican Cinema

### MARVIN D'LUGO

> Beyond its reactionary content and its schematic
> formulation, cinema is going to connect with the hunger
> of the masses to make themselves socially visible.
>
> Jesús Martín-Barbero

### Mexican Mothers in Melodrama

At the center of Luis Alcoriza's award-winning 1971 film *Mecánica nacional* (National Mechanics) we find a scene that self-consciously parodies one of the prominent tropes that historically have shaped Mexico's movie melodramas: the cult of the iconic maternal figure. Set in a rural locale on the outskirts of Mexico City, the scene involves the makeshift lying-in-state of the family matriarch, Doña Lolita (Sara García), who, the night before, had come with her family to view the final laps of a national car race but died suddenly after overeating and drinking. A television crew assigned to cover the racing event captures the improvised ritual of mourning for the lavishly adorned corpse as they await their real job, the race's finale. In this way, a scene of family bereavement is transformed into a theatrical event in which the savvy television director even orders Doña Lolita's grieving son, Eufemio (Manolo Fábregas), to look upward in a pious gesture that mimics the convention of religious paintings of supplicants praying to heaven. This insertion of the television "gaze" mockingly reminds Alcoriza's audience of the connectivity of certain melodramatic tropes that cross popular visual media, blurring the distinction between experiences that are lived and those that are performed.

Jesús Martín-Barbero has argued that the key to the obstinate persistence of melodrama lies in part in its adaptability to changing technological formats. Through its circulation across cultural and political borders, melodrama interpellates an ever-increasing mass audience, enabling individuals to bear witness to a collective "total spectacle" in which they may see themselves as part of a unified social and cultural whole otherwise denied them by hierarchical, class-bound society (125). Instead of naturalizing staged emotional gestures, however, the scene from *Mecánica nacional* exposes the very artifice of melodrama's appeal, showing us how individual feelings are reshaped by recognizable performance codes and circulated by mass media so that the experience and its representation become indistinguishable.

By self-referentially staging the multiple planes of imagery in this scene, Alcoriza reveals the double project of his film: first, to engage his audience in the recognition of the artifice of their seemingly natural responses to Doña Lolita's unceremonious death; then, to deflate the quasi-religious cult of the mother by staging the death ritual as a parody of sacred maternity. Alcoriza's deconstructive impulse is aided in a conspicuous way by his choice of casting. The deceased matriarch is, of course, not just any old lady. Doña Lolita is played by "The Mother of all Mexicans," Sara García (Mora 1985, 230), an actress whose career portraying the long-suffering maternal figure in dozens

Sara García as suffering mother

of Mexican films began in 1933 with her performance in this stock role in Jorge Bell's *El pulpo humano* (*The Human Octopus*). Over the years her increasingly more clichéd appearances as the self-sacrificing mother and later as the grandmother became fixtures in Mexican melodramas.[1]

The cult of the mother that is the brunt of Alcoriza's parody is rooted in a critical conflation of maternity with sainthood that, as Julia Tuñón reminds us, was one of the rhetorical axes of Mexican cinema's golden-age melodramas (185). The sacredness of maternity, as played out endlessly in Mexican films of the 1930s and 1940s, explicitly aligned melodramatic gestures with Catholic religious iconography (Mora 1985, 229). By joining this "classical" movie trope with its updated television version, Alcoriza calls into question both the melodramatic stereotype and the community's dedication to the hoary cultural sensibility embedded in the cliché. He explains his conception of the film's project this way: "I mock symbols. I think it is very legitimate to love one's mother. I love mine very much, but this has nothing to do with Mother with a capital 'M.' What terrifies me—I repeat—are symbols of Mother, of Father. . . . The taboos, the authorities, respect for everything" (Reyes Nevares 71).

*Mecánica nacional* is especially noteworthy in this regard because its development of a topical Mexican satire also reveals the ways in which presumed genre-restricted dramatic and narrative formulas have transcended their historical periods, geographic location, and even their original ideological meanings, by means of successive media interventions into a persistent cipher of underlying features of Latin American social ethos. The objective of this essay is to explore Luis Alcoriza's metacinematic approach to the questions posed by the persistence of a melodramatic imagination as it evolved during the crucial decade of the 1960s. Unlike the cohort of Latin American filmmakers and commentators of the New Latin American Cinema of this same period (such as Cuba's Enrique Colina and Daniel Díaz Torres and Argentina's Fernando Solanas and Octavio Getino, all of whom stood outside the mainstream film industries that they critiqued), Alcoriza poses a sustained self-conscious assessment of melodrama from within the very industry he mocks. As we shall see, through the dynamics of displaced images such as that of the sainted mother, Alcoriza effects his deflation of the melodramatic imagination.

The trajectory of Alcoriza's career reflects in a striking manner the filmmaker's particular engagement with and eventual disengagement from the cultural construction of the Mexican melodramatic sensibility. As a member of his family's acting troupe, he arrived in Mexico in 1940 at the age of twenty, a political refugee from the Spanish Civil War. With his prior training as an actor, he made an easy transition into theater and, later, film, specializing in playing the role of Christ in various biblical films. By the mid-1940s, he had embarked on a new film-related career as a screenwriter; in the following fifteen years he compiled a prodigious list of credits for original scripts and adaptations.[2]

His early years in Mexico coincided precisely with a crucial period in which Mexican cinema was forging its status as the preeminent national and transnational film industry in the Spanish-speaking world (López 1994, 7). An engaged observer of the industry's construction of a Mexican cultural imaginary built around melodramatic forms, he soon found himself an active participant in the forging of that imaginary as an actor. Ironically, as a successful scriptwriter, he would even become a generator of the very cultural narratives that must have seemed contrived and false to him (Pérez Turrent 10–11).

He turned to directing in 1960, in part, as he noted, to prevent other directors from mutilating his scripts (González Casanova 92). His first directorial project, *Los jóvenes* (The Young Ones, 1960), though praised in some quarters, proved a limited success. This was followed by national and international acclaim for the "Three Ts": *Tlayucan* (1961), *Tiburoneros* (Shark Fishers, 1962), and *Tarahumara* (1964), three films that brought him critical acclaim and commercial prominence as a new talent in Mexican cinema. The decade of the 1960s, culminating with *Mecánica nacional,* constitutes Alcoriza's period of greatest acclaim. *Tlayucan,* in fact, was nominated for an Oscar in the Best Foreign Film category. It is in the context of these critical high points in his career—*Tlayucan* and *Mecánica nacional*—that my discussion of Alcoriza's critique of melodrama is framed.

## Sacred Images

By the 1930s, Mexican movie melodrama had already become "a purveyor of collective conventions and provided a sort of sentimental education of the tribe, with roots in the schematic rhetoric and theatricality of popular spectacles" (Hernández Rodríguez 102). Its rhetorical features, derived from a variety of popular media (Mora 1985, 228), were built on a series of simple Manichaean polarities—good-bad, saint-whore—and an aesthetic of visual and emotional excess often commented on by critics.[3] Yet recent critical reevaluation of Mexican melodrama has suggested that what we are speaking of is less a genre than a broad cultural sensibility not contained by geopolitical borders, social class, history, or specific technologies (Burton-Carvajal;

García Canclini; López 1991). As an aesthetic and social phenomenon, melo-drama has thus eluded simple reductive classification. During the first three decades of the sound era, the three most highly developed Latin American film industries, those of Argentina, Brazil and Mexico, insistently exploited particular clusters of narrative, dramatic, and visual tropes in ways that sug-gested that what critics and audiences were calling melodrama was really a facet of collective unconscious for Latin American audiences (Paranaguá 1996, 238–42). This view is reinforced by the seemingly extravagant apprais-als by various commentators of Latin American film and culture: Martín-Barbero has argued that "the way [Latin Americans] live and feel finds its most open expression in melodrama" (243). Carlos Monsiváis, speaking of the sensibility of various generations of Latin Americans, describes how they extracted from their formation in melodramatic culture a certain sense of identity (2000, 61). In that same vein, Carlos Fuentes calls melodrama "the central fact of private life in Latin America (*Homenaje a Juan Rulfo,* quoted in Podalsky 57).

Trying to explain the relation of the rise of mass culture and the diffusion of melodrama as one of the privileged forms of popular cinema, Néstor García Canclini argues that, during the early decades of sound cinema, the appeal of the melodramatic sensibility to much of the Latin American movie audi-ence was as a form of mediation between individual and collective identities within an age of relatively rapid urbanization and the development of mass culture (189). Martín-Barbero takes that argument one step further when he questions why there should be such an appeal within Latin American cul-ture for an expressive mode long dismissed as a low form of commercialized mass-oriented culture (131). He sees melodrama's transgeneric, transhistoric force as lying precisely in its power as an affective bridge between collective historical experience and the lives of individuals during periods of extreme social and ideological crisis.

In its Latin American cinematic incarnation, melodrama provided what Martín-Barbero has called in his case study of Mexican melodrama "un cine a la imagen del pueblo" (a cinema in the image of the nation, 180). The force of the image, as he argues, is grounded in the power of certain visual strate-gies to move the audience to "see itself," to position itself within a particular emotional and ideological framework. That process of mirroring was aided by the recurrence of visual and musical tropes that transcended the verbal and seduced the popular audience into seeing its own likeness in the obses-sions and desires of fictional characters (182).

With obvious indebtedness to the writings of Peter Brooks and Thomas

Elsaesser, Martín-Barbero traces the origins of melodrama to the popular theatrical forms that arose in the aftermath of the French Revolution, which, in turn, were rooted in earlier popular theatrical forms, including pantomime and dance. As a popular spectacle, theatrical melodrama relied heavily on images, sounds, and gestures rather than on words and the development of complex ideas (125–26). In the early decades of the twentieth century, however, with the advent of sound-recording technologies, melodrama became more and more closely identified with an auditory imagination that conditioned the responses of listeners to melodramatic scenarios in lyrics and music. Martín-Barbero contends that "[t]he functionality of music and the creation of auditory effects that one would find in the splendor of the radio soap opera (radionovela) had in the nineteenth-century melodrama not only its antecedent but the paradigm of its very form" (126).

Yet the auditory cues associated with melodrama were, apparently, subservient to the power of melodramatic iconography. Even before the advent of sound cinema, as film historians have noted, the power of film imagery engaged the imagination of movie audiences and mediated collective identity by means of the spectacle of a story told in moving pictures. Monsiváis sums up the force of this attraction of the image on the individual and collective psyche of Mexican popular audiences in an essay appropriately titled "All the People Came and Did Not Fit onto the Screen" (1995, 145–51). In it he speaks of the democratizing impact of the institution of cinema on ordinary Mexicans, especially those of the marginal classes: "[A]nyone could go the cinema, and this unexpected democratization flew in the face of the exclusivity of 'high culture,' whose representatives were either enthusiastic or worried about the phenomenon" (145). Monsiváis even describes the appeal of images of stars, speaking of "cinema and the religion of the facial image" ("El cine" 1995, 23).

The "sacredness" of facial images in a culture such as Mexico's proves ultimately to be more than a facile metaphor in understanding the versatility of melodrama. Within the historical contexts of the early decades of the twentieth century, which saw the political upheaval of Mexico's decade-long revolution followed by the advent of modernization, motion pictures came to hold a special cultural value. Perceived in one context as the tangible embodiment of modernity, for many audiences motion pictures assumed an ironic countermeaning, that is, a kind of sacredness akin to the patterns, structures, and rhetoric of the all-embracing culture of Catholicism that was being displaced and replaced by the revolution. Serge Gruzinski speaks of a cultural imaginary built around the very power of images to construct a bridge between traditional culture and modernity in early sound cinema.[4] Tracing the elaborate refiguration of cultural images in Mexico, from "Columbus to *Blade Runner*," he underscores a striking historical constancy in the transformation of cultural images at times of political and social upheaval. In the concluding section of the historical trajectory that he traces, he notes the curious way movie imagery parallels the patterns of appropriation of Christian iconography seen in the colonial period. Just as images had been part of an ideological project to advance the subjugation and conversion to Catholicism of native populations in Mexico, movie images in the crucial decade of the 1930s became cultural markers as much as they were "instruments" for deciphering new experiences through the grid of an already constructed cultural imaginary (28). In each period he observes, Gruzinski notes a dual process: both the controlled production of images used for ideological goals and the interpretive act of viewing images, which involves the viewer's practice of decontextualization, "the blurring of references, the confusion of ethnic and cultural registers, the overlap of life and fiction" (226).

Following a line of associations that Marsha Kinder had earlier delineated in Spanish melodrama, Gruzinski underscores the Catholic sadomasochistic discourse whose appeal lay in its implicit assumption that "suffering always ennobles the martyred losers" (Kinder 73). The kind of Catholic imagery that was intended to hold sway over native populations often involved the erotics of suffering and compassion as embodied in the iconography related to Christ and the Virgin Mary and closely aligned with the emotional excesses that would later be identified with melodramatic representation (157–58).

Confirming Gruzinski's general argument about the conflation of religious iconography and melodrama, Julia Tuñón exhaustively details the specific narrative and visual practices associated with the maternal figure in golden-age Mexican melodramas. She points to the repeated device of staged maternal self-sacrifice within which maternity itself coalesces with saintliness (185). If in general, as Tuñón notes, the characterization of women was aligned with the religious axis, with either Eve or the Virgin Mary (288), the plots and images that were most powerfully associated with the good mother in Mexican cinema were usually those of the Virgin. In obvious ways, this scenario connects broadly with the reinforcement of melodramatic scenarios: "The peculiarity of this maternal essence is shared with the deity, in particular, with the Virgin of Guadalupe, which is clearly evident in many films, but always in limit situations, in scenes of dramatic excess, in moments of catharsis" (187).

In all of these discussions, it is important to note that commentators expand the concept of the image on-screen beyond the mere cinematic "shot."

García Canclini, for instance, speaks of the way melodrama gives importance to "primordial forms of sociality such as kinship, neighborhood, territorial and friendship solidarities" (147). Alcoriza's critical approach to melodrama, as we shall see, focuses on the narrow sense of the sacred image as a discreet framed shot and also as the broader narrative mise-en-scène depicted on-screen as it variously affirms or contravenes the spectator's sense of identification with a traditional community within the broader scenario of modernity.

## *Tlayucan;* or, Questioning the "Splendor of the Image"

In a revealing statement made shortly before his death in 1992 about his own early attraction to Mexican cinema, Alcoriza spoke eloquently of the evocative power of the cinematic image in Emilio "El Indio" Fernández's *Pueblerina* (Country Girl). This power derived, he claimed, as a lesson from Sergei Eisenstein's cultivation of Mexican cinematic imagery: "I was impressed because it was pure; there was never any intention as to dialogue or phrases, never any ideas. It was simply the image in all its beauty and splendor" (93).

One of the brilliant concepts guiding *Tlayucan,* his first international success as a director-screenwriter, is, as the film's opening credits suggest, the recycling of Mexican cultural iconography in an effort to debunk the "splendor of the image" of folkloric traditionalist Mexico. That credit sequence opens on a view of a picture-postcard indigenous village with a backdrop of billowing clouds that recall the signature elements of Gabriel Figueroa's cinematography, which had been used abundantly since the 1930s to connote an idealized rural Mexico (Ramírez-Berg 16). In combination with the indigenous name of the village, which is superimposed on this image, the audience's introduction to the space of the fiction appears to foretell a fairly conventional if somewhat dated version of the familiar narrative of national folkloric culture drawn from the essentialist vocabulary that privileged rural, traditional community and *indigenismo.* These are the well-known marks of what Alex Saragoza aptly terms the "performance of authenticity" (96). As the plot will reveal, these images and the story they enunciate are characterized by persistent reminders of the historical operations of Mexican melodramatic practices now refigured as parody.

Linda Hutcheon's classic discussion of parody defines the strategy as "repetition with a difference, an imitation with critical ironic distance, whose irony cuts both ways . . . from scornful ridicule to reverential homage" (32). As the narrative of *Tlayucan* progresses, there is little doubt that the director plays that double edge of parody to great advantage, leading some critics to mistakenly read the film's treatment of "folkloric, rural culture" as "an un-deformed vision of the melodrama of a rural Mexican community" (Ayala Blanco 10).

The theatrical plot eventually debunks that view as it brings us to the narrative heart of the film, the altar of the church depicted in the credits, at the center of which is a statue of the local Virgin to which various characters pay homage. This sacred figure becomes the pivot point of the film. In Alcoriza's script, an idealized *campesino* couple, Eufemio (Julio Aldama) and Chabela (Norma Angélica), are plagued by economic problems that intensify when their son Nicolás (Juan Carlos Ortiz) takes ill. After various efforts to obtain the money for urgently needed medicine, the desperate Eufemio goes to the altar and asks the Virgin for a sign of help. At the exact instant of his supplication, a flash of light appears before him, which he takes as a sign from the Virgin. He climbs up to the altar and removes a pearl from the statue's crown just as another flash is seen. In a quick cutaway to the terrace overlooking the altar, we see the source of these mysterious flashes of light: a group of American tourists has been admiring the interior of the church and taking Polaroid photographs of the altar and then of Eufemio's theft. The erstwhile hero is thus literally "caught in the act" by the modern technology of the instant camera.

The insertion of this technologized image is first seen by the audience from Eufemio's perspective as a sign from the saint, then immediately transposed by an establishing shot to the site of the tourists perched at the terrace window looking into the church and down to the altar. Through the agency of the photographic flash, Alcoriza disrupts the audience's identification with the illusion of a storybook Mexico framed by the timeless Manichaean polarities of good and evil by transforming the miraculous into the mundane. In this way, both the hero and his presumed Mexican audience are transposed into a political and economic world within which such images are trafficked as commercial "merchandise," here literalized by the tourists' gaze, which turns religious melodrama into cultural commodity.

Seemingly a gag played for comic effect, the introduction of a group of foreign tourists to disrupt the plot is an effect that had been used previously in Alcoriza's script collaboration with Luis Buñuel, most hilariously in *Ensayo de un crimen* (The Criminal Life of Archibaldo de la Cruz, 1955). It is, however, considerably more complex in its thematic import here, as it folds back on questions of the ideology of the melodramatic image. The centerpiece of the scene is, of course, the instant camera's visual assault on the revered religious figure that depicts a melodramatic version of Catholicism. The melodramatic treatment of the Virgin is not an original move by Alcoriza but merely a cross-reference to a trope that had been amply worked over in Emilio Fernández's *María Candelaria* (1943) and *Enamorada* (1946). As in those films, the appeal of the iconography of the Virgin lies in the emotional force of its compassion for her abject subjects. As in the ecclesiastical staging of the figure of the Virgin in Mexican churches during the colonial period, this meaning is underscored by the saint's religious aura, which is foregrounded by the statue's placement at the center of the altar (Gruzinski 47). The icon thus conveys nonverbally to the believer, in this case the innocent campesino, a message of compassion that is metonymically conflated with the notion of divine maternity, implicitly aligned for Mexican audiences with the cult of the Virgin of Guadalupe (Radcliffe and Westwood 142).

The American tourists provide a secularized gaze embodied in the new technology of the image they possess, which challenges the very premise of the old religious and melodramatic iconography. The camera flash, in effect, transposes "Deep Mexico" (*México Profundo*)[5] into the modern commercial world, thereby exposing the anachronism of Eufemio's story by aligning it with the Mexican government's "selling" of the folkloric (and, by association, melodramatic) Mexico to tourists.

The satire of sacred melodrama embodied in the staging of the theft of the pearl is buttressed by an intertextual parody of elements of two films from Mexico's golden age: Emilio Fernández's *María Candelaria* and *La perla* (1945).[6] The story line of *Tlayucan* openly parodies these Fernández-Figueroa texts, beginning with the idealized rural family, played, of course, by nonindigenous actors. Eufemio and Chabela are humble campesinos struggling under financial burdens. As in *María Candelaria,* the plot involves the heroine's affection for the pigs that she raises. Chabela does not take ill with typhoid as does Dolores del Río in Fernández's film; it is her son who develops a fever and must have expensive penicillin treatment. At this point, the plot apes *María Candelaria* by having the noble Eufemio, the good farmer-husband-father, steal a pearl from the crown of the statue of the Virgin to pay for the medicine.

The plot of *Tlayucan* then shifts to the Steinbeck text and the comic fetishization of the pearl. Alcoriza mischievously builds in hilarious plot twists when he has the townspeople believe that the pearl has been eaten by one of the pigs. In order to retrieve the precious object, the men must induce diarrhea in the pigs and pick through the feces. What had started out as a sublime evocation of rural Mexico becomes in this way a gross parody of Fernández's melodramatic plots. To add to the underlying critique of melodrama's falsification of human experience, Alcoriza's script continually plays with the audience's expectation of melodramatic clichés of plot and character, only to reverse them at key moments. He takes a stock character such as the saintly mother and presents her as almost ready to sell her body to save her son; he then subverts that voyeuristic pleasure by having her reject the indecent proposition of Don Tomás (Andrés Soler), the lewd old man who lusts after her. But, to further build the audience's voyeuristic desires, Chabela eventually agrees to "perform" her sexually provocative daily bathing for the old neighbor as her thanks for his having provided her family with the needed money.

Perhaps no other character in the film so perfectly embodies the undoing of the Manichaean moral values at the root of Mexican melodrama as does the blind man Matías (Noé Murayama), a character that apparently was inspired by the blind man in Buñuel's *Los olvidados.* This coincidence of blind men as protagonists led one critic to call Alcoriza's film "Buñuel without Buñuel" (Ayala Blanco 111). It is telling that Matías is the first human figure presented in the film after the credits. Alcoriza has him begin the narrative as though to guide us through the mise-en-scène of the idealized village. Even in the early characterization of this seemingly stock character, we note a striking ambivalence in his portrayal, as if to suggest that the audience's interpretive act of reading this picturesque scene needs to be realigned with social reality. Matías is variously shown begging for his breakfast, praying to the Virgin, and bringing flowers to an old spinster, yet also mocking Chabela for talking to her pigs as though they were human beings and fighting with other blind people.

Matías functions as Alcoriza's double in the film. He understands the melodramatic meaning derived from the reverential gaze of the viewing subject and knows how to manipulate that gaze. He cleverly "stages" his abjectness for his on-screen audience because he cynically believes that Christian charity is merely a script designed according to the dictates of the Mexican melodramatic genre to maneuver his audience toward compassion (Aviña 133). From this self-conscious manipulation comes a difficult realization for audiences: Matías is neither good nor bad. Initially, he appears to be only a stock character, easily identified with a call for sympathy and Christian charity. Very quickly, we see him as a cynical, unlovable figure.

Matías is a key presence in two of the major comic sequences of *Tlayucan* that work to disrupt the iconography of the audience's melodramatic imagination. In the first, after the religious ceremony commemorating the Virgin, he is seated on the steps outside the church along with other blind beggars. A verbal dispute erupts, and Matías begins to strike another blind man. The scene quickly becomes a melee, with all of the blind characters assaulting each other on the church steps. In the second comic scene, Matías has encouraged the workers and the priest to purge the pigs so that their feces can be examined for the missing pearl. He even provides the appropriate elixir and force feeds it to one of the pigs. When the pigs finally begin to defecate in the church courtyard, the men grovel to search the excrement for the pearl. Both of these scenes function to juxtapose the aura of divine space against the real world, where living beings defecate. By inserting into the narrative characters who move outside the scripted identities of melodrama, Alcoriza shatters the illusion of wholeness of the melodramatic image.

In a very transparent way that, ironically, was misunderstood by critics at the time, *Tlayucan* seeks to explode via parody the sanitized and sacralized image of people that, as Martín-Barbero contends, had been secured by Mexican cinema's obsessive reliance on melodrama (182). The confusion about the film's cultural and artistic meanings may well have led Alcoriza to abandon the kind of soft parody that shapes *Tlayucan* when, a decade later, he made *Mecánica nacional,* a film that intensifies the parody of the melodramatic sensibility but does so without the ironic nuances of *Tlayucan.*

## The Mechanics of National Identity

In an effort to advance its standing as an independent leader in regional politics, the government of Luis Echeverría, which took power in 1970, was eager to cultivate the impression of a vibrant and socially relevant cinema. Film would be a vehicle with which to express a "reopening" of Mexican society after the repressive regime of Echeverría's predecessor, Gustavo Díaz Ordaz, and would serve to promote the sense of Mexico as an independent, nonaligned leader in Latin America politics (Maciel 201). It is in this context of official tolerance of a socially critical cinema that Alcoriza's next send-up of the melodramatic imagination emerges. In this respect, it is useful to view *Mecánica nacional* not only in the metacinematic context of its critique of Mexican melodrama but also in broader regional contexts in which it is juxtaposed against new Latin American cinema from Cuba and Brazil.

Just as *Tlayucan* recycles a comic trope of the tourists invading pristine Mexican space, in *Mecánica nacional* Alcoriza reworks another formula that he used in three scripts for Buñuel: *La ilusión viaja en tranvía* (Illusion Travels by Tram, 1953), the French-Mexican collaboration *La mort en ce jardin* (Death in the Garden, 1956), and his last collaboration with Buñuel, *El ángel exterminador* (The Exterminating Angel, 1962). All of these films developed plots that had been constructed as choral works that focused on a varied group of members of a single social class enclosed in a confined space and a limit situation. *Mecánica nacional* works on the same premise and involves another couple who ironically bear the same names as the protagonists of *Tlayucan*. Eufemio, his wife, Chabela, Eufemio's mother, Doña Lolita, two daughters, and their compadres, Güero and Dora, set out in a festive mood for the countryside in hopes of catching the conclusion of a "national" race from Acapulco to Mexico City. The women have prepared large quantities of food because the group plans to spend the night in the area adjacent to the finish line. The outbound trip to the campsite occasions a massive traffic jam as the family converges on the highway with other vehicles with a similar intention. This cross-section of contemporary Mexican society finally arrives at its destination and sets up camp, and the festivities soon begin.

The film has overt, even heavy-handed allegorical overtones that are apparent from the very choice of a title, which may refer either to Eufemio's automobile repair shop or to the mechanics of national identity. Indeed, it becomes clear as the narrative evolves that the characters are drawn as symbolic representations of the contemporary Mexican population (Mora 1989, 121; Reyes Nevares 63), which is composed of Mexicans motivated by movement and speed as embodied in race cars. Like the characters in *The Exterminating Angel*, they find themselves trapped in a symbolic space that leads them to reveal the atavistic marks of a social identity that they presumably had left behind. By invoking the rural mise-en-scène, Alcoriza is able to underscore the tension between tradition and modernity that has long been recognized as the back story of melodramatic cinema's popularity (Rubenstein 220–21). Part of the intertextual parody at the root of the film is precisely this reemergence of the myth of "Deep Mexico." Indeed, Alcoriza's decision to repeat the name of the hero and heroine of *Tlayucan* suggests an essential link between the conception of the two films as narratives of cultural traditions under attack by the incursion of modernity and the response in the appeal to patriarchal melodrama's moral structures.

Martín-Barbero observes that one of the keys to the seductive force of Mexico's cinematic melodrama is the power of the industry's star system: "The stars—María Félix, Dolores del Río, Pedro Armendáriz, Jorge Negrete, Ninón Sevilla—provide faces and bodies, voices and even tonality to the people's hunger to see themselves and to hear themselves" (182). The two lead characters of *Mecánica nacional* were played by well-known entertainment personalities who, as Carl Mora notes, were cast in roles that were the antithesis of their established personae (1989, 121–22). Manolo Fábregas was from a well-known stage family and had an established career as a serious actor who seldom played proletarian characters such as Eufemio. Lucha Villa

(Chabela), the most popular ranchera singer of the period, ironically references her own off-screen celebrity when, under the influence of alcohol, she begins to croon ranchera songs off-key. In this manner, as with his casting against type of Sara García as Doña Lolita, Alcoriza uses the cult of stardom to emphasize the fact that the melodramatic dramatis personae played by these actors are, in fact, mere constructions.

Once the chorus of characters arrives in the countryside, they form a convenient temporary community and settle down for a night of carousing before the finale of the race. At this point, the action pauses to focus on a mosaic of characters that juxtaposes Eufemio's generation with a band of youthful revelers who represent the emerging generation of modern Mexicans. The presence of these youths helps bring into focus by contrast the real protagonists of *Mecánica nacional:* the middle-aged generation of males for whom the shock of modernity is most threatening. Fast cars, youth culture, and the omnipresence of the symbols and cultural power of the gringos—music, drugs, and sexual freedom—bring Eufemio and Güero (Pancho Córdova) to recognize that they can only envy the social, economic, and sexual success of a younger and therefore more truly modern generation of Mexicans.

Traditional masculinity in crisis had been underscored at the start of the film. The sign at the front of Eufemio's auto body shop reads "Sólo damos servicio a clientes muy machos" (We only provide service to very macho customers). After spouting the conventional platitudes about the women who make up his family (his mother, wife, and daughters), Eufemio chides a deliveryman by calling him a *maricón,* a "queer." Eufemio and Güero, the two aggressive and outspoken machos who rule their women, are the first to assert their own moral superiority by virtue of their social position as heads of families, and by recourse to the patriarchal code that enables them to deauthenticate the men around them (by saying they are not real men) and treat the women around them as either saints (Eufemio's mother, Doña Lolita) or whores (Chabela and Dora [Gloria Marín]).

In his development of the character of Eufemio, Alcoriza launches his strongest attack on the collusion of melodrama with the defensive patriarchal mindset. Unlike his namesake in *Tlayucan,* a folkloric peasant character, this Eufemio is a presumably a modern Mexican. Initially, his social identity is vaguely tied to modernity as symbolized by his professional dedication to automobiles, yet his sexual and social aggressiveness seems strikingly misplaced in this community of modern Mexicans. Eufemio thus suggests the unfinished work of modernization. The early image of the famous Torre Latinoamericano, Mexico's symbol of Latin American modernization, for instance, becomes the occasion for him to boast that this is the tallest building in the world. By having his daughter try to correct his misplaced chauvinism, Alcoriza introduces to us the threat of the unseen American "other" as a force that drives the characters' embrace of the defensive patriarchal and melodramatic sensibility. Later, when two English-speaking Americans appear in the merry-making, it has the similar effect of reminding the characters and the audience alike of the broader transnational forces that melodrama seeks to keep out.

The true "national mechanics" of the film's title, however, is not the isolated symbol but rather the social dynamics of contemporary social interactions. That dynamics is revealed at what appears to be the high point of sexual frolic in the film. Eufemio and Güero attempt to seduce a neighbor's wife when, in the confusion of bodies strewn about in a dark wooded area, they discover Eufemio's daughter and Güero's son *in flagrante*. To intensify Eufemio's shock and outrage, he next sees Chabela engaged with another man in the back seat of a nearby car. This moment of emotional confrontation coincides with the announcement of his mother's final agony. The crisis of masculine identity played out as a melodrama of patriarchy in crisis is framed by the symbolic space of the countryside, now recognized as a hybrid space, the mythical place of tradition but also the site of modernity, where sexual and social roles break down.

The mechanics of the national allegory that Alcoriza has mounted leads inexorably to the final sequence, in which Eufemio's family brings Doña Lolita's

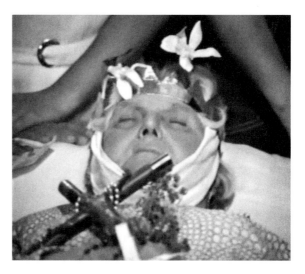

The death of the mother in *Mecánica nacional*

corpse back to the city in a grotesque manner. With no ambulance or hearse available, they have been forced to cram her upright body into the front passenger seat of the family car. Inevitably, the car is now stuck in the middle of a repeat of the traffic jam that had initiated the original outing. When the other drivers discover that Eufemio's vehicle is carrying his mother's body back to the city for burial, they offer their condolences. Looking upon the image of the now "saintly" Doña Lolita becomes a quasi-religious epiphany for the irate drivers. As they gaze upon the old woman's face, they become miraculously calmed. One member of the crowd calls for a minute of silence out of respect for the departed. Amid the macabre new traffic jam caused by the minute of silence, a policeman on motorcycle appears and offers to lead Eufemio's car through the traffic.

Everyone now returns to their respective vehicles, and the slow entourage moves forward with Eufemio's car now flanked by two motorcycle officers. Eufemio speaks the final words of the film, which are directed to the corpse seated beside him: "You never thought you would have a funeral like this one, right, Mamacita? Just like a government minister." The camera then cuts away from the interior of the car and, from a high-angle position, pans across the massive line of cars slowly proceeding back into the city as if in a funeral cortège. The familiar chords of "La negrita," the classic mariachi melody, are heard as the urban mise-en-scène is held in a freeze-frame. Playing with the clash of opposing cultural mindsets that makes up modern Mexico, the film's final image and sounds underscore as parody the resurgence of the traditionalist folkloric Mexico that subsumes the preposterous picture of unbridled modernization.

## Conclusion: The Return of the Repressed

As the foregoing discussion has emphasized, the national mechanics of both *Tlayucan* and *Mecánica nacional* lies in the critical coalescing of religious iconography with melodrama and the dispersion of that pairing within contemporary society. Despite their apparent differences of plot and setting, both films focus metacinematically on the power of iconic images to hold sway over the actions and beliefs of those who view them. Of particular importance in this regard is the way Alcoriza takes a culturally specific Mexican situation and, through the parody of *Marianismo,* the cult of the Virgin Mary as a stand-in for the more Mexicanized Virgin of Guadalupe, breaks it out of the confines of the national to pose a broader critique of melodrama in Hispanic contexts.

The textual dynamic of the two films is shaped around "intrusive" gazes, those of foreign tourists and of new technologies that have shifted the melodramatic ethos into new cultural spaces. In each film, the outsider becomes the agent of modernity whose presence disrupts the process of the characters' and the spectator's identification with the images of melodramatic self-projection. It is telling that, in both films, the technological gaze of the instant camera and the television lens disrupt the self-contained and self-authenticated illusion of coherent traditionalist society within which Mexican melodrama has long resided.

What is perhaps most original in Alcoriza's approach to the undoing of melodrama's aura is that it relies on a complex interrogation of representation rather than on a deflating of melodrama's presumed psychological inauthenticity. The implicit message that arises from the formulation of both films is the residual reverence of the community's response to an image linked iconographically to the atavistic social values of the pre-modern community. This recurrent motif, in effect, folds back on the conception of the Mexican community (and, by extension, the Latin American community) as the audience for melodrama. Faced, as Eufemio is, with the outward trimmings of rapid economic and cultural modernization, theirs is a fragile, surface disguise that still masks the trace of traditional cultural values that serve at moments of crisis to reaffirm traditional identities, if only as a fleeting moment of nostalgia in the face of the onslaught of modernity.

## Notes

Except where indicated, translations from the Spanish are my own.

1. In describing the generic characteristics of the maternal figures that reappear throughout Mexican melodramas of the first two decades of the sound era, Julia Tuñón frequently refers to features that are insistently identified with roles originated by Sara García. See Tuñón 190–97.

2. In 1946 Alcoriza developed his first produced script for the self-exiled Hollywood director Norman Foster. It was a melodramatic ranchera film titled *El ahijado de la muerte* (The Godchild of Death), starring Jorge Negrete. Over the course of the next seventeen years, he wrote scripts for more than fifty Mexican films, including collaborative scripts for twelve films that he made with Luis Buñuel.

3. Carlos Monsiváis deciphers some of that Manichaean rhetoric in a genre that he identifies as the "family melodrama," one of the dominant and recognizable expressions of that sensibility: "In the first half of the 20th century, morality was what the church, family, state and society accepted. Immorality was what lay outside their domain. The melodrama seemed to be an excellent vehicle for securing the hege-

mony of traditional values. However, the ghosts of disunity also circulated among the familiar melodramatic sets and sounds: honour, adultery, separation. Before the essential message of all cinema was clearly understood (that is to say, the irrefutable power of modern life), the film industry exalted the repression of instincts in favour of moral servitude" ("Mythologies," 1995: 119).

4. Gruzinski describes the phenomenon of the audience confronting their self-image during the first decades of sound cinema in Mexico: "The image of Mexican cinema, during its Golden Age in particular, prepared the farmer and town masses for the trauma of industrialization of the 40s; they carried an *imaginaire* that, in league with the radio, either undermined or actualized traditions by initiating the crowds to the modern world through its mythic figures, such as Pedro Armendáriz, Dolores del Río, María Félix and many others. From the late 30s on, the flood of cinematographic images wove a new consensus centered on the new values of city, technology, illusions of consumerism, and even at times the assimilation of the most denigrating stereotypes" (222).

5. This concept alludes to the notion not simply of pre-modern traditional culture, but, as Claudio Lomnitz remarks in terms of the broader debate about the modernization process of Mexican society, to "formulating Mexican nationalism in a way that preserves the sense that the nation has its own internal system of value production. As a result, the opposition between the state and nation, between a 'deep Mexico' and a commercial, international, and superficially modernizing elite, emerges as a common image of the national situation" (122). This is precisely the conflict that the plot of Alcoriza's film poses, albeit with a decided bias in favor of modernization.

6. In historical terms, the circulation of the Fernández-Figueroa films from the mid-1940s onward constituted a privileged aesthetic rendition of Mexico for the outside world. With the recognition of *María Candelaria* at the 1946 Cannes Film Festival and the more general appreciation of Figueroa's cinematography (dating from his recognition at the 1937 Venice Film Festival), the Fernández-Figueroa paradigm for the cultural promotion of Mexico abroad had achieved the status as the quasi-official version of cinematic Mexico. If *María Candelaria* holds a special preeminence owing to its artistic recognition, *La perla,* Fernández's version of the John Steinbeck novella, which was scripted, in fact, by the novelist, provides an even closer link to the all-important U.S. cultural market. Just as Alcoriza's collaboration as co-screenwriter of Buñuel's *Los olvidados* challenged that status in 1950, a decade later, in *Tlayucan,* he takes up the seemingly timeless rhetoric of the persistent Fernández-Figueroa model.

## Works Cited

Alcoriza, Luis. "Splendor of the Image." *Artes de México: Revisión del cine mexicano* no. 10 (1990): 32, 93.

Aviña, Rafael. *Una mirada insólita: Temas y géneros del cine mexicano.* Mexico City: Conaculta/Cineteca Nacional, 2004.

Ayala Blanco, Jorge. *La aventura del cine mexicano.* 2d ed. Mexico City: Editorial Posada, 1979.

Burton-Carvajal, Julianne. "Mexican Melodramas of Patriarchy: Specificity of a Transcultural Form." In *Framing Latin American Cinema: Contemporary Critical Perspectives.* Ed. Ann Marie Stock. Hispanic Issues, vol. 15. Minneapolis: University of Minnesota Press, 1997. 186–234.

Elsaesser, Thomas. "Tales of Sound and Fury: Observations on the Family Melodrama." In *Film Genre Reader.* Ed. Barry Keith Grant. Austin: University of Texas Press, 1997. 350–80.

Fuentes, Carlos. *Homenaje a Juan Rulfo.* Mexico City: Instituto Nacional de Bellas Artes, 1980.

García Canclini, Néstor. *Consumidores y ciudadanos: Conflictos multiculturales de la globalización.* Mexico City: Editorial Grijalbo, 1995.

González Casanova, Manuel. *Luis Alcoriza: Soy un solitario que escribe.* Badajoz, Spain: Disputación de Badajoz, Festival Ibérico de Cine, 2006.

Gruzinski, Serge. *Images at War: Mexico from Columbus to Blade Runner (1492–2019).* Durham: Duke University Press, 2001.

Hernández Rodríguez, Rafael. "Melodrama and Social Comedy in the Golden Age." In *Mexico's Cinema: A Century of Film and Filmmakers.* Ed. Joanne Hershfield and David R. Maciel. Wilmington, Del.: SR Books, 1999. 101–21.

Hutcheon, Linda. *Theory of Parody: The Teaching of Twentieth-Century Art Forms.* New York: Methuen, 1985.

Kinder, Marsha. *Blood Cinema: The Reconstruction of National Identity in Spain.* Berkeley: University of California Press, 1993.

Lomnitz, Claudio. *Deep Mexico, Silent Mexico: An Anthropology of Nationalism.* Minneapolis: University of Minnesota Press, 2001.

López, Ana M. "Celluloid Tears: Melodrama in the 'Old' Mexican Cinema." *Iris* 13 (Summer 1991): 29–51.

———. "A Cinema for the Continent." In *The Mexican Cinema Project.* Ed. Chon A. Noriega and Steven Ricci. Los Angeles: UCLA Film and Television Archive, 1994. 7–12.

Maciel, David R. "Cinema and the State in Contemporary Mexico: 1970–1999." In *Mexico's Cinema: A Century of Film and Filmmakers.* Ed. Joanne Hershfield and David R. Maciel. Wilmington, Del.: SR Books, 1999. 197–232.

Martín-Barbero, Jesús. *De los medios a las mediaciones: Comunicación, cultura y hegemonía.* Mexico City: Ediciones G. Gili, 1987.

Monsiváis, Carlos. *Aires de familia: Cultura y sociedad en América Latina.* Barcelona: Editorial Anagrama, 2000.

———. "All the People Came and Did Not Fit Onto the Screen: Notes on the Cinematic Audience in Mexico." In Paranaguá 1995: 145–51.

———. "El cine y la religión del rostro." In *Un siglo de cine.* Ed. Edgar Soberón Torcha. Mexico City: Cinememoria, 1995. 23–35.

———. "Mythologies." In Paranaguá 1995: 117–27.

Mora, Carl J. "Feminine Images in Mexican Cinema: The Family Melodrama; Sara García, 'The Mother of Mexico,' and the Prostitute." *Studies in Latin American Popular Culture* 4 (1985): 228–35.

———. *Mexican Cinema: Reflections of a Society, 1896–1988.* Rev. ed. Berkeley: University of California Press, 1989.

Paranaguá, Paulo Antonio. "América Latina busca su imagen." *Historia general del cine.* Madrid: Cátedra Signo e imagen, 1996. 10:205–393.

———. *Mexican Cinema.* Trans. Ana M. López. London: British Film Institute, 1995.

Pérez Turrent, Tomás. *Luis Alcoriza.* Huelva: Semana de Cine Iberomamericano, 1977.

Podalsky, Laura. "Disjointed Frames: Melodrama, Nationalism, and Representation in 1940s Mexico." *Studies in Latin American Popular Culture* 12 (1993): 57–73.

Radcliffe, Sarah, and Sallie Westwood. *Remaking the Nation: Place, Identity and Politics in Latin America.* London: Routledge, 1996.

Ramírez-Berg, Charles. "The Cinematic Invention of Mexico: The Poetics and Politics of the Fernández-Figueroa Style." In *The Mexican Cinema Project.* Ed. Chon A. Noreiga and Steven Ricci. Los Angeles: UCLA Film and Television Archive, 1994. 13–24.

Reyes Nevares, Beatriz. *The Mexican Cinema: Interviews with Thirteen Directors.* Albuquerque: University of New Mexico Press, 1976.

Rubenstein, Anne. "Bodies, Cities, Cinema: Pedro Infante's Death as Political Spectacle." In *Fragments of a Golden Age: The Politics of Culture in Mexico Since 1940.* Ed. Gilbert Joseph, Anne Rubenstein, and Eric Zolov. Durham: Duke University Press, 2001. 199–233.

Saragoza, Alex. "The Selling of Mexico: Tourism and the State, 1929–1952." In *Fragments of a Golden Age: The Politics of Culture in Mexico Since 1940.* Ed. Gilbert Joseph, Anne Rubenstein, and Eric Zolov. Durham: Duke University Press, 2001. 91–115.

Tuñón, Julia. *Mujeres de luz y sombra en el cine mexicano: La construcción de una imagen (1939–1952).* Mexico City: El Colegio de México/Instituto Mexicano de Cinematografía, 1998.

# 8

# Weeping Reality

## Melodramatic Imagination in Contemporary Brazilian Documentary

**MARIANA BALTAR**

A middle-aged man faces the camera in his living room. An off-screen voice asks him about family matters and everyday life until he gradually begins to recount episodes from the labor struggle of the late 1970s, during Brazil's military dictatorship. Led by union president Luis Inácio Lula da Silva, who had been a metalworker, this struggle ultimately resulted in the creation of the Partido dos Trabalhadores (Workers' Party) and, much later, the election of "Lula" as the president of Brazil in 2002. João Chapéu, the man being interviewed on-camera, participated in the workers' strike. When the dictatorship squashed the movement, he, like many others, lost his factory job, and during the interview he tearfully recalls the aftermath of his dismissal: "My son was sad, you know, because he was . . . he was proud to say to me when he saw a Mercedes truck: 'Dad, you made some part of that truck.' So I felt that . . . he was proud of me, because he used to say: 'Look, dad, you made some part of every Mercedes truck we see.' And I'd say: 'You're right, son.'"

This scene is from the 1994 documentary *Peões* (Peons) by Eduardo Coutinho, which is about the late 1970s labor movement in the ABC, or industrial areas, of the state of São Paulo. *Peões* consists of interviews with workers who were under Lula's union leadership or, as the director puts it, the "anonymous" agents of that struggle. Coutinho, one of Brazil's most prominent filmmakers, is known for the strength of his interactions with his subjects. The sense of intimacy in his films, which gives his documentaries legitimacy, is achieved by means of a number of unusual acts on the part of the director. These practices include making himself and the camera visible in the frame and asking intimate questions in order to discuss political and other public issues. In this essay I argue that there is a melodramatic quality in *Peões* and in other contemporary Brazilian documentaries, but not one that simply adheres to the conventions of the genre. What we see in Coutinho's documentaries in particular is an appropriation of the melodramatic imagination rather than melodramatic narrative per se.[1]

Brazilian documentaries take up the melodramatic in nonconventional ways in order to call attention to urgent contemporary issues, and they do so by focusing their narratives about public life on the private stories of individuals and inviting spectators to affectively engage with these stories. It is this affective engagement that leads the way toward the addressing of public issues. The documentary's dialogue with the melodramatic imagination becomes a way of dealing with the tensions of a world characterized by an ever-increasing modernity, a modernity that gives centrality to the private sphere in social and political relations and that produces a visual regimen involving the growing spectacularization of private life.

Several documentaries seem to establish this critical dialogue. In addition to *Peões* and other films by Coutinho such as *Edifício Master* (Master Builder, 2002), one might include José Padilha's *Ônibus 174* (Bus 174, 2002), Sandra Kogut's *Um passaporte húngaro* (2003), Roberto Berliner's *A pessoa é para o que nasce* (Born to Be Blind, 2004), Marcos Prado's *Estamira* (2004) and Cristina Grumbach's *Morro da Conceição* (Conceição Hill, 2005). Although not entirely based on the mode of excess that characterizes melodrama, these films appropriate its elements in order to strengthen the viewer's affective engagement and identification with their subjects.

A number of contemporary Brazilian documentaries focus on individual interviews in order to explore public life through the telling of private stories. This public-private correlation is not always foregrounded, but it is noticeable in the intimate portrayal of those interviewed. The melodramatic emotional matrix serves to reinforce the feeling of the public within the private, thus raising questions related to a certain hypertrophy of the private in contemporary times. It is important to stress, however, that the dialogue with melodrama is only partial. Each of these films is in tension with the melodramatic, if only through a process of intertextual reappropriation. The moral patterns traditionally associated with the universe of melodrama are slightly altered, leading to a certain de-dramatization and restraint.

This relation between some contemporary Brazilian documentaries and melodrama is roughly similar to what we find in the work of such directors as Rainer Werner Fassbinder in the 1970s and Pedro Almodóvar in the 1980s. They saw in masters of the melodrama such as Douglas Sirk and Emilio Fernández an ironic and critical potential. Their political reevaluation of the melodrama as a narrative genre was accompanied by theoretical discussions, the most prominent of which are those by Thomas Elsaesser (1987) and Peter Brooks (1995), who discuss the public nature of the private sphere. They emphasize the pedagogical value of feelings, giving new importance to the centrality of the domestic, of everyday life, of the feminine, and of emotional expression. These theorists contend that the melodramatic imaginary, which serves as the basis for melodrama as a narrative genre, has a privileged place in the context of modernity, where intimacy and morality seem increasingly intertwined as regulators of social life. Ultimately, their argument suggests, melodrama serves a privileged form for a moralizing pedagogy, which is necessary for new social and public relations in a secular and market-oriented society. The argument that connects melodramatic narratives to sociohistorical scenarios can also be seen in the works of Ben Singer and Ismail Xavier, though they do not use the term "melodramatic imagination." All these writers recognize the value of melodrama in the regulation of sociability under an increasingly secularized modernity. Nevertheless, Brooks, in particular, with his notion of melodramatic imagination, enables us to extend the universe of the melodramatic to different kinds of narratives or modes, including the documentary.

Brooks's argument is organized around the notion that the imagination forms the genre. In other words, between the late eighteenth century and the beginning of the nineteenth century, the institutionalization of a genre defined as melodrama responded to the necessities of modern subjectivity, which ultimately is structured by the melodramatic imagination. Therefore, narratives outside the domain of melodramatic fiction can be determined by a melodramatic impulse. Where Brazilian documentary is concerned, the melodramatic imagination enables the private sphere to be brought into the public, and with it a moralizing pedagogy—but this is accomplished in a way that also fosters social engagement. These films often capture exactly what is most interesting about melodrama, which is, according to Brooks, "the emphatic articulation of simple truths and relationships, the clarification of the cosmic moral sense of everyday gestures. We are near the beginnings of a modern aesthetic in which Balzac and James will fully participate: the effort to make the 'real' and the 'ordinary' and the 'private life' interesting through heightened dramatic utterance and gesture that lay bare the true stakes" (13–14).

To engage emotionally with the narrative is to put oneself in a state of "suspension" and to be connected to it in a sentimental and sensory way. Most of the material in the narrative must have an obvious quality if the spectator or reader is to be guided through the action and the implicit pedagogy. According to this logic of obviousness, characters become personifications of social conditions and are subject to a public gaze that is morally judgmental. The gaze leaves the characters exposed, but it also provokes spectators into identification with the characters on the basis of empathy and pathos. This recourse to melodramatic imagination is rarely explicit or perceived at first glance. When analyzed, however, it brings to light certain issues concerning tensions between the private and the public spheres, the representations of memory and intimacy (as themes and as strategies), and the authority of the subject when it embodies the public and the social. In both functional and documentary forms of melodrama, the putative dichotomy between the private and the public is undercut—especially in moments when individuals start to talk about themselves and summon their stories and most intimate memories, which constitute the organizing elements of the narrative.

What I am describing as the affective engagement with figures in a documentary has a good deal in common with Paula Rabinowitz's concept of a "sentimental contract." In an article aimed at analyzing American documentaries about labor issues such as Barbara Kopple's *American Dream* (1980) and *Harlan County USA* (1976) and Michael Moore's *Roger and Me* (1989), Rabinowitz calls attention to the "rhetoric of sentimentality" that runs through stories about labor struggles. This rhetoric, which is considerably in debt to melodrama, creates the emotion necessary to the act of political mobilization. It depends on references to the private experiences of subjects, on the articulation of a moral logic in speeches that bring to light shared feelings, and on a process of identification with the subject and engagement with the issue. It seems to me that what Rabinowitz calls a rhetoric of sentimentality is closely related to the concept of the melodramatic imagination. Both concepts refer to an expressive economy that regulates the public expression of private feelings, and both help form group identity, whether of class or nationality. Affective engagement and the sentimental contract are powerful strategies for achieving political ends, and they are nearly always dependent on the performances of people who reveal emotions in public (a strong tendency of contemporary Brazilian documentary).

A documentary such as *Peões,* and, to a certain extent, a considerable part of Eduardo Coutinho's work establishes a very special kind of dialogue with the melodramatic imagination based on an intimacy that is created between the director and his subjects. Their relationship evokes a feeling of both direct simplicity and complicity between the individuals and Coutinho. I call this effect the *intimacy pact,* and especially in *Peões* it produces emotion and legitimization of the documentary. In this film the intimacy pact also serves to create an idea of community based on the memories of its subjects. In order to understand how this works, it is necessary to analyze the family-based, sentimental approach to experiences of the labor struggle. On one hand, there is a sense of shared morality and collective memory in the experiences of each of the participants in the Brazilian strike in the late 1970s; on the other, there is personification of this morality—and of its values—in individual testimony. The speeches of the subjects interviewed in the film reveal a hope for the election of their former leader, who, at the time the documentary was being produced, was making a strong run for the presidency as the candidate of the Workers' Party. *Peões* also makes a very special and sentimental use of images taken from earlier documentaries about the strike.[2] These images are used to trigger memory in the subjects and enforce the sentimental aspect of their experiences. They also serve as exacerbated symbols of community because they affirm a homology between the subjects' individual experiences and the collective memory manifest in the archival images.

In *Peões,* the interviewees watch archival footage on a television set that faces the camera. The archival images are used not as unmediated evidence but as accessories to the encounter between director and subject. What we see is a person who is watching historical footage and recognizing himself and others. Thus, the archival images have not only the value of truth but also the value of sentiment. In the end, an individual recognizes himself as an agent of history. In other words, the collective memory is embodied by the interviewee, who, on viewing the images, is constantly asked by the director about his emotions and feelings during that moment in history. Public and private become, in this moment, *obviously and symbolically* part of the same sphere. In the encounter with history, the subject recognizes himself as part of the public sphere based on documentaries of the period. There are two fundamental consequences of this situation: public images trigger private, intimate feeling and create an idea of sharing, and they forge an intimate relation between the subjects and the director. Throughout, the dialectic between private and public is marked by the director's questions about feelings and emotions.

Coutinho's particular use of archival images complements the development of a sentimental contract. The melodramatic treatment of archival images is particularly evident at the beginning of the documentary, during an encounter between the director and an unnamed interviewee, whose detailed information about former co-workers seems to put the development of the documentary on hold. The sequence cuts back and forth between the face of the interviewee and the faces in photographs that he handles and then uses to jot down names and telephone numbers, saying, "This guy here, you have to interview this guy. He's dying, literally. His name is Marimbondo. . . . Oh, you can also talk to Contreiras, I think that this is him, Sônia has his telephone number." This scene, which takes place in the first fifteen minutes of the film, introduces a series of interviews in which other participants—always interviewed in the living rooms or kitchens of their homes—recall the years of the labor movement. The domestic setting of the various interviews is symbolic of the emotive speech of the subjects. Eduardo Coutinho is regularly visible, and this tends to create an identification between spectators and the director, whose questions provoke various emotional memories. One might say that Coutinho embodies the "public gaze" of the melodramatic imagination. The individual "performances" are directed outward toward him as well as to the spectator, who, in turn, feels a greater proximity to and intimacy with the interviewees.

The testimonials make clear that there is a sense of community among those interviewed, which results in what might be called "affective sharing." The main concern of *Peões* is to make us perceive the emotional bond that forms this community. True to this aim, the questions that Coutinho asks seek to encompass the moral code of the laborers as represented by their references to struggle, pride, and honor. The use of archival images also promotes the idea of an affective community and the sharing of a common memory. By means of the images, individuals recognize themselves as participants in the collective archival memory. This recognizing of oneself and one's colleagues reaffirms the feeling of community that gradually builds during the course of the film.

We can see this same emphasis on the collective in a scene where a hand is shown going through a stack of photographs while Coutinho, off-screen, asks, "What about this one?" The camera focuses on the photograph and a second voice says, "This guy looks like me." Cut to the man who has just spoken. Coutinho remarks, "You were handsome, huh?" The man, whose name is Avestil, laughs, "Oh, yeah, I was. But I still am, right? Take a gander!" Off-screen, Coutinho asks, "You tell your kids, hoping that they feel proud, the memory that lingers, don't you?" The camera focuses on another picture in which Avestil appears alongside co-workers. Avestil replies, "Every time I tell the story of the strikes, which is something that I even like to talk about, I hope that they feel proud and say: 'Wow, my father was a metalworker.' And this is not so far in the past. In the future, this story will be much more distant. . . . Yeah, this is history, right?"

Avestil's testimonial introduces a long sequence of interviews that deal with the theme of family and honor. In a way, his performance anticipates the major concerns of the documentary and evokes the feelings produced by political struggle. Invariably, the testimonials refer to a sense of pride, to the thrill of being a metalworker, and to the dreams fulfilled through work and struggle. These topics are raised by Coutinho's questions, which are voiced mostly off-screen: "You told me that you dreamed of being a metalworker; would you explain that to me?" asks Coutinho in the first interview of the film, which is conducted with a woman called Dona Socorro. Other questions are similar in tone; they deal with the issue of work and the labor struggles as social and personal fulfillment and as growth and victory, though permeated by grief. Throughout, *Peões* emphasizes the domestic sphere and the sentimental. The testimonials tend to be filmed in moderate close-ups, but occasionally a medium shot shows the surrounding domestic space. A good example involves the testimonial by the man called Seu Antônio. The scene begins with a shot of a table filled with books and the figure of an old man sitting in the center of the frame. Coutinho says off-screen, "Seu Antônio, we are in the pantry, but there are books everywhere." The film cuts to a closer shot of Seu Antônio, and Coutinho starts the conversation by posing questions about the present: Does Antônio live alone? Who cooks for him? and so on. The theme of marriage is privileged: "Was she also a metalworker?" Coutinho asks. Antônio answers that no, his wife worked at a macaroni factory. Coutinho then asks, "Why did you become involved in the strikes?" "Oh, because I liked it," answers Antônio. "And your wife wasn't upset with it?" asks Coutinho. From this point on, the conflict created in the marriage by the strike becomes central to the interview, until Antônio's daughter Maria Angélica is invited to participate in the conversation. Speaking off-screen, she recalls the family's daily routine. She refers to music played in the house and to her father's habit of singing to her mother as signs of their happiness.

Seu Antônio in *Peões*

At this moment, father and daughter, filmed in a medium shot, sing a song by Roberto Carlos. The daughter now takes over the conversation: "The songs, all this was part of our everyday life, but the central issue of his life was always discussing rights and politics. When I was a kid, the fact that he was so involved in politics, and that my mother was so afraid of it. . . . I didn't understand it very well. So I think that there was a time when I was kind of repulsed by it. Jeez, my father was more interested in politics than in my mother; more interested in politics than in us." Her words evoke the past but also call the present into question by contrasting Antônio's recollection of his militancy with the on-screen image of his apathetic and sad figure. By contrasting his daughter's memory of the past with the present, we can also see the social and affective losses and gains. Antônio's family gathers around the table in the pantry to remember for the camera his political and personal lives. The singing of Roberto Carlos's song by Antônio and his daughter is thus a remembrance of things past, and it invites an emotional response.

Like several of Coutinho's earlier films, *Peões* is a low-budget production in which camera movements are kept to a minimum and a musical score is absent. The simplicity of his films is perhaps best described by the critic Consuelo Lins, who speaks of Coutinho's "Franciscan" approach to filmmaking. But the melodramatic imagination is neither antithetical to nor impossible in this kind of film. In the case of *Peões*, the melodramatic is consciously applied and helps shape the way the subjects present themselves to the director in their performance. A similar dialectical relation between melodrama and social history seems to me to be present in other Brazilian documentaries.

Father and daughter in *Peões*

They are ultimately related to the increasingly influential idea that political and public issues should be approached via the individual and the personal sphere. I believe that Brazilian documentaries such as *Peões* are "barbaric" in the positive and propositional sense that Walter Benjamin gives to the term. They use the ruins of a world controlled by public display of the private to create an intersubjective experience that provides not only a sense of the personal and the sentimental but also, and perhaps more important, a better understanding of the political and the public.

## Notes

1. I thank Professor João Luiz Vieira for his comments on this essay, which was supported by a Capes fellowship.
2. The documentaries are *Linha de montagem* (Assembly Line) by Renato Tapajós, *ABC da greve* (ABC of a Strike) by Leon Hirszman, and *Greve* (Strike) by João Batista de Andrade. *Peões* also uses photographs from the news.

## Works Cited

Benjamin, Walter. *Obras escolhidas: Magia e técnica, arte e política.* Vol. 1. 7th ed. São Paulo: Brasiliense, 1994.

———. *Selected Writings.* Vol. 2, pt. 1, 1927–30. Cambridge: Belknap Press of Harvard University Press, 1999.

Brooks, Peter. *The Melodramatic Imagination: Balzac, Henry James, Melodrama, and the Mode of Excess.* New Haven: Yale University Press, 1995.

Elsaesser, Thomas. "Tales of Sound and Fury: Observations on the Family Melodrama." In *Home Is Where the Heart Is: Studies in Melodrama and the Woman's Film.* Ed. Christine Gledhill. London: British Film Institute, 1987. 43–69.

Gledhill, Christine, ed. *Home Is Where the Heart Is: Studies in Melodrama and the Woman's Film.* London: British Film Institute, 1987.

Lins, Consuelo. *O documentário de Eduardo Coutinho: Televisão, cinema e vídeo.* Rio de Janeiro: Jorge Zahar, 2004.

Rabinowitz, Paula. "Sentimental Contracts: Dreams and Documents of American Labor." In *Feminism and Documentary.* Ed. Diane Waldman and Janet Walker. Minneapolis: University of Minnesota Press, 1999. 43–63.

Singer, Ben. *Melodrama and Modernity: Early Sensational Cinema and Its Contexts.* New York: Columbia University Press, 2001.

Xavier, Ismail. *O olhar e a cena: Melodrama, Hollywood, cinema novo, Nelson Rodrigues.* São Paulo: Cosac and Naify, 2003.

# 9

## Televisual Melodrama in an Era of Transnational Migration

### Exporting the Folkloric Nation, Harvesting the Melancholic-Sublime

CATHERINE L. BENAMOU

Over the course of the past few decades, film scholars North and South have found in the themes, audiovisual styles, popular archetypes, casting, and settings of screen melodrama fertile terrain for an investigation of the social dynamics and aesthetics of "national" cinemas in Latin America. Yet during the same period, telenovelas have carried most of the cultural burden of "narrating the nation" (López 261–66). This burden derives not only from the genre's proven ability to attract advertising revenue at home and abroad but also from its consistently high ratings—its ability to reach and attract millions of viewers who, because of their socioeconomic standing or their geographic location, have had limited access to urban movie theaters and the Internet. The relatively high production values of telenovelas (especially those produced for export) compared to other forms of television programming have also transformed them into a showcase for national media industries, concepts of social identity, and cultural expression, thereby boosting the producing nations' cultural capital abroad. A crucial companion to economic and technical capital, this nonmaterial capital, which translates into "respectability" in the marketplace, provides national media industries with the symbolic clout needed to penetrate global media markets and channels of distribution, garner major commercial sponsors and investors, and recruit international talent and technical expertise.

When placed in a broad historical and industrial context, however, it is difficult to speak of either popular film melodrama or telenovelas as pursuing distinctly "national" paths of development. From the 1930s onward, there was an intense circulation and adaptation throughout the region of melodramatic narratives in cinematic and other mediated forms such as *fotonovelas* and radionovelas, and since the 1970s, commercial television, in particular programming destined for export, has been fueled by a regional cross-fertilization of generic formats, technical crews, writers, and production processes (Espada; Hamburger 84; Mazziotti 43–53). Moreover, it is the international rather than the national geographic reach and economic power of Latin American television industries, emblematized in the highly mobile and stylistically malleable telenovela, that has attracted the attention of the critical and the trade press to these industries, with an eye on the three largest exporters of the genre—Brazil, Mexico, and Venezuela. Thus it is as easy to speak of melodrama as a unifying factor in Latin American—and more broadly, Ibero-American—cultural and political relations as it is possible to speak of melodrama (whether cinematic or televisual) as a discursive keystone in modern nation building and a means to the projection of the nation abroad.

Today, as Latin American television is becoming increasingly globalized in its economic reach and applications of new technology, telenovelas are the preferred site where national popular and commodified (or appropriated) vernacular forms are "negotiated" with global mass cultural values and aesthetic trends.[1] National media capital has become increasingly mobile, investing in U.S.-based enterprises (even as the latter have capitalized handsomely on neoliberal economic policies); the Latin American region has also become increasingly intertwined with the European Union, thanks to Spain and Portugal. In response to these investment and marketing trends, telenovelas are able to catapult their loyal viewers, near and far, into the charmed space of global travel and exchange while bringing them home to their psychocultural roots.

As compared to "ratings-busters" such as the Colombian RCN's *Yo soy Betty, la fea* (1999–2001, the program that led to both the 2006 Mexican Televisa remake *La fea más fea* and the ABC prime-time series *Ugly Betty*), relatively little has been said about the contribution to the televisual melodrama and the enterprises that produce them for those who travel and dream of becoming more than a cog in this global exchange: migrant and emigrant workers and artists. This essay is an effort to compensate for this industrial bias by exploring the fate of the new transnsational televisual melodrama—its industrial underpinnings, narrative discourse, audiovisual aesthetics, and ideological potency—at the intersection of two contemporaneous processes:

the migration of Latin American television and of its national viewers north-ward in search of new markets, lifestyles, and sources of employment.

Embedded in this task are several questions that are growing in impor-tance: (1) What is the degree to which migration and emigration are actually facilitating the global success of the telenovela and the enterprises that it sustains? (2) What is the degree to which this success is causing a reduction in the "national identity" and the national social relevance of the telenovela? That is, in their zeal for the development of exportable products, are televi-sion producers elaborating a postnational form? (3) What is the degree to which there are "built-in" characteristics that allow telenovelas to appeal simultaneously to global, transnational, and national audiences—their cul-tural translatability? (4) Even if the telenovela retains its distinctive cultural (because still "national") resilience, what is its transnational niche, and is it capable of meeting the competing demands of that niche? Or are emerging forms of melodrama filling the gaps left by what might be called the global overextension of the telenovela?

In order to begin answering these questions, it is necessary to identify the forces acting on the transnational melodrama at three distinct sites of elaboration and cultural articulation: the mode of its production within na-tional television industries, the extent of transnational zones of transmis-sion, involving textual changes and marketing strategies tailored to suit the importing countries, and its diasporic Latino/a sites of reception. In the last regard, I will rely on the opinions of viewers of Spanish-language television that I surveyed in Los Angeles and Detroit. These opinions have been culled from audience surveys conducted as part of a multimethod, longitudinal research project concerning the transnational transmission of Spanish- and Portuguese-language television and its meanings for diasporic viewers in the United States and in Spain.

## Keeping the Passion Alive: Telenovelas and the Television Business in an Expanded Transnational Environment

In her well-informed comparative study of the telenovela industries in Ar-gentina, Brazil, Mexico, and Venezuela, Nora Mazziotti identifies three key facets of cultural and economic articulation: the national, the continental, and the transnational (24; see also Martín-Barbero 282–83). Although the telenovela has operated simultaneously in all three arenas for decades, these articulations delineate distinct temporal phases of discursive orientation and industrial focus. Roughly speaking, the genre can be seen as evolving from an early experimental and nation-focused phase to an industrial maturation in which nationally oriented programming is exported and imported throughout Latin America and, finally, into bouts of strategic and stylistic shapeshifting in the effort to keep up with the geopolitical extension and increased cultural and economic interconnectivity created by global trade and investment partnerships.

Historically, the steady growth of telenovela exports—at times bringing in revenue as great as that garnered by other national industries (Mazziotti 53)—has been made possible in the diegetic realm by effective product differentiation (including "national" markers in terms of stylistics, thematics, settings, and shooting techniques) while retaining a high degree of transparency in its narrative encoding, permitting its decodification by a wide cultural range of spectators from Krakow to Tierra del Fuego and from Tokyo to Dakar. This narrative transparency has been facilitated by continual recourse to "universal" themes and plot patterns, in the Proppian sense,[2] along with the repetition of individual scenes through flashbacks and semiotic redundancy so that a single sentiment or idea tends to be conveyed on various "tracks" of enunciation, and characters and settings are identified as much by themes on the musical track as by dialogue and costuming. Slender plotlines have made room for heavy emotion, as well as for the calibration—and addition during shooting—of turning points in order to extract the maximum effect from the predetermined structural elements.

The telenovela's global success has also depended heavily on the relative stability of commercial television industries—most are now media conglomerates, thanks to deregulation—even in the absence of political and economic stability or steady growth in other national sectors. Organizational and economic stability are essential for branding to succeed—the logos of Venevisión, Televisa, and Rede Globo de Televisão, which "seal" each telenovela broadcast, are probably better known around the world today than the colors of the flags of Venezuela, Mexico, and Brazil. As Fox and Waisbord have argued, organizational stability in these countries derives from the relative autonomy of near-monopolistic television enterprises, even when the state undergoes substantive changes in leadership (Fox and Waisbord 3–5). The climate of industrial stability in Brazil, Mexico, and Venezuela has permitted innovations in writing and shooting techniques, a degree of predictability in production methods, acceleration of production to meet external demand, diversification of consumption formats, sustenance of "quality," and familiarity within a multi-episode form that extends on average from 120 to more than 200 episodes (Mazziotti 35, 39). In this way, telenovelas have permitted the acquisition of symbolic capital for medium- to major-producing nations even in the absence of sustained economic growth or social cohesiveness at home. Without exaggeration, it can be said that the telenovela has become an essential ingredient (together with sports, migration, sociopolitical movements, and natural and cultivated resources) in the glue that keeps several Latin American nation-states functioning as such while participating in a rapidly changing world order.

Paradoxically, a new type of global market has been created, one that urges a return to national and continental frames of historical reference and semantic inscription at precisely the moment when telenovelas are being adjusted to a wider geocultural range of consumers: Europe, East Asia, Eastern Europe, China, Mongolia, and several African nations have become regular clients. This situation is complicated by the fact that Latina and Latino diasporic viewers are not confined to a specific market; they are found in the northern part of the Western Hemisphere and in the interstices of European and Asian migratory destinations. Emigration has been paralleled by the tendencies of the major television industries to invest in the industries or set up modes of transmission in neighboring nations, thereby contributing further to the "Latinization" of media hegemony in the region, as well as the cultural hegemony of certain nations over others, much as occurred with national film industries at the height of their development (Fox and Waisbord 12–13).

Within this scenario—the dependency of televisual melodrama on the conversion of televisual industries into transnational enterprises—are two built-in challenges that have spurred television exporters to push the genre into a materially and discursively hybrid, potentially self-contradictory stage of development. The first challenge to national television networks has been a material one: the turn of the new millennium has witnessed an increasing dependence on the part of major media enterprises—especially the "hegemonic" ones based in Brazil, Mexico, and Venezuela—on foreign markets in order to retain their competitive edge in a global arena where U.S. media conglomerates have expanded their reach. In this they are aided by new transmission technologies and a lowering of investment barriers in the wake of neoliberal policies. For example, the digital compression technology used in transnational satellite transmission allows for a single channel to be transmitted in more than one language, amplifying the global transmission potential of English-language and other international broadcasters. It also opens an opportunity for more channels to enter the global airspace than ever before (Sinclair 131). Competition is increasing for Latin American producers and exporters of telenovelas and their broadcast partners in the United States (namely, Univisión and Telemundo), precisely because U.S. networks and cable enterprises (such as Showtime, ESPN, MTV, HBO, and Twentieth Television) are trying to break into a transnational space already conquered by Latino American networks thanks to the telenovela (see Speight). The U.S. "Hispanic" market is only one of the arenas being vied for by globally oriented broadcast enterprises, with the domestication—and hence Anglification—of the telenovela (as distinct from the U.S. soap opera) as one of the weapons of choice. This highly competitive environment has been intensified by the deregulation of the European television market, as well as the new interest of Anglo-American enterprises in adapting and creating programs that have a telenovela feel and in using television to experiment with narrative form and digital aesthetics, including high-definition formats. The continual raising of the technological and stylistic bar for televisual programming and related services (such as Internet download sites) has meant an increase in production costs in order to meet the expectations of media buyers in terms of quality *consistently, over time* (Mazziotti 35).Thus far, only the Mexican, Brazilian, and Venezuelan industries have been able to consistently achieve this aim—because of the size of their advertising markets or because of the relative stability of sources of advertising revenue.

The second new sociocultural challenge is that posed by accelerated emigration. The growth of the Mexican population outside Mexico has allowed new networks such as TV Azteca to function in a tight national economy by tapping diasporic as well as home-front audiences. The increasing diversification of television during globalization has also spurred the segmentation of markets into "high-end" (pay TV, cable) and "low-end" (satellite or analog) signals. Telenovelas are available at the high end for diasporic and elite viewers but have tended to butter their bread with the working and underemployed sectors, as reflected in a selective use of working-class characters and an equally selective critique of power elites. A disparity could emerge between home and foreign or diasporic audiences not only in terms of advertising but also in relation to the socioeconomic and political realities that viewers confront and bring to the task of textual interpretation.

Each of these challenges has had a profound quantitative and qualitative impact on programming, refiguring what might be described as national narratives or national audiences. Beyond the skewing of programs toward emigrant Latinas and Latinos, the growing links between media and migrant flows raise specific questions regarding the "burden of representation" carried by major media enterprises. To what extent are they beholden to a national audience? How does the pressure to compete successfully with other exporters affect audiovisual style, production techniques, casting, and other cultural and economic considerations? On both counts, one finds significant variations in the response of exporting televisual industries that produce telenovelas. Judging from the cultural profile and aesthetic attributes of programming that originates in each of the three major exporting countries, it can be argued that there is a positive correlation between the presence of emigration and the retention of substantive cultural nationalism.

For example, although it has suffered the lowest level of emigration among these three countries, Venezuela has had the most at stake in exporting its product, owing to the effects of politics on national broadcasting control and content in a relatively small domestic market (in 2005, it had an estimated population of 26.6 million but only 5.8 million television households, compared to 19.7 million television households in Mexico and 37.2 million in Brazil; see Motion Picture Association 2005). Reflecting this extroversion in market strategy, Venevisión, the largest Venezuelan media enterprise, which is owned by the Cisneros Group (which also owns the Miss Venezuela beauty pageant shown yearly in the United States), has been aggressive in its global outlook, buying and retransmitting Mexican- and Brazilian-produced telenovelas and retaining a major foreign interest (14 percent) in Univisión, the largest Spanish-language broadcasting system in the United States (Venevisión, "Programación"; Mazziotti 45).[3] The parent company's objectives in transcending the confines of a Venezuelan audience are clear from the introductory statement found on its Web site:

> The Cisneros Organization has captured Ibero-America as *a unified market, based on the cultural trends and patterns of consumption that are common in markets where Spanish and Portuguese is spoken in America and Europe.* In the first decade of the new millennium, economic integration and the consolidation of the industry in this market has created a variety of new commercial opportunities. In this sense, the Cisneros Organization is producing *cosmopolitan Latino entertainment;* associating itself with televisual productions in Latin America; expanding its investments in *the Hispanic market of the United States;* promoting Spanish content in the United States and internationally; and investing in market niches, such as the beer market and baseball. (Organización Cisneros, "Introducción," emphasis added)

Globalization in the case of Venevisión, then, has signified an increase in its capability to act as conduit for transnational Latinoamerican media, and in its contribution to global standards for the telenovela, lowering the premium placed on national and local culture in favor of a more diffuse *latinidad*. Locations in Venezuelan telenovelas that are made for export tend to be nonspecific—an apartment, a street, a beach, and so on—and are less essential in their semantic value as settings for plotlines, as compared with settings for Mexican programs, which carry dense historicocultural associations and are designed to infuse the telenovela with a dose of national flavor for foreign audiences and authenticity for diasporic and domestic audiences. Apparently, the Cisneros strategy of "essence without specific reference" has not only secured a promising niche for Venevisión in the global marketplace—with the United States as a significant outlet for its product—but it has also permitted the network to avoid clashes with Hugo Chávez because it has replaced critical news programs that focused on national politics and aired on domestic television in the evenings with telenovelas of various national origins.[4]

By contrast, the telenovelas produced by Mexican Televisa and its strongest rival, TV Azteca, have remained strongly "national." By "national," I am referring not only to a particular style of performance or design of dramatic mise-en-scène such as "weepiness" on the part of male as well as female protagonists and "baroqueness," which have been cited as Mexican trademarks (López 261–62), but also to Mexican folk iconography and handicrafts in the décor, the dramatizations of watershed moments in Mexican national history (for example, *Amor real* [Real Love, 2003] and *La esposa virgen* [The Virgin Wife, 2005]), and insistence on Mexican "national" (*chilango*) and regional or colloquial accents, including dialogue spoken by foreign actors (especially Puerto Ricans and Venezuelans). This continued projection of *mexicanidad* in association with a melodramatic narrative form in an age of rampant televisual globalization can be attributed partly to Mexico's preexisting cultural hegemony in the region after World War II—greatly boosted by the golden age of Mexican cinema and Latin America's early receptiveness toward Mexican telenovelas (hence the confidence to continue projecting Mexican culture abroad, even as far as China). As early as 1970, eighteen Latin American countries were importing seven hundred hours of Mexican programming on a monthly basis (Mazziotti 47–48).

Of more direct importance, however, is the burgeoning of the Mexican diaspora in the wake of the North American Free Trade Agreement (NAFTA), making it possible to capitalize on transnational transmission while still targeting a "national" audience. More than 30 million Mexicans currently reside abroad, most in the United States, and remittances to Mexico, now totaling more than $20 billion yearly, have topped oil exports as the largest source of revenue. In other words, at present, human labor power is Mexico's most lucrative export, and the wish to earn dollars instead of pesos makes for a desirable—and possibly essential—transnational audience.[5] This attractiveness is reinforced by the fact that in California, a key destination for Mexican migrants (who make up the majority of the Hispanic immigrant population), "over 99 percent of Hispanic households have a working television set in their homes" (de Sipio et al. 62). Thus, to a significant extent, Televisa's continued expansion of its exports has occurred in tandem with the formation of a "greater Mexico" abroad.

As a producer of programming destined for the global market, the largest Brazilian private network, Rede Globo de Televisão (Globo), is positioned somewhere in between its Mexican and Venezuelan counterparts in terms of its negotiation of a national and global cultural profile, if not the volume of programming that it exports. Enjoying the largest domestic market in Latin America, Globo has been exporting telenovelas since 1975, beginning with Portugal (where it launched *Gabriela,* which was adapted from the Jorge Amado novel *Gabriela, Cravo e Canela [Gabriela, Clove and Cinnamon]*) and extending outward to other Portuguese-speaking territories in Asia and Africa, eventually reaching a total of 128 countries on four continents (Mazziotti 43–44). But Globo has only been transmitting directly abroad by satellite since 1999 through TV Globo Internacional (TVGI) and currently reaches roughly 5.5 million viewers, mostly in Lusophone countries, with selected national programming in Portuguese.[6] Globo's success at home and abroad has been achieved by combining a polished look (luminous high-key lighting, virtuoso editing, and so on) with innovative plot structures and compelling contemporary as well as national historical content.

The relative size of Brazil's internal market potential, based on a population of roughly 189 million in 2006, or almost double Mexico's population of roughly 105 million (UNCTAD 54, 53), still dwarfs the size of any single foreign market for Brazilian television, including the diasporic and greater Lusophone market. Paradoxically, the same domestic competition that reinforces a sustained focus on the national is placing pressure on Globo to cultivate opportunities for export beyond Lusophone territories (Sinclair 133–34). Besides Globo's hearty domestic market, what counts now are the returns from lucrative markets that are primarily located in the United States and Europe and that include Spanish- as well as Portuguese-speaking viewers.

Indeed, while the Brazilian-born population of the United States remains small compared to the number of immigrants from Mexico and the Spanish-speaking Caribbean, almost three million Brazilians already live abroad (Rohter), and the itineraries and challenges that they face are beginning to resemble those of other Latin American migrants: more than 17,400 Brazilians were apprehended along the U.S.-Mexican border during the first four months of 2005 alone (Luiz).[7] Demand for Portuguese-language media with national content has skyrocketed in the United States as the Brazilian diaspora, especially in Georgia, Miami, New York, and Boston, has reached unprecedented levels, last estimated at 1.3 million (quoted in Luiz). Recent arrivals have more "staying power" (in part because of their increasingly undocumented status) than did earlier Brazilian immigrants and more media-buying clout than they had when residing in Brazil. In addition to regularly consuming Spanish-language television—which occasionally features Brazilian telenovelas dubbed into Spanish—Brazucas in growing numbers are purchasing satellite dishes to receive programming transmitted directly from Brazil via TVGI.

Before I shift my analytical vantage point, a few summary observations are prompted by this industrial comparison. First, although there has always been an intracontinental flow of trade in programs and talent, the recent period has witnessed an acceleration of continental cross-fertilization in style, themes, casting, and modes of audience address as well an increase in telenovela-friendly audiences across the globe. This cross-fertilization has alternately entailed each of the following:

1. The "Brazilianization" of style and technique, including the move toward a more high=gloss aesthetic in Mexico and Venezuela, thanks to the mobile contributions of Brazilian technicians from Globo along with a seemingly contradictory return to the historical epic (once the mainstay of cinematic melodrama in the region) and heightened realism in telenovelas set in the present. This thematic and representational realism is frequently infused with populism, as is the case with the Mexican depictions of immigration discussed below.

2. Venezuelan telenovelas as a renewable resource or "gene bank" for stories and themes—especially the "rags to riches" Cinderella template (Mazziotti 51)—as evidenced in the RCN original *Yo soy Betty la fea* (I Am Ugly Betty, 1999). Televisa has also frequently undertaken remakes of earlier Venezuelan telenovelas such as *El derecho de nacer* (The Right to Be Born, 1966) and *Esmeralda* (Emerald, 1997–87), a version of *Topacio* (Topaz, 1984, in turn authored by Cuban screenwriters and in some cases initially adapted from Cuban radionovelas).

3. Colombia has emerged as an incubator for woman-centered narratives, which, having been popularized, have become grist for successful Televisa exports to the United States. In addition to *Yo soy Betty la fea,* Televisa has "Mexicanized" RCN's *La potra Zaina* (Zaina the Colt, 1992, retitled *Apuesta por un amor* [Betting on Love, 2005]) and *Café* (retitled *Destilando amor [Distilling Love, 2007]*).[8]

4. The overall Mexicanization of Spanish-language productions, given Televisa's continued dominance of the airspace of other Latin American nations, its stronghold in the United States via Spanish-language networks, its successful "domestication" (through the use of Mexican geographic locations, character types, and iconography, such as the ubiquitous Nuestra Señora de Guadalupe) of stories from elsewhere in the region, and the "acculturation" of non-Mexican (especially Hispanic Caribbean) actors by endowing them with roles and accents heavily coded as Mexican.

5. Conversely an element of "neo-Cubanization" in Mexican telenovelas: the exodus of Cuban talent during the *periodo especial* of economic austerity following the Soviet Union's collapse has been especially beneficial to the Mexican television industry as new Cuban stars, such as the *galanes* (male romantic leads) César Évora Díaz, Francisco Gattorno, and Ninón Sevilla's heir apparent, Niurka Marcos, freely regale viewers with both their Cubanidad and life stories on telenovela-related talk shows broadcast in the United States.

Second, as telenovelas have become glossier and their plotlines more fluid and multilayered, they have also had to appeal to divergent cultural constituencies—a "foreign" non-Spanish and non-Portuguese speaking audience, a "traditional" national audience that transects class and regional differences but increasingly is weighted toward the working class, and a transnational audience of devoted (and often homesick) viewers. Rather than leading to the homogenization of Latin American programs made for export, the tricentric cross-fertilization has contributed to a pan-Latina/o rather than a trans-Latina/o sensibility, while foregrounding the increasingly "hybrid" nature of transnational televisual programming and of the telenovela in particular. Hybridity in this context is more than a toolbox of rhetorical devices to ensure that there is something for everyone; it is the manifestation of specific practices, from the transnational transfer and adaptation of source material to international casting to set dressing and editing techniques. On the textual level, hybridity is manifested in occasional disjunctures between naturalistic (or traditionalist) set design and stylized or convention-breaking camera and sound work, occasional pastiche in performance and characterization, and multiaccented and multilingual dialogue. While in the past Brazilian and Mexican telenovelas have shown particular resistance to linguistic "impurities" (see López 262–63; Mazziotti 50), the producers have recently yielded to the diversification of regional accents in Portuguese and Spanish to include Argentinian, French, and Cuban accents as well as French, Italian, and Portuguese phrases in Mexican telenovelas, and to the incorporation of English phrases and colloquial expressions. Although some observers might see the latter as merely another sign of U.S. cultural hegemony, some thought should be given to the way in which the heterological character of the transnational telenovela is beginning to resemble the multiaccented and multilingual social universe currently experienced by those living in border cities in the United States and Europe, as well as in Latin American urban centers. Would not a Brazilian living in Miami or a Spaniard living in Madrid hear Argentinian- and Cuban-accented Spanish? Would not a Mexican living in Arizona hear northern Mexican accents, central rural dialects, and Spanglish more often than a *chilango* (Mexico City) accent? Would not a migrant returning to Mexico or Brazil be likely to use English phrases out of habit or to demonstrate migratory achievement?

In positing the continuity and greater self-consciousness of national expression and continental cross-fertilization in the transnational telenovela, I am disagreeing with Jesús Martín-Barbero's position that the entrance of national television enterprises into the global marketplace ultimately "signifies . . . the tendency for Latin American audiovisual businesses to mold the image of their people in terms of audiences which are more and more undifferentiated, the tendency to dissolve cultural difference into cheap and profitable exoticism" (283–84). I would also hesitate to label the textual results of this global televisual trend "postmodern"; if anything, the transnational telenovela is "neomodern," albeit packaged in a glittery, deracinated wrapper: many telenovelas are conservative at heart, and they continue to stress sociocultural continuity through language, character interaction, and mise-en-scène. There is a stress on the ability of national societies to *absorb* the crises that accompany modern change (as if modernity were still something new), the ability of patriarchal structures to restore order while accommodating feminine ambition and desire and the possibility of cultural authenticity—and hence, of preserving national identities by escorting the viewer back to foundational moments in the formation of the nation-state. This is not to say that the telenovela is impervious to postmodernity—one can certainly find strong instances of postmodernism in the more technically and artistically sophisticated productions, especially in Brazil. If anything, the hybrid construction and appearance of the telenovela, together with the industrial and social phenomena that subtend its hybridity, provide special insight into how postmodernity, within the new framework built by global trade, investment, and marketing, consists, as George Yúdice has suggested, of "a series of conditions variously holding in different social formations that elicit diverse responses and propositions to the multiple ways in which modernization has been attempted in them" (7).

Finally, other industrial players have become increasingly involved in the process of transnational transmission. Unless it arrives directly by satellite (as in the case of Globo's TVGI), transmission from Latin America to the United States is principally a two-step process involving the filtering and insertion of telenovelas into programming flows that are locally packaged and include programs produced in the United States. Three networks—Telemundo (owned by NBC, that is, Time-Warner), Univisión, and Telefutura (both owned by Univisión Communications, Inc., a consortium of foreign and domestic media capital firms)[9]—are primarily responsible for the transmission of Spanish-language programming to local communities via satellite and via urban owned-and-operated stations. Univisión, the largest of these networks, currently has twenty-two owned-and-operated stations in the United States, with WUDT Detroit (2005) being the latest addition.

There are specific ways in which Spanish-language networks such as Univisión, which cater primarily to the Latina and Latino diaspora, have helped to shape the marketing, modes of viewer engagement, and cultural orientation of telenovelas. Through U.S.-produced talk, gossip, variety and awards shows, viewers come into closer contact with the actors while obtaining insight (via backstage shots) into the industry. Such shows are especially important because they permit live audience interaction with performers. By supporting the publicity agenda of telenovela producers, U.S. Spanish-language networks help place telenovelas at the center of the Latina and Latino transnational imaginary. Thus far, priority on Univisión has been given to Televisa's telenovela talent, given the strong ties between the two companies. Yet because those telenovelas increasingly feature actors of various national backgrounds, the paratextual discourse emanating from these shows favors a pan-Latina/o rather than a strictly Mexican form of identification and engagement.

Moreover, the transmission through Univisión does not work unidirectionally, downlinking Latin American programming and funneling it to U.S. audiences. Shows such as *Cristina* and *Sábado gigante* (Giant Saturday), produced in Florida, not to mention awards shows, are also transmitted transnationally to Spain and to Latin America. The U.S.-based SLTV networks not only work together with Latin American networks to configure Ibero-America as "a unified market," to quote the Cisneros Organization's Web site, but also have encouraged the formation of a *pan*-Latino rather than a simply trans-Latina discursive paradigm, largely in response to the diverse national and ethnic composition of U.S. native and diasporic Latinas/os who make up their first-tier audience.

Televisual melodrama, then, is not only a site where the tensions among the national, the local, and the global are articulated and made manifest, it is also a communicative bridge that links viewers across national, expanded regional, and global realms of transmission and reception, working to shape new cultural and intercultural communities. The pressure on Latin American television networks to appeal to these audience types and locations simultaneously—allowing them to compete on the global stage while staying loyal to their home audiences—has led to a juggling act in programming flow and textual construction, an exercise made more delicate by the spread of diasporic audiences, who reside at the interstices of the national and the global. As a result, the national as a category of differentiation and identification is not dissolved, but is necessarily redefined in the course of transnational transmission and of pitching to local pan-Latina/o audiences in the United States.

## The Diversification of Television Melodrama in Response to International Migration

Beyond its hybrid composition and pan-geographic reach, what are the attributes of televisual melodrama that invest the transnational telenovela with relevance for the diasporic viewer? The answer to this question resides in part in the potential offered by the arduous process of migration itself, carried out in increasingly dangerous and hostile conditions, to supply melodramatic material for a range of transnational television programming, including news coverage.

In the wake of stepped-up migration, and complications and abuses of enforcement, SLTV networks in the United States have increasingly made use of the testimonial form, which is characteristic of most Latin American investigative news reports (in contrast to the U.S. "sound bite"), to get the stories of migrants out into the public sphere. These human interest stories, featured mainly in such news magazines as Univisión's *Primer impacto* (First Impact) and *Aquí y ahora* (Here and Now), are geared toward revealing the impact of immigration policy and exposing the current condition of many migrants, undocumented and documented, living in the United States. Such reports often have a didactic function: they explain the pitfalls of immigration legislation and warn about mistakes and injustices that plague many migrants, including criminal activity that has been fueled by the criminalization of border crossing and the corresponding vulnerability of migrants to *coyotes* and labor contractors, petty thieves, pimps, con artists, and vigilante groups such as Ranch Rescue and American Border Patrol in the southwestern states.[10] In these prime-time television reports, those with direct experience of migration testify to the facts as they know them, show signs of their suffering, and denounce their deception at the hands of abusive authorities or opportunistic criminals, occasionally with their faces hidden to protect their identity, while an empathetic reporter-interviewer prods them to talk about their experiences in a style closer to that of a psychoanalyst or social worker than an investigative reporter.

The delivery of key information by both interviewer and interviewee is facilitated by a strong dose of pathos, which is accessible to the viewer, if not through direct identification with the migrant as protagonist and victim, then vicariously through a compassionate interviewer. The posture of the latter is pitched to indicate that factual information alone does not yield the full story. For example, in the October 4, 2007, episode of *Aquí y ahora*, Univisión reporter Victor Hugo Saavedra interviewed a group of forlorn parishioners at an evangelical church along the Texas-Mexico border. Several had given their life savings to a con-artist "preacher" named Webber who claimed to be "Grand Chief Thunderbird IV" of a fictional Native American "Kuweah Nation" in exchange for tribal membership that would allow them to "freely enter" the United States and would protect them from deportation, only to discover that the certificate, when presented to Homeland Security agents, was fraudulent. Instead of trying to ascertain the exact amount of the victims' monetary loss, Saavedra asks emotionally provocative questions such as "Did you believe him [the impostor] more because he preached in your church?"

Thus news programming that appears to be infused with documentary techniques is infused with melodrama. One can expect to find in this coverage tales of frustrated desire, the unraveling of unconscionable injustice, acts of transgression or bad choices by well-meaning or innocent subjects, the interrogation of a modern system that so easily and unjustly metes out discrimination, the possibility of empathizing with a traumatized subject at a safe remove from the action, dramatic reenactments of the traumatic events, and audiovisual excess (that is, electronically distorted voices or chiaroscuro lighting ostensibly helping to preserve the interviewee's anonymity). There is also a sense that larger forces are at work that will continue to impinge on unsuspecting individuals until they are fully accounted for and reined in, which adds an element of suspense and hooks the viewer into hoping for a resolution that is rarely achieved in news programs. As in fictional melodrama, the somatic wounds are visibly apparent to the viewer, even if the full truth or ultimate causes of the incident are not.

Just as a melodramatic sensibility informs the presentation of biographical material and the confessional mode, news reports of migratory misadventures and injustices have provided plot material for more conventionally melodramatic telenovelas such that the pairing of migration with melodrama transects different programming formats within the transnational and national SLTV flow. The thematic and rhetorical continuities within this flow, combined with the augmented realism of telenovelas, increases the chances for a "cross-reading" of texts in the talk, telenovela, and news formats.

As a form of melodrama, the telenovela is, as Esther Hamburger has suggested, a genre well suited to addressing national crises that affect a wide cross-section of citizens (7–12, 131–47). By personifying the crisis through the dramatic relations of a few characters, for whom national and transnational dilemmas are among a larger set of problems, telenovelas distill what are in reality complex situations with numerous protagonists and competing rather than unified power structures. Thus, they provide just enough of a psychoideological buffer so that the plotline is injected with a dose of reality, without forcing the viewer to take up a position in relation to the crisis being referenced, and thereby avoid bursting the diegetic bubble that makes telenovela viewing so pleasurable. On one hand, the viewer is relieved of having to shoulder the crisis, which in any case has its roots in structures and agencies outside the viewer's range of control. On the other, even if the melodramatic text does not depict the crisis from an emigrant's perspective (this is usually done by news stories), it can obliquely chronicle the types of hardship or disenchantment experienced by significant sectors of the national population and, through well-timed placement of culturally charged iconic signs, allow access, albeit indirect, to the deeper sociohistorical roots of the characters' dramas. The solutions to these interpersonal dramas can therefore work synecdochically to deliver implicit, prescribed solutions to the crisis. These solutions are tied to character arcs and appear initially as a means of individual advancement or deliverance from suffering at critical turning points in the plot.

Faced with these allegorical scenes and situations, the viewer who is engaged with the protagonists' fate yet safely removed by at least a degree is able to work vicariously through the knottier contextual entanglements rooted in political and economic forces. When it does enter the telenovela plot, the migration story becomes a third or auxiliary line of emplotment that, in forcing a glance at the parallelism between the personal and the national, can foreground the work of the genre in bridging fiction and lived experience. Thus, whether central or peripheral to the plot, the migration narrative has become a pivotal site for the delivery of ideological content regarding national identity, class, and gender relations, especially since many of the featured emigrants are working-class women.

The feminization of migrant protagonists in telenovelas not only reflects the increasing proportion of women to men in the migrant stream (a 2006 United Nations Population Fund study revealed that 69 percent of internal and international migrants from Latin America were domestic workers; Lindo), but, working ultimately within, rather than against, the predominantly conservative ideological codes of the telenovela, it also enhances the vulnerability of the migrant subject to various forms of aggression and deceit, providing the pretext for various forms of rescue and a trajectory of repatriation, often with a happy ending. If one takes the plot resolutions of these telenovelas as well as news reports of the pitfalls of border crossing together, migration provides the key to a future in the host country that is dubious, at best; the third line of emplotment thus assists in the task of the primary diegesis to restore a sense of confidence, or at least attachment to the homeland, in spite of the persistent injustices to be found there.

Notwithstanding the feminine emphasis in the migration plotline, one must be careful not to collapse the ostensible protagonist into focalization, especially given the vulnerability of the migrant to masculinized threats and her need to be rescued, preferably by a masculine agent. One is encouraged to sympathize with the female migrant, who represents the vulnerability of the collectivity abroad, but one can easily engage in this sympathy from a "masculine" protective position. Often the viewer's textual identification ideologically, if not affectively, with masculine agency in the migration narrative is buttressed by the patriarchal resolutions and the resilience of patriarchal institutions in the face of both external and internal threats. This, together with the scheduling of telenovelas as prime-time fare in the United States and in Latin America, points to the inclusion of more than one gender, as well as more than one generation, in the pool of viewers. Although migration is a gendered experience from the decision to migrate to the border crossing and the socioeconomic future that awaits most migrants, for transnational programming to be successful it must reach a wide range of viewers and let go of gender specificity in marketing and mode of address. In the surveys that I conducted in Los Angeles and Detroit, I have found no significant gender-based pattern of telenovela viewing that would privilege women over men as captive viewers, and, ironically, women, not men, tended to be most critical of the type of entertainment that telenovelas provide.

Another relevant attribute of the transnational telenovela (as contrasted with the U.S. soap opera) is that it depicts the necessity of collaborative if not collective action of sympathetic characters with the hero(ine) to resolve situations that are not reducible to interpersonal dynamics. It is the co-worker or the com(p)adre who helps the momentarily blind and unwise protagonist to "see" and who works assiduously to pull the protagonist out of the crisis. Of course, it is through just such collective action that Latin American immigrants have coped with the obstacles they experience in the United States. A media survey that I have been conducting in the Detroit metropolitan area has also shown television viewing among Latinas and Latinos to be a group activity rather than an individual one. Although this allows for the possibility that programming content can be an object of public rather than private reflection and debate in telenovelas, collective action is avoided in favor of cultural alienation and social isolation for predominantly female protagonists.

Aside from incorporating the migratory experience as a plot element, Mexican telenovelas in particular are able to convey meaningful messages to diasporic viewers simply by devoting the camera's attention to readily identifiable locations in rural Mexico (often the same locations that have experienced high levels of emigration), as well as the reiteration of icons of *mexicanidad* in the mise-en-scène. The shift toward rural settings, where land is struggled over much as it was fought over during the Mexican Revolution and thereafter, has been accompanied by another type of geosocial de- (or re-)centering—the increasing emphasis on *norteño,* or northern culture, music, and accents. This is not surprising, given the increasing references in Mexican telenovelas to hypothetical and actual journeys made by characters to the United States, not to mention the polysemic power of the borderlands as a site where Mexican sovereignty was fought for and relations with the United States repeatedly negotiated. The final episode of the Mexican program *La fea más bella* (The Prettiest Ugly Woman), whose theme song was composed and performed by the norteño Banda el Recodo, takes the cast out of the studio and into a street parade and live stage performance before a massive audience in Monterrey, Nuevo León (broadcast in the United States on June 25, 2007).

The telenovela's referencing of norteño culture, including songs that are more commonly filled with tales of border crossing and contraband than of homely secretaries turned glamorous executives, allows the solidity of the geopolitical border to be contested by practices and memories that transcend arbitrary definitions of cultural difference and political sovereignty. That this space is being reclaimed by telenovelas and other types of television programming is not surprising given that, prior to the 2006 presidential election, the Mexican government not only recognized the Mexican citizenship of Mexican emigrants who had become U.S. citizens, but also gave Mexicans residing in the United States the right to vote.

Collectively, these traits—reminders of home for the nostalgic, representations of struggle that both resemble and depart from the actual migratory experience for the realist—illustrate how the folkloric dimensions of the telenovela work across audience groups in different ways, providing a scenic view for the global audience, a happy ending that does not require extensive strategizing and collective struggle for the working-class migrant, and an emotional release through empathy and identification for the regional and diasporic viewer. In particular, the migration narrative and its referencing through allegory generate a Gramscian type of folklore "which in the form of melodramatic excess, validates one's sense of suffering while making that suffering appear beyond one's control" (Landy 14). Implicit in this type of folklore is compassionate suffering in solidarity with others, but also a process of simultaneous referencing—the trace of the "real"—and evading the historical "real," a working through for the spectator at a distance.

Beyond creating safe spaces, both diegetic and extradiegetic, in which migrant viewers can make an imaginary return to a land of origin, recent Mexican telenovelas inscribe migration by various means, including a subplot or minor character who returns home for the sake of becoming symbolically reconciled with family and former neighbors. The allegorical representation of migration may be as diffuse as depicting the loss of love interests who leave for lengthy periods of time, are then presumed dead or remarried, and return in disguise to do battle with the evil meddlers who have impeded the continuation of the relationship. Or it may be as palpable as the figuration of border crossing, concealed identity, and detention set in another context. This is the case in the popular historical epic *Amor real,* which on the surface appears to reiterate the formula of an inheritance dispute between rightful and fraudulent heirs to a hacienda. The narrative is set in fictitious Ciudad Trinidad (referring to the port where Cubans and their Spanish colonizers did battle with English pirates) during the period leading up to the Cinco de Mayo (1862) victory, when

Mexican patriots were able to rout French occupying forces led by Napoleon III and their Mexican collaborators. Manuel Fuentes Guerra (Fernando Colunga) is a patriot who has inherited his late father Joaquín Fuentes Guerra's landed estate and who marries the daughter of a fellow hacienda owner, hoping to repair the family's rapidly dwindling fortune. Halfway through the serial, Manuel's birthright to the estate and to his name is challenged when an impostor forges an altered version of his father's will and rumors erupt about the former profession of his biological mother, who up to that point has served as his maidservant. Upon being "excommunicated" from Trinidadian society and dispossessed of his home, Manuel flees with his biological mother (Ana Martín) in a horse-drawn carriage back to his rural town of origin, where a priest can be enlisted to testify to his identity and his mother's virtue in the eyes of God. En route, they attempt to cross a river and are discovered and chased along the riverbank by troops sent by Mexican (*criollo*) traitors, who are set on destroying Manuel's personal life and professional reputation (he is an authentic but, to them, intolerably upwardly mobile *mestizo*). The carriage is overturned; left for dead, Manuel escapes with his mother to an encampment of impoverished patriots that resembles much more closely a redoubt of Pancho Villa's rag-tag army than a garrison of homespun Mexican troops preparing to defend their national turf. The chief officer of the garrison, and, we discover, of the Mexican resistance, is a "people's leader" who lives among his troops and is committed to the achievement of justice, as well as Mexican sovereignty. The encampment seems improvised enough—it is set up in the ruins of an old hacienda, and food is scavenged and shared—that it could just as well be one of the camps set up by border crossers as they make their way into Texas or Arizona, looking for work. This is a turning point for Manuel, who comes to accept his mother's silence about her past and goes from being a silk-stockinged patrician to a grassroots, poncho-wearing combatant who is accepted and trusted by the rag-tag army. After a violent clash with the criollo and *gachupín* traitors who have taken over the town and are clinging to Manuel's wife's home like barnacles, the telenovela ends with Manuel returning to claim his rightful place in his family and in local and national society.

In these sequences we see a transhistorical dynamic at work in which, in spite of the elaborate attention to historical detail, it is possible to recall a string of Mexican popular struggles formed in response to neocolonialism and inequity. The possibilities of allegorical readings are usually triggered by such things as the ambiguous mise-en-scène of the garrison. Modeled after revolutionary photographs of Zapata's and Villa's armies rather than pictorial representations of the Cinco de Mayo revolt, it is anachronistic, as is the appeal, in the dialogue of the patriot leaders, to communal rather than individualistic or oligarchical values, and the figuration of border crossing, punctuated by the slow-motion and repeated shots of the carriage overturning in a shallow river.

On a much more modest historical scale, migration narratives have figured in telenovelas as life-transforming detours along the arcs of nationally delineated characters, usually single working class women, who encounter danger and misfortune *al otro lado* (on the other side of the border) and return more worldly-wise, albeit wounded, to their hometowns. Such is the case in *Amigas y rivales* (Friends and Rivals, Televisa, 2001) of the secondary character Nayeli (Angélica Vale), a maid who works in a wealthy household in Mexico City and dreams of romance with the bachelor son Roberto (Arath de la Torre) of the benevolent patriarch, Don Roberto de la O (Eric del Castillo). Her future seems palatable, if not for the neighborhood toughs who harass her and try to rape her on her return home from work one night. Nayeli flees to Los Angeles, where she rooms with a young Mexican migrant who helps her to obtain work as a waitress in what appears to be a strip joint near Los Angeles Airport. Unfortunately, her roommate is not so benevolent; he attempts to rape her one evening, whereupon she knocks him unconscious. Believing that she has killed him (which she hasn't), she takes refuge in the apartment of a new friend, Johnny Trinidad (Johny Lozano, a Puerto Rican actor and former member of the band Menudo), who helps her return to Tijuana and who decides—with the best of intentions—to follow her to Mexico City. Johnny is an aspiring boxer, a Spanglish-speaking Mexican American from New York City, who manages, through boxing contacts, to land a role in a telenovela in Mexico City. Johnny is all Nayeli needs to protect herself from the neighborhood thugs, even though the two never consummate their relationship. In an interesting twist on the repatriation narrative, Mexico is portrayed as the land of opportunity for young U.S. Latinas and Latinos. True to generic form (and then-dominant Mexican state discourse), Los Angeles is a perilous, immoral place, full of false promises and abusive relationships, both employment-related and personal. Although Mexico clearly has its social problems and poor living conditions for hard-working people, it offers a web of protection and trust through family and work relations (Don Roberto sends Nayeli home with his chauffeurs) that is clearly absent from Los Angeles, where one's human value is brutally diminished by untamed desire.

An alternate yet ideologically consonant portrayal of feminine migration is given in *Destilando amor,* a highly Mexicanized remake of the Colombian transnational hit *Café con aroma de mujer* (Coffee with the Scent of a Woman, 1994), broadcast by Telemundo in 1995 and based on an actual scandal involving fraudulent coffee exports (for an extensive discussion of the latter, see Venegas 63–64, 67–69). In the regionally popular remake, Teresa Hernández (Angélica Rivera) is a young *rimadora,* or agave harvester, working on a hacienda near Tequila, Jalisco, who falls madly in love with Rodrigo Montalvo (Eduardo Yañez), the handsome heir to the hacienda. Teresa, whose nickname, "Gaviota," evokes her circular migrancy as a farmworker, discovers that she is pregnant with Rodrigo's child. He has returned to London to complete his studies as an agronomist, which will allow him to take tequila-making into the twenty-first century. Desperate to inform him of this good yet socially compromising news, Teresa accepts the dubious offer of a local "fashion photographer" to work as a model in Europe. Bearing a false passport with the name Mariana Franco, she arrives in Paris only to discover that the fashion house is in fact a brothel, and what awaits her is a miserable existence as a sex slave. Teresa escapes without tarnishing her sworn fidelity to Rodrigo, and, with the help of a benevolent Italian restaurant owner, makes her way to London. After a fruitless search in Oxford, she spots Rodrigo (who is enrolled at Cambridge University) on a London street, and in her rush to reach him, she is struck by a double-decker bus, severely injured, and knocked unconscious. Saved by the Virgen de Guadalupe (like Nayeli, she is alone and unprotected by family or friends), she awakens in a Catholic charity hospital to find that she has lost her baby and contact with Rodrigo, yet has received spiritual encouragement from an English nun. During her months of rehabilitation, Teresa learns English, French, and European history, in addition to reading and writing. Lacking the money for a return ticket to Mexico, and having overstayed her European visa, she has herself deported back home. But instead of finding a beaming Rodrigo waiting for the spring agave harvest and ready to take her hand in marriage, she finds a deeply disillusioned man who, unaware of her pregnancy and having discovered abandoned "test shots" of a coquettish Teresa, has taken a Mexico City slicker as his wife.

Several features link these stylistically and historically distinct telenovelas. First, migration (or exile, in the case of *Amor real*) is figured as a rite of passage in which the protagonists, male or female, must lose everything of value, especially their social identity, in order to appreciate what they have left behind. The ineffability of this loss exceeds the nostalgia one might expect from a tale of migration, and thus acts as a deep structural clue to the allegorical operation. Loss is invariably followed by reconciliation with the family and local community and by extension, the nation-state. In keeping with the didactic function of the Mexican telenovela, the rhetoric of self-improvement and good citizenship tends to trump any narrative of social progress or political reform, notwithstanding the (feeble) referencing of social ills, lack of opportunity, even persecution, on the home front as a cause for departure. There is more than simply a lesson here on how to succeed in a globalized capitalist society, for there is often a tendentious note—and an occasional hammering—of Mexican state discourse within the didacticism.

The theme of alienation and betrayal, material and spiritual impoverishment, and in some cases, death, experienced by migrants abroad can be traced to Mexican film melodramas of the fifties and the seventies, such as Alejandro Galindo's *Espaldas mojadas* (Wetbacks, 1955) and Arturo Ripstein's *La ilegal* (1979). In the newer versions, which border on Harlequin romance, migration is equated not only with the betrayal of one's national origins—Mexican nationalism is clearly preferred to other forms of *latinidad*—but also, in the woman-centered subplots, with a departure from the physical and emotional safety provided by an autochthonous, timeworn form of patriarchy and a "Latin," or more humane, form of capitalism. Outside of this framework, one finds only the most barren modes of existence; spatial mobility (an apt metaphor for sociocultural mobility) is shown to be a fading illusion for the undocumented, and the only available avenues of survival for women involve the commodification of one's body, and with that, the consequent impact on one's future. Although both Nayeli (*Amores rivales*) and Gaviota (*Destilando amor*) utilize their free will to craft their departures from Mexico, significantly, their agency in resolving their employment difficulties or the dangers encountered on arriving abroad is curtailed, whereas the power of paternalism, and, in the latter case, the state and the Catholic Church as beneficent institutions, is restored.

Because the integrity of the nation-state is at stake, there is no transcendence in the migratory effort or in global investment; there is only the possibility of a lateral move homeward, for those wise enough to choose it. Mexico is depicted as a viable, even attractive, space of return, where remunerations and career expectations are modest, yet where one is certain to find the protection and support of one's boss, coworker, family, and true love, not to mention one's authentic self: imperfect yet visibly improved by exposure to global challenge. In the process, privatized versions of the paternalistic state, along with diplomacy that protects the nation's interest—such as the National Tequila Regulatory Council in *Destilando amor* or Manuel Fuentes Guerra's sheltering of patriot fighters on his hacienda in *Amor real*—prevail. Years later, when she returns to London as a successful public relations executive, Teresa succeeds in negotiating a trade agreement between Mexican tequila producers and their

G8 counterparts in London because she is able to fuse the proud memory of her rural origins with her metropolitan skills, while her love interest, the Cambridge-educated Rodrigo, must keep returning to his hacienda to save the family legacy. The two can only be reunited at their place of origin. *Amor real* sends the same message, albeit in a different way.

Although the migration sequences in telenovelas are hardly ahistorical, especially given the growing attention to the plight of women during migration with particular attention to sex slavery, and notwithstanding their Los Angeles and London locations and naturalistic audiovisual style, the dramatic circumstances and characters' responses have been configured to conform to the broader arcs in the serial plotline, as well as to the ideological imperatives of each text. Migration is acknowledged as an unavoidable feature of Mexican contemporary reality, but it does not represent a stake or a prevailing context for the plot, nor are migrant viewers necessarily addressed by its sanitized rendering in these texts.

Other programming initiatives, involving the conversion of actual stories into televisual melodrama, have been more adept at exposing the social and familial consequences of migration, thereby historically grounding the dystopian rendering of life al otro lado. They also explicitly attempt to appeal to migrant viewers by inscribing mostly feminine migrant voices without speaking through their elite benefactors and detractors or harnessing viewer empathy to a patriarchal positioning. The weekly Televisa series aired on Univisión, *Mujer: Casos de la vida real* (*Woman: Stories from Real Life, 1985–2008*), hosted by the veteran telenovela and stage actress Silvia Pinal, tends toward the sensational, dramatizing reported incidents such as sexual captivity of young rural women in return for money paid to their father; a selfish mother who leaves her children with their grandmother in northern Mexico so she can work in the fields in the United States, only to start a family with a new husband and never return; con-artist employment brokers who set up an office in Mexico to process "applications" from aspiring migrants and after collecting hefty visa fees, disappear; and the sobering tale of a woman who, after many months of awaiting word from her husband, who has gone to work in New York, discovers that he was one of the many service workers who died in the 9/11 World Trade Center explosions, with no repatriation of the body or pension forthcoming. Unlike telenovelas, the series does not aspire towards seamless, naturalistic representations of characters and settings, nor does it interweave multiple plotlines around a central tale of heterosexual romance; rather, its own "aesthetic of hunger," in the words of Glauber Rocha, seems to resonate with the usually modest circumstances of its protagonists, and the intensity of emotion is geared to compensate for the technical limitations of the camerawork and editing work.

*Mujer: Casos de la vida real* is constructed on the basis of stories relayed to the producers by viewers(the veracity of all of the stories, and the modifications made in the staging of them are difficult to ascertain), but the selection and dramatization of the stories are unabashedly designed to morally instruct the audience. At the end of each half-hour episode, Silvia Pinal returns (much in the style of Robert Osborne on TMC) to deliver a few words of caution before opening the next "letter."

Less heavy-handed in its didacticism, but equally dedicated to socially responsible programming and based on actual events, is the melodrama-crime miniseries *Al filo de la ley* (On the Edge of the Law), developed for Univisión by the U.S.-based Plural Entertainment and aired on Univisión in May and June 2004. The series boasts much higher production values than the longer-running *Mujer: Casos de la vida real* because it was shot on film and did not hesitate to experiment with unconventional angles, lighting, or unusual cuts and dissolves, as well as the interrelation of parallel plotlines during editing. The microdrama of the law office is fused in each of these plotlines with the cliffhanging suspense of detective work and courtroom battles. The visual style borders on that of film noir, as low-key lighting is often combined with spartan sets and cityscapes, and a predominantly realist approach (with noticeable dramatic departures anchored in subjective viewpoints) is taken toward casting, characterization, and the staging of events. The production of the series in the United States both introduces the possibility of U.S. television influence—it has the feel of a Latino *Law and Order*—and gives it a pro-active pan-Latino approach to casting and characterization. Principal actors, who play attorneys working in downtown Los Angeles, speak in Mexican, Cuban, and Colombian accents, while episodic actors and characters exhibit a range of backgrounds, from Mexican American to South American. The narrative matrix on which each episode is built consists of the arrival of a young, single attorney Valeria (Ximena Rubio) at a law firm where her ex-boyfriend Andrés (Jorge Aravena) and his new love interest Bárbara (Natalia Ramírez) both work. Hence the series offers a rare middle-class vantage point from which to portray diasporic Latinas and Latinos in the United States.[11]

In a pivotal episode (aired on May 25, 2004), Valeria takes on the case of Susana Montalbán, who came to the United States from Mexico after marrying Rogélio, a U.S. citizen. The couple met while Susana was working as a waitress in Cancún, where Rogélio (who, as an "*agringado,*" prefers to be called "Roger") was vacationing. Although the couple had a child after arriving in Los Angeles, Susana is still waiting for the residency papers that Rogélio promised her. What makes the wait worse is that Susana is tormented by her potentially violent and psychologically abusive husband, who regularly commands her to engage in involuntary sex. She faces a choice between obtaining the residency papers to which she is entitled and recovering her self-esteem and peace of mind by returning with her child to Mexico. After consulting Valeria and Andrés about the possibility of obtaining a divorce, Susana returns home, feeling empowered enough to leave temporarily with her son until her situation is resolved.

Valeria begins to investigate the status of her residency application just as Roger, witnessing his wife's arrival home from across the street, calls the INS. As he warns Susana not to leave, the INS agents enter and apprehend Susana. In the meantime, Valeria discovers that no application was ever filed for Susana, and, after an information-sharing session at the detention center, Valeria and Andrés decide to take the case to court. Armed with a private male lawyer, Roger (now clearly a "gringo" who is not to be trusted) challenges Susana's accusations, claiming that she married him for residency papers and had abandoned the home. Valeria makes the difficult decision to give the final summation, motivated by her desire to confront her memory of being raped by a masked stranger, which, in effect, had interfered long ago in her romantic relationship with Andrés. Note that rather than emphasizing the tensions emerging between Valeria, Andrés, and Barbara, which would be expected in a star-driven telenovela, the focus remains on the immigration case. The lawyers and Susana are essential to the central ideas of compassionate Latina

Valeria listens to Susana's experiences of spousal abuse in *Al filo de la ley*.

and Latino professionals who can assist the less fortunate members of their urban community and the benefits of seeking help rather than silently struggling against an abusive husband or immigration regulations.

The program emphasizes the way in which, by focusing the drama on Susana, the show lets Valeria assume a supportive position as a listening

The INS comes for Susana in her home.

Valeria and Andrés interview Susana in the detention center.

professional and as a woman who has experienced male aggression. The viewers' sympathy for Roger is severely compromised by his willingness to deport his own wife; it seems that he and the INS agents are "out to get her" and that Roger's ability to bully Susana derives from his citizenship status and sense of masculine entitlement rather than from any physical prowess or moral superiority. During the interview the camera emphasizes the ensemble of lawyers and their client, in which the telephone lines, emphasizing communication between free and incarcerated subjects, transect the frame and the only character whose face is fully lit and in view is Susana's.

Interesting from the formal standpoint is the resemblance in discursive strategy between the narrative focalization in *Al filo de la ley* and the interviewing techniques used in the news magazine *Aquí y ahora*: a sympathetic Latina professional facilitates the revelation of Latina migrant experiences to a pan-Latina audience. These latter examples point to the synergistic relation between recorded images of the historical plane and the use of melodrama to attract spectators and involve them in the pathos of the migratory experience; more work needs to be done to explore the new directions taken by televisual melodrama as it is brought into close or interactive contact with documentary or testimonial story sources in a didactic and expository, rather than sensationalist, discursive frame.

## Diasporic Latina and Latino Viewers Respond

I would like to briefly expand on the responses of Latina and Latino viewers whom I interviewed in 1998 in Los Angeles and in 2005 in Detroit, Michigan, regarding their programming preferences and viewing habits.[12] The respondents at both locations were from a wide range of national backgrounds and included fairly even numbers of men and women (and in Los Angeles, those of alternative sexualities). First, although migration is often, and has been represented as, a highly gendered experience, the only positive correlation found between gender identification and telenovela viewing was that women in Detroit tended to express a preference for *Mujer: Casos de la vida real* as well as the focus on "social issues" of some prime-time Televisa telenovelas, because they showed women's problems "as they are" and one could "learn from them." Men at both locations were just as likely to express a desire to watch certain telenovelas, especially in Los Angeles, where proportionately more male than female respondents listed the genre as their most-watched type of programming. Men and women mentioned the pleasure of narrative involvement as a reason for watching or, as one viewer put it, "being carried away to happiness." On the other hand, a respondent from Costa Rica said that he watched telenovelas because "the stories are based on real events."

Women were the most likely to openly express criticism of Spanish-language telenovelas. One respondent from Guatemala said that she did not "watch television because everything is repeated; the telenovelas are the same stories." In Los Angeles, by contrast, where Telemundo has a local station, most of those who preferred to watch the network did so in order to see Brazilian telenovelas such as *Xica da Silva* (2000) because they were refreshingly different. Other telenovelas that were popular in Los Angeles (on the Univisión channel) were *Esmeralda* (1997–1998), which was based on the Venezuelan program *Topacio,* and *Tres mujeres* (Three Women, 1999–2000), which concerns a young woman (Karyme Lozano) who goes to New York to study painting. The Detroit favorite in 2005 was *Apuesta por un amor,* in addition to *Mujer: Casos de la vida real.* At both locations, male respondents who said they enjoyed watching telenovelas gave reasons such as the ability to see the rural landscape they had left behind and to ogle the pretty female stars. (The latter response tended to come from single men who had migrated alone to the United States.)

What I found most striking is that many of those who showed a preference for telenovelas also preferred to watch news programming. When asked what they would like to see more of on Spanish-language programming, they answered overwhelmingly in favor of news and educational programming, including programs about immigration issues, domestic violence, English-language instruction, and environmental justice. In fact, most of the respondents in both cities showed a strong preference for news reports over other types of programming. One Los Angeles respondent reported wanting news programs to "last two hours." Many Detroit viewers clamored for access to information about public services and news coverage of local events in Spanish (a demand that has, in large part, been met by the introduction of WUDT-Univisión). Finally, in both Detroit and Los Angeles, access to information about the situation and rights of immigrants in the United States was very high on the list of reasons for watching television overall. The salient desire among many of the migrants for innovations within the telenovela needs to be taken into account when evaluating the efficacy of transnational and local Spanish-language programming in the United States.

Although it is difficult to speak with any certainty of the degree of fit between transnational telenovelas and diasporic as well as national audiences, there are signs that the turn towards realism, along with aesthetic and cultural hybridity, is helping to correct the disjunction that historically has occurred between the industry's perceptions of its audience and the actual demographic and ideological profile of the viewers that consume its product. Viewed from another angle, telenovelas have been somewhat effective in chronicling the decentering of Latina and Latino subjectivity in the wake of domestic crisis and emigration, while proffering the tools with which diasporic audiences can feel as though they, and the nations they left behind, are being "recentered."

Nevertheless, the comments of survey respondents indicate an inclination toward programming that increases viewer agency and a critical understanding that far exceeds the impressions of the "spectator in the text" obtained from many of the populist and more illusionistic renderings of the national in a world where the nation's boundaries have come unpegged for migrant viewers and for the media institutions whose products they consume. Although there is little doubt as to the impact of emigration on the orientation and packaging of televisual melodrama, the degree to which the relation between documentary and fiction can be effectively shaped to address the issues encountered by ex-citizens and repatriated citizens (that is, to treat them as more than an attractive market), remains to be seen.

## Notes

1. For the distinction between national and vernacular popular forms, see Canclini.

2. Vladimir Propp was a Russian folklorist whose highly influential book *The Morphology of the Folktale* (1928) introduced the notion that folktales, which tend to vary in the telling and have been linked to cultural tradition, share certain basic plot elements and formal dynamics that remain constant across cultural boundaries and over time. Propp provided the theoretical basis for observing the ways in which new cultural content could be inserted into older plot structures and character "functions." Telenovelas operate in much the same way, injecting new context-sensitive content into existing plots and character configurations (hence the propensity for remakes), and are able to speak in seemingly familiar terms to a wide cultural and linguistic range of viewers. See Propp xxvi–xxx, 12–13, 41–46, 73–79.

3. See also Organización Cisneros, "Trasmisión, programación, producción y entretenimiento"; Associated Press.

4. See Romero.

5. It is known that most of the 44 million Hispanics residing in the United States are of Mexican origin; even within the undocumented population (around twelve million), approximately 56 percent are Mexican nationals; Rumbaut, n.p.

6. The satellite service is available throughout the Americas and Europe, Australia, Japan, and most of Africa and the Middle East. See TV Globo Internacional, "Assine

o Canal," and "Sobre a TV Globo Internacional." I thank André Markon for direct-ing me to this site.

7. According to Luiz, in 2005, Brazilians made up the fourth-largest group, after Mexicans (80 percent), Hondurans, and Salvadorans, to be apprehended at the U.S.-Mexico border.

8. For an analysis of the Colombian originals, see Venegas 63–65.

9. The partners in this consortium are Texas Pacific Group, Inc., and Thomas H. Lee Partners (major firms), Madison Dearborn Partners, LLC, Providence Equity Partners, Inc., and Haim Saban. Grupo Televisa S.A. owns 11 percent, and Venevisión owns 14 percent (Associated Press 1).

10. See Sang and Menjívar.

11. Latina and Latino characters on prime-time English-language television pro-grams tend to be accorded a lower socioeconomic status than do African Americans and "white" Anglo characters; Mastro and Behm-Morawitz 113, 117–88.

12. One hundred fifty-six two-page surveys were conducted at various locations in the Los Angeles metropolitan area between March 1998 and December 1999, and 117 four-page surveys (replicating most of the L.A. questions and entering into greater biographical and programmatic detail) were conducted in southwest Detroit between March and August 2005. Mike Casas assisted with the design and administration of the Detroit surveys, especially in the areas of news programming and viewer preferences.

## Works Cited

Associated Press. "Univisión Board OKs Sale." MSNBC.com, http://www.msnbc .msn.com/id/13566655/ (accessed July 5, 2007).

Canclini, Néstor García. *Las culturas populares en el capitalismo.* Mexico City: Edito-rial Nueva Imagen, 1982.

De Sipio, Louis, et al. "Talking Back to Television: Latinos Discuss How Television Portrays Them and the Quality of Programming Options," study conducted by the Tomás Rivera Policy Institute, 1998. In *The Future of Latino Independent Media: A NALIP Sourcebook.* Ed. Chon A. Noriega. Los Angeles: UCLA Chicano Studies Research Center, 2000. 59–97.

Espada, Carolina. *La Telenovela en Venezuela.* Caracas: Fundación Bigott, 2004.

Fox, Elizabeth, and Silvio Waisbord. "Latin Politics, Global Media." In *Latin Politics, Global Media.* Ed. Elizabeth Fox and Silvio Waisbord. Austin: University of Texas Press, 2002. 1–21.

Hamburger, Esther. *O Brasil antenado: A sociedade da novela.* São Paulo: Jorge Zahar, 2005.

Hussain, Farhana. "Net Flow," "Snapshot: Global Migration" [graphics], *New York Times.* Data compiled from United Nations Population Division, the World Bank, and the International Monetary Fund, June 22, 2007. http://www.nytimes.com/ref/world/20070622_CAPEVERDE_GRAPHIC (accessed July 17, 2007).

Independent Spanish Broadcasters Association. "Immigration Bill Would Benefit Hispanic Media." June 12, 2007, http://www.spanishbroadcasters.com/email/Assets/isba-email.gif (accessed July 7, 2007).

Landy, Marcia. *Film, Politics, and Gramsci.* Minneapolis: University of Minnesota Press, 1994.

Lindo, Róger. "Mujeres, la mitad de los migrantes." *La Opinión Digital,* September 7, 2006, http://www.laopinion.com/print.html?rkey=00060090622542519200 2 (accessed April 26, 2007).

López, Ana M. "Our Welcomed Guests: Telenovelas in Latin America." In *To Be Continued . . . Soap Operas Around the World.* Ed. Robert C. Allen. London: Routledge, 1995. 256–75.

Luiz, Émerson. "Brazilians in America: 1.3 Million and Growing Fast." *Brazzil-Brazil,* May 29, 2006. http://www.brazzil.com/index2.php?option=com_content&do_pdf=1&id=9294 (accessed July 9, 2007).

Martín-Barbero, Jesús. "Memory and Form in the Latin American Soap Opera." In *To Be Continued . . . Soap Operas Around the World.* Ed. Robert C. Allen. London: Routledge, 1995. 276–84.

Mastro, Dana E., and Elizabeth Behm-Morawitz. "Latino Representation on Primetime Television." *Journalism and Mass Communication Quarterly* 82, no. 1 (Spring 2005): 110–30.

Mazziotti, Nora. *La industria de la* telenovela: *La producción de ficción en América Latina.* Buenos Aires: Paidós, 1996.

Motion Picture Association, Latin American Regional Office. "Estatísticas 2005 All Media Sheet—Latin America." http://www.mpaal.org.br/estatísticas.htm (accessed December 11, 2006).

Organización Cisneros. "Introducción," under Información Corporativa. http://www.cisneros.com/esp_lite/corporate/default.asp (accessed July 3, 2007).

———. "Servicios y productos de consumo masivo," under Compañías. http://www.cisneros.com/esp_lite/companies/company.asp?idcompania=4 (accessed July 7, 2007).

———. "Trasmisión, programación, producción y entretenimiento," under Compañías. http://www.cisneros.com/esp_lite/companies/default.asp (accessed July 3, 2007).

Oroz, Silvia. *Melodrama: O cine de lágrimas da América Latina.* Mexico City: Universidad Autónoma de México, Dirección General de Actividades Cinematográficas, 1995.

Propp, Vladimir. *Theory and History of Folklore.* Trans. Ariadna Y. Martin and Richard P. Martin. Ed. Anatoly Liberman. Theory and History of Literature, vol. 5. Minneapolis: University of Minnesota Press, 1984.

Rohter, Larry. "Brazilians Streaming into U.S. Through Mexican Border." *New York Times,* June 30, 2005, http://www.nytimes.com/2005/06/30/international/americas/30brazil.html?ei=5090&en=e31a4c782e490298&ex=1277784000&partner=rssuserland&emc=rss&pagewanted=print.

Romero, Simon. "Media Mogul Learns to Live with Chávez." *New York Times,* July 5, 2007. http://select.nytimes.com/mem/tnt.html?tntget=2007/07/05/world/americas/05venez.html&tntemail1-y&emc-tnt&pagewanted=print.

Rumbaut, Julio. "U.S. Immigration Law Changes and Their Effect on Hispanic Media." *Radio Business Report,* June 2007. http://www.spanishbroadcasters.com/docs/RBR-June07.rtf.

Sang, Hea Kil, and Cecilia Menjívar. "The 'War on the Border': Criminalizing Immigrants and Militarizing the U.S.-Mexico Border." In *Immigration and Crime: Race, Ethnicity, and Violence.* Ed. Ramiro Martínez Jr., and Abel Valenzuela Jr. New York: New York University Press, 2006. 164–88.

Sinclair, John. "Mexico and Brazil." In *Latin Politics, Global Media.* Ed. Elizabeth Fox and Silvio Waisbord. Austin: University of Texas Press, 2002. 123–36.

Speight, Kimberley. "American TV Viewers Getting Taste of Telenovelas." *Reuters/Hollywood Reporter,* posted at *Yahoo! News* Wednesday, December 14, 2005, http://news.yahoo.com/s/nm/20051214/en_nm/telenovelas_dc_1;_ylt.

Spener, David, and Kathleen Staudt. "The View from the Frontier: Theoretical Perspectives Undisciplined." In *The U.S.-Mexico Border: Transcending Divisions, Contesting Identities.* Ed. David Spener and Kathleen Staudt. Boulder, Colo.: Lynne Rienner, 1998. 3–33.

TV Globo Internacional. "A Programação." http://200.220.30.196/AProgramacao.aspx (accessed July 7, 2007).

———. "Assine o Canal." http://tvglobointernacional.globo.com/AssineOCanal.aspx (accessed July 7, 2007).

———. "Sobre a TV Globo Internacional," http://tvglobointernacional.globo.com/SobreTVGI.aspx (accessed July 7, 2007).

United Nations Conference on Trade and Development (UNCTAD). "Population and Labour Force of Countries and Geographical Regions." In *UNCTAD Handbook of Statistics 2006–07.* New York: UNCTAD, 2007, sec. 8.4.1., http://www.unctad.org/Templates/webflyer.asp?docid=8612&intItemID=1397&lang=1&mode=toc.

Venegas, Cristina. "Land as Memory in the Transnational Telenovela." *Spectator* 19, no. 1 (Fall–Winter 1998): 58–71.

Venevisión. "Programación," http://www.venevision.net/programacion/index.asp (accessed July 3, 2007).

Yúdice, George. "Postmodernity and Transnational Capitalism in Latin America." In *On Edge: The Crisis of Contemporary Latin American Culture.* Ed. George Yúdice, Jean Franco, and Juan Flores. Minneapolis: University of Minnesota Press, 1992. 1–28.

# Contributors

**LUISELA ALVARAY** is an assistant professor in the College of Communication at DePaul University, Chicago. Her work has appeared in *Film & History, Emergences, Cinemais,* and *Objeto visual,* among other journals. She is the author of *Las versiones fílmicas: Los discursos que se miran* and *A la luz del proyector.*

**MARIANA BALTAR** received a Ph.D. in 2007 from the Universidade Federal Fluminense in Rio de Janeiro. Her essay in this collection is based on her work on contemporary Brazilian documentaries and the melodramatic imagination.

**CATHERINE L. BENAMOU** is an associate professor of film and media studies at the University of California at Irvine. Her articles about media have appeared in film journals and several collections, including Jonathan Rosenbaum's *Movie Mutations* and Diana Robin and Ira Jaffe's *Redirecting the Gaze.* She is the author of *It's All True: Orson Welles in Pan-America.*

**MARVIN D'LUGO** is a professor of Spanish and adjunct professor of screen studies at Clark University. A contributor to various critical anthologies concerning Spanish and Latin American cinema, he is also the author of *The Films of Carlos Saura, Guide to the Cinema of Spain,* and, most recently, *Pedro Almodóvar.*

**PAULA FÉLIX-DIDIER** teaches film at the Center for Experimentation and Research in Film and Video Production in Buenos Aires and at the Universidad de Buenos Aires. She is finishing a degree in moving-image archiving and presentation at New York University.

**ANDRÉS LEVINSON** is a graduate student in history at the Universidad de Buenos Aires and teaches Argentine Cinema at the Center for Experimentation and Research in Film and Video Production in Buenos Aires.

**GILBERTO PEREZ** is a professor of film studies at Sarah Lawrence College and author of *The Materialist Ghost: Films and Their Medium.*

**DARLENE J. SADLIER** is a professor of Spanish and Portuguese at Indiana University and the author of *Nelson Pereira dos Santos* and, most recently, *Brazil Imagined: 1500 to the Present.*

**CID VASCONCELOS** received his Ph.D. in 2007 from the Department of Sociology at the Universidade Federal de Ceará. His thesis focused on Brazilian melodramas of the 1940s. He is an assistant professor of audiovisual and new medias at the Universidade de Fortaleza.

**ISMAIL XAVIER** is a professor in the Department of Cinema, Radio, and Television in the School of Communications and Arts at the Universidade de São Paulo. He is the author of numerous articles and several books, including *Allegories of Underdevelopment* and, most recently, *O olhar e a cena.*

# Index of Names and Titles

Walerstein, Gregorio, 44
Walerstein, Mauricio, 44, 45, 47, 48n9
*Wara Wara* (Maidana), 9
Ward, Humphrey (Mrs.), 3
*Way Down East* (Griffith), 3, 20, 21
"Ways of Melodrama" (Durgnat), 16n3
Welch, David, 75–76n4
"The Woman's Film" (Doane), 16n3

Xavier, Ismail, 132
*Xica da Silva,* 167

Yañez, Eduardo, 160
*Yawar mallku* (Sanjinés), 11
*Yo soy Betty la fea,* 140, 148, 149
Yrigoyen, Hipólito, 62n4, 62n9
*Y tu mamá tambien* (Cuarón), 15

Zacarías, Alfredo, 7, 11
Zavarce, Néstor, 103
*Zona roja* (Fernández), 12
Zubarry, Olga, 38

The University of Illinois Press
is a founding member of the
Association of American University Presses.

———————————————————————

Composed in 10.5/13 Adobe Minion Pro
by Celia Shapland
at the University of Illinois Press
Manufactured by Sheridan Books, Inc.

University of Illinois Press
1325 South Oak Street
Champaign, IL 61820-6903
www.press.uillinois.edu